THE UMPIRE
STRIKES BACK

THE UMPIRE STRIKES BACK
by Ron Luciano
& David Fisher

Bantam Books
Toronto · New York · London · Sydney

THE UMPIRE STRIKES BACK
A Bantam Book / April 1982

Library of Congress Cataloging in Publication Data

Luciano, Ron.
The umpire strikes back.

1. Luciano, Ron.   2. Baseball—United States—Umpires—
Biography.   3. American League of Professional Baseball
Clubs.   I. Fisher, David, 1946-   II. Title.
GV865.L8A37   796.357′092′4 [B]   81-15059
ISBN 0-553-05010-9   AACR2

Published simultaneously in the United States and Canada

Bantam Books are published by Bantam Books, Inc. Its trademark, consisting of the words "Bantam Books" and the por-
trayal of a rooster, is Registered in U.S. Patent and Trademark
Office and in other countries. Marca Registrada. Bantam
Books, Inc., 666 Fifth Avenue, New York, New York 10103.

PRINTED IN THE UNITED STATES OF AMERICA

0 9 8

To my mother, Josephine, who taught me the difference between safe and out.

THE UMPIRE STRIKES BACK

1

HOW I BECAME AN UMPIRE

OR Finally Bad Enough for the Regular Season

"**R**eady, Ron?" asked the disembodied voice in my ear.

I looked at the microphone in front of me, and nodded.

Merle Harmon, my old friend with whom I would be broadcasting Major League Baseball's Game of the Week, leaned over and said gently, "You'll have to speak up, Ron. They can't hear you when you nod."

I nodded firmly. "Ready."

Mike Weisman, the voice in my ear, was producing the telecast from NBC's mammoth communications van parked outside the Texas Rangers ballpark. "Okay, good," he replied. "We've got ten minutes. Let's rehearse."

Rehearse? A baseball game? I'd spent my entire life in sports. I'd been an All-American football player in college, I'd played four years of professional football, I'd umpired in the major leagues for 11 years. Rehearse? In all that time I'd never heard of rehearsing a sports event. But as I soon learned, this wasn't sports. This was sports broadcasting, and it was a whole new ballgame.

Normally, at that moment I would have been in the umpires dressing room, desperately trying to squeeze my winter body into my summer uniform.

Instead, I was sitting in the broadcasters booth trying not to smear my make-up. I squirmed uncomfortably in my chair, and wondered what I was doing up there. I was supposed to be down on the field exchanging compliments with Reggie Jackson, screaming at Orioles manager Earl Weaver, letting the fans behind first base call the plays for me, telling Rod Carew how to hit. Who was Yankee third baseman Graig Nettles going to have to complain about if I weren't there? What would American League President Lee MacPhail do if I weren't there causing problems for him to solve? How could Billy Martin possibly turn the Oakland A's into winners without me there to advise him? Who was going to make pitcher Tommy John break into laughter in the middle of his wind-up?

My new career wouldn't begin officially for almost two hours, and already I was thinking about retirement.

Three days earlier I'd been packing my umpires gear and preparing to fly to California to open the 1980 baseball season. I was looking forward to it. I was scheduled to work the World Series and I was probably going to get the All-Star Game. In addition, I'd recently been elected to a second term as President of the Association of Major League Umpires, so people *had* to listen to me. But in those three days I'd auditioned for NBC Sports and been hired to assist Merle Harmon as color man on the regional Game of the Week. Suddenly, sitting in the announcers booth in Arlington, Texas, the insanity of the situation hit me. Including four years in the minor leagues, I'd spent the past 15 years on the playing field. When I was home during the off-season I was usually out in the woods hunting or bird watching. Incredible as it sounds, I had no idea what a color commentator was supposed to do.

Fortunately, Weisman did. He wanted us to rehearse the opening of the program. "First," he told me, "talk about the Yankees. Can they come back from their disappointing 1979 season? They've got a rookie manager, Dick Howser, talk about him. Mention their new centerfielder, Ruppert Jones, and their new catcher, Rick Cerone. Can Cerone replace Munson? Don't forget to mention that they picked up Bob Watson and Rudy May as free agents over the winter. Do you think their pitching is sound enough to win? Do they have enough hitting . . ."

I was nodding furiously, trying to remember all of this.

". . . then go to the Rangers. Fergie Jenkins is their starting pitcher, so talk about his long career. What was it like being behind the plate when he was on the mound? Better mention that their manager, Pat Corrales, is in trouble if they don't get off to a quick start. Then run down their line-up. Got it?"

"Right," I said, nodding. "How much time do I have?"

"Thirty seconds."

Thirty seconds! I can barely say my name in 30 seconds, even without including a middle initial. I started sweating, causing my make-up to run. Never being a person satisfied to create a small disaster when I could just as easily create a catastrophe, I realized I was about to embarrass myself on national television. There are people who claim I didn't know what I was doing as a football player. They're wrong. There are people who claim I didn't know what I was doing as an umpire. They're wrong. But I knew I didn't know what I was doing in that booth, and within ten minutes the entire nation was going to find out.

I glanced over my shoulder. A burly sound technician was blocking the door. There was no way out.

I had never wanted to be a television broadcaster.

My voice is perfect for mime and my face is made for radio. But I had never wanted to be an umpire, either. (With the exception of my friend Bill Haller, no one ever grew up intending to be an umpire. But Haller's brother Tom wanted to be a catcher, so an affinity for masks must run in that family.) My ambition as a child was to spend a quiet adult life sleeping late, hunting and fishing, and somehow getting paid a lot of money to do it. Instead, I became a professional football player.

I was born in Binghamton, New York, in 1937. My father and his two brothers had immigrated to America from the tiny Italian village of San Giovanni about twenty years earlier. They split up when they got here and bought train tickets to wherever their money would take them, because they couldn't believe that any one town would be large enough to have three jobs available. My father's ticket took him to the small town of Endicott, in upstate New York. His brothers ended up in Pennsylvania.

With my mother, who was born in America, he opened Perry's Grill, a ninety-seat restaurant across the street from the IBM clock factory. We served about 350 meals a day. Eventually the restaurant became a parking lot. IBM became a conglomerate.

We lived over the bar and the jukebox would be blasting until 1:00 A.M. every morning, so even today I can recite the lyrics of any song written between 1945 and 1955 and sleep through absolutely anything. The bar had one of the first television sets in the city and I thought it was the greatest invention in the world. Back in 1949 the networks used whatever was available and inexpensive to fill time. Weather forecasts lasted a half hour. I didn't care. I would sit in front of that set, absolutely mesmerized. I might go to school the next day without having done my homework, but I knew the temperature in Honolulu.

I had a normal childhood, except perhaps for the largest gangland bust in history. When your name is Luciano, and you're living in a community of seventeen thousand Italians, there is no such thing as a gangster. The Mafia was considered a local fraternal organization. There were perhaps fifty families in Endicott thought to be "connected," and they were among the most respected people in town. In fact, when *The Untouchables* went on the air, none of us could understand its appeal. The wrong side always won.

Two of my closest friends were Joe and Pete Barbara. Their father, Big Joe, owned the local Canada Dry bottling plant and was one of the wealthiest men in town. They lived in a big, lovely house, with stables and a pool, in the nearby village of Apalachin, and most weekends I would go up there to get thrown off horses with them.

By 1957 I was at Syracuse University. We had some time off so I drove home and called them, hoping to get together during the weekend. But they told me not to come up because their father was having company. When I opened the newspaper Sunday morning, I learned that his company had included every crime boss in the country. Later I found out that the Barbaras' telephones had been tapped and all of my conversations with Joe and Pete had been recorded. The FBI knew which girl in my class I had a crush on. They interviewed me a number of times in the next few years, but all I could honestly tell them was that I kept falling off the horses.

My father died when I was eleven; my mother raised me and my two sisters. She is a very special woman. She's small and wiry, and was always very athletic. Even today, at age eighty, she can stand on the foul line and sink six out of ten baskets. Of course, she's real slow getting back on defense, so she's usually the last one picked.

I was a good student in school, particularly in mathematics, but athletics were the most important aspect of my childhood. My uncle, Nick DiNunzio, had gone through Syracuse University on a football scholarship and was assistant coach of the high school football team, so my mother appreciated the value of sports. Even though there was always work to be done at the restaurant, I was allowed to stay after school to play ball.

Being bigger and taller than most of the other kids, I was a decent basketball player and a very good football player. If I made contact with the baseball I could really drive it, but I had difficulty hitting the thing. When I realized it was easier to hit a two-hundred-pound lineman than a five and three-quarter ounce baseball, I began concentrating on football.

There was never any question in my mind where I wanted to go to college. Uncle Nick had been a quarterback at Syracuse—I wanted to go to Syracuse. The day Coach Ben Schwartzwalder offered me a scholarship was one of the happiest days of my life. (I was two years behind Jimmy Brown and three years ahead of Ernie Davis, so you can say it was Brown, Luciano and Davis at Syracuse—but you have to say it fast.)

Jimmy Brown was the single greatest athlete I have ever seen. Even then he was the same shy, unassuming person he is today. Except for the white silk suits and the big cars, you'd hardly even know he was there. But on the football field or lacrosse field he was unstoppable. Our lacrosse team revolutionized the sport. Our opponents had elaborate plays, involving skillful stick handling, crisp passing and patterned blocking. Jimmy just put the ball against his chest and ran through everybody. (That strategy would still work today. All an ambitious coach would have to do is build a team willing to work together and make sacrifices together, then go out and find a young Jimmy Brown.)

Actually, we had a nice friendship. He called me "Hey, you," and I called him "Mr. Brown." Years later, after both of us had finished our playing careers, I bumped into him in Los Angeles. At first he pretended not to know who I was, but then he said, "Hey, you, move over please." It was nice to see that even after all his success he still remembered his old teammate.

When I was being recruited by Syracuse they guaranteed me a job on campus so I could earn some spending money. As I later found out, all scholarship players were given jobs. The specific job depended on your status on the team. The "greenies," or fourth-team players, actually had to work. In my sophomore year I swept out the laundry room, but by my senior year I had graduated to a responsible job befitting my position as a potential all-American tackle.

I was the bench watcher. There was a two-and-a-half-ton cement bench on the quadrangle. I was paid twenty dollars a week to make sure nobody stole it. Sure, it was hard work, but somebody had to do it. And I did a good job, too. That same bench is there today and there isn't a chip out of it. Ironically, watching that bench proved to be better training for my pro football career than playing in the games.

Our big game my senior year was against the Pittsburgh Panthers. I had been sick all week with a virus and right up until Saturday the newspapers listed me as a doubtful starter. But I really wanted to play because I knew pro scouts were evaluating my ability, and so I suited up. Later, I was told that Pitt's game plan that day was to run at me until I was worn down, then bury me. That's exactly what they did. By the fourth quarter I was so woozy I could barely hold a three-point position, but I refused to quit. I'd never walked off a field during a game in my life and I didn't intend to start that day. We were winning by less than a touchdown with seconds left in the game, but Pitt drove down to our three-yard line. They ran three off-tackle plays in a row. I stopped them cold each time. They didn't gain an inch. On fourth down they passed into the end zone and we intercepted to win the game. That was probably the finest game I ever played.

In the pro football draft that year I was chosen in the second round by the Baltimore Colts, but the Colts immediately forwarded me to the Detroit Lions to complete an earlier trade for the great quarterback Bobby Layne. I was a player-to-be-named-later. That didn't bother me. As far as I was concerned, I had yet to play my first pro game and already had been traded for one of the greatest quarterbacks in football history. The fact that the Colts included thirty-five other players and forty million dollars in the deal didn't bother me. In my mind it was Luciano for Layne.

Detroit offered me ten thousand dollars to sign with them. In those days athletes didn't have agents and I had no idea who to turn to for advice. I finally asked Rocky Pirro, the line coach at Syracuse, if he thought it was a good deal. Rock considered it for a moment, then said, it sure beats twenty bucks. So I was satisfied.

The following August I was selected to play in the annual Pro-College All-Star Game. Not only would I have a chance to show the world champion Baltimore Colts the mistake they'd made trading me, I'd have an opportunity to see how well I stacked up against the best college players in the nation. Actually, I was nervous, I wondered if I was good enough to play pro football.

The All-Star team trained outside Chicago. At one of our first practice sessions the coaches asked each of us to describe the offensive system we had used in school, so they could design a system we could all understand. We'd had nine different play series at Syracuse, I explained. When the quarterback called the play he would first name the series, then the number of the back carrying the ball, then the number of the hole in the line he was going to go for, then a descriptive word afterward. If the play was a reverse or a double-wing, the first number would change. Although it sounds difficult, mathematically it worked perfectly, and I loved it.

Next the coaches asked Bob Reifsnyder, an all-American tackle from Navy, to describe the system they used at Annapolis. Reifsnyder used to tell us stories about life as a football player at the Naval Academy. One night, he said, some of the players had dates and couldn't get passes. So they got some dynamite, blew holes in the wall and went out. Navy's play-calling system was pretty basic, he said. Two numbers to designate the play and a word afterward.

Finally, the coaches turned to the man who had been the leading small-college running back in the country. He furrowed his brow and thought about it. Finally he shrugged. "I just told 'em, gimme the ball and stay outta my way." As soon as I heard that, I knew I could play pro football.

It was during a practice session that I met Richard Nixon. I didn't just meet him, I sort of fell over him.

At that time he was Eisenhower's vice-president, and he had come to watch us work out. I was looking forward to meeting him. Here I was, the son of an

Italian immigrant, meeting the vice-president of the United States. But I was determined to be cool.

Nixon came into the locker room just before we went out on the field. I was already in uniform, wearing steel cleats. When he walked over to my locker, I stood up to shake his hand. But as I stood up, my cleats started sliding and I started to fall. I grabbed the first thing I could get hold of, which turned out to be the vice-president, and we both went down together.

After the Secret Service men untangled us, Nixon smiled graciously and shook my hand. From a distance.

Everybody laughed and thought the incident was finished. It wasn't. A few minutes later he was standing on the sidelines watching us scrimmage. I was on defense, and the offense tried an end run. I ran across the field and threw a perfect cross-body block at the runner, knocking him off his feet. Unfortunately my momentum kept me going, right out of bounds, and I cut Nixon's legs right out from under him. I was mortified. I figured I was already in trouble with the FBI because of my friendship with the Barbaras; now I had to tackle the vice-president.

Nixon took it well. While we were still lying there on the ground he looked at me and shook his head in disbelief. Then he said, "You've just got to be a Democrat!"

The game itself was played in Chicago's Soldier Field on a magnificent August night. I was really pumped up for it. This was the fulfillment of a lifelong dream. I didn't start, but in the middle of the first quarter went in to play offensive tackle. I was so excited I barely heard the quarterback call the play. I ran up to the line of scrimmage and got down in my stance and looked up. Looking right back at me was Eugene "Big Daddy" Lipscomb. He was about 6'72", one of the biggest, toughest, strongest and meanest linemen in pro football. I gritted my teeth and got ready. I was going to tear into him. I was going to show him how tough I was. He smiled.

The first play was a run to the other side of the line. My assignment was to brush by Lipscomb then move downfield to block. The play went perfectly. I just nudged him out of the way and went downfield.

The quarterback called for a pass on the next play. That meant I had to hold Lipscomb back to give the quarterback time to set up. It was strength against strength. I was confident, but not cocky. I'd success-fully blocked two rushers before, and he wasn't any bigger than two men. The ball was hiked and I snapped out of my stance and hit him. I bounced right off him, so I had to charge into him again. I think it was that second hit that got him angry. Like a great grizzly bear he reached over and grabbed my arm, and just threw me out of the way.

I landed right on my ego. Thunderbolts of pain were shooting through my shoulder. For the first time in my life I walked off the field in the middle of a game. I knew my shoulder was in serious trouble because as I walked to the sidelines I kept tripping over my hand.

They rushed me to the hospital and tried to stuff my arm back in its socket, just as you might try to push a cork back into a wine bottle. It wouldn't go back in. Finally they had to operate.

When I woke up they told me I wouldn't be able to play pro football that season. I was devastated. My entire career was about to end even before it had be-gun. I was determined not to let that happen. Not without a fight. So I reported to the Detroit Lions' training camp at Cranbrook, Michigan, with my arm in a sling.

Today I may joke about my pro football career, but

that's really not necessary. I can let my accomplishments speak for themselves.

Until the time I reported, the Lions had been one of football's great teams. Tobin Rote was still there, and Yale Lary, Hopalong Cassady and Darris McCord. I'll never forget the first time I met McCord. I was walking toward the locker room and he was coming toward me. He was about 6'7" and built much the same way as Jimmy Brown except, of course, that Brown had muscles in his body that don't exist on other people. McCord was the anchor of the Lions' defense and I wanted to impress him, so I straightened my shoulders (as best I could), stood up ramrod tall and sucked in my gut. I wasn't exactly small. I was 6'4" tall and weighed 220 and was in good shape. As he walked by he glanced at my body. "Hi ya, kid," he said, then stuck the knife in. "Halfback?"

My gut just fell out.

My bad shoulder didn't respond to treatment that fall, so I had to accept the fact that I wasn't going to be able to play football that season. The Lions were very understanding about it, paying me full salary and allowing me to stay with the team. At first it was incredibly difficult for me to watch from the sidelines, but then I began to realize it wasn't such a bad deal. I was sleeping late, doing pretty much whatever I wanted, and getting paid. This was about as close to fulfilling my childhood ambition as I was likely to get.

It was during that first season that I discovered my real football talent. The key to my entire career was quick reflexes in the audio-visual room. On a pro football team, I quickly learned, quarterbacks are like God, except more powerful. They can hire you or fire you. The quarterback doesn't like you, you're gone. So my first move was to make friends with the Lions' quarterback corps. If they wanted something done, Luciano was there to do it for them.

Each Monday morning the quarterbacks were supposed to watch the films of the game played the day before and chart the plays. It was a simple but tedious job: on a diagram of the playing field they had to indicate the line of scrimmage, what play had been called, where it ended and who made the tackle. The quarterbacks hated to do it, so I volunteered to do it for them.

They loved me for it. "Hey," they'd tell any club official who questioned my value to the team, "that Luciano's some player." What they really meant was that I was some plotter. When my shoulder had healed they still protected me. If the team was scrimmaging, they would take me to a far corner of the practice field and use me to center the ball for them. When the rest of the team was doing calisthenics, I was usually off running some errand.

Even after night curfew, if anyone on the squad needed something I was the man to see. They'd be playing cards or dice and want a hamburger, and I had no objection to going out to get it. I'd buy it, put it under my arm to keep it warm, and bring it back to the complex. Of course, I never mentioned the under-the-arm part. At ten thousand dollars a year in 1959 money I didn't mind running errands. As Rocky Pirro had wisely told me, it sure beat twenty bucks.

Just to be on the safe side, I used any excuse I could invent to hang around the Lions' front office. Quarterbacks get traded; secretaries don't. I needed paper clips. The signature on my check was smudged. Perhaps the windows needed cleaning? I was so happy to be in pro football I would have done anything to stay there.

I still thought of myself as a football player. After spending a year watching the Lions win four, lose seven and tie one, I was convinced I could play in the National Football League and I hadn't lost my desire to play. I believed that being a professional athlete was the best possible job in the world, next to doing nothing. So if my shoulder healed and I was no longer able to do nothing, I really wanted to play.

By hanging around the front office I got to know the club officials. Spike Briggs owned the Lions, as well as the Detroit Tigers baseball team, and he was a terrific man. George Wilson, the head coach, was an absolute sweetheart. A rotten coach, but a decent and fair man and everybody liked him. We might have had the ball on our opponents three-yard line and he'd call for a thirty-yard pass play, but nobody complained because he was such a good guy. They'd just shake their heads and say, "That's George," and run whatever play they wanted to run.

Whatever I did for the Lions that first year I must have done it well, because they gave me a two-thousand-dollar raise for the 1960 season. I was determined to prove I could play pro football. I was going to establish myself as a force on the offensive line. I was going to earn every penny they were paying me.

I tore up my shoulder again during our third pre-season game. It was my fault. The shoulder had been bothering me during the winter, but I was afraid to tell anybody because I thought the Lions would fire me. So instead of working out and strengthening it, I did nothing, and it just couldn't take the beating.

After my second operation the Lions wanted to send me home on half salary. I refused, claiming to be the audio-visual coach, so they kept me with the team at full salary. Although I was bitterly disappointed that I couldn't play, I was getting to like the situation. I was getting paid a lot of money for not playing. In retrospect, I might not have been a great football player, but I wasn't dumb.

The Lions were 7—5 in 1960 and it became apparent at the end of the season that they could do just fine without me. I heard some rumors that they were going to move me from tackle to guard, or even center. Before going home for the summer I went to see Coach Wilson and told him I thought Detroit had been very fair to me, and that I was willing to play wherever he felt it would do the Lions the most good.

It turned out to be in Minnesota.

Detroit traded me to the newly created Vikings for a low draft choice. I didn't want to go there at all. Minnesota was an expansion team and anyone who could describe a football in ten words or less was going to be in their training camp. People were literally going to be fighting for jobs, and I couldn't afford to get hurt before I had a contract.

So I contacted Buster Ramsey, the Lions' defensive coach, who had taken the job as head coach of the Buffalo Bills of the fledgling American Football League. "Come on," he said happily. "You know the plays. I don't."

I brought my playbook with me and we installed the entire Lion offense at Buffalo. It didn't work as well there as it had in Detroit. We were 6—8.

I finally made it into the regular season without being hurt. Two games. I was on the suicide squad, the group of players who can't get life insurance because their job is to smash the wedge. The wedge is another group who can't get life insurance because their job is to block for the player who runs with the ball on kickoff and punt returns. I was charging downfield on a kickoff and got blocked cleanly. Trying to protect my shoulder, I tore up my knee.

An injury that keeps you out of football for one year is an accident. An injury that keeps you out of football a second year is a shame. An injury that keeps you out of football the third year is a message.

For the first time in my life, I began to realize I wasn't going to grow old playing football. In fact, if I continued trying to play, it was apparent I wasn't going to get to grow old. It had become obvious I wasn't going to have the kind of career I had always dreamed about. It's easy to make jokes about it now, to pretend it didn't make any difference, but it did. It made all the difference in the world. I desperately wanted to play football. I loved the game. I had been a star in high school and college and honestly believed I was capable of playing in the pros. But my body kept breaking down on me.

I had to think about doing something else with the rest of my life. It was frightening. The world of athletics is heavily insulated against reality. Like so many other young athletes, I believed I was destined for fame and fortune on the field, and then I could open a bar. When I was one of the first forty players chosen in the pro draft I was sure of it. It just didn't turn out that way.

Three years on the disabled list hadn't convinced me I was too fragile to play pro ball. I thought it was a long streak of bad luck. So I reported to Buffalo for the 1962 season and survived until the third preseason game. Then my shoulder went again. By unanimous agreement of every general manager in pro football, I retired. The Bills paid me off, about ten thousand dollars, and I went home. It was a difficult time. Not only did I have to deal with the end of my dream, I had to find a means of making a living.

I had been going to graduate school during the off-season and gotten my master's degree from Syracuse in education administration, so I decided to try teaching. I had no problem getting a job. Everybody in Endicott knew me. My Uncle Nick was a teacher and football coach at the high school. His wife was teaching. Another aunt was on the school board. In all, about twelve relatives were working in the district. It wasn't too difficult to slip in another one.

It was a tremendous letdown. After doing nothing for four years and making good money doing it, I had to work twice as many months for half the salary. Instead of hanging out with the team at Lindell's AC Bar in Detroit, I was sitting home at night marking seventh-grade math tests. I wasn't getting hurt anymore, but I had to get up at 7:00 A.M.

I started as a substitute teacher. Admittedly, I wasn't very good at it, but I was an excellent bluffer. I'd fake my way out of any problem. They had me teaching woodshop, for example. I can't even change a light bulb without written instructions. All I knew about working with wood was that you had to sand it. So whatever the problem, my answer was "sand it." When the kids asked for advice, I'd run my hand over the board, nod, and say, "Looks pretty good. Why don't you just sand it a little more?"

Except for a hammer, screwdriver and pliers, I didn't even know what the various tools looked like. If one of the boys asked me where a certain number file was, I'd shake my head in utter frustration and growl, "Well, where'd you leave it?" Or I'd grab one of the class leaders and say, "Do me a favor. Show this guy where the file is. He can't find it for himself."

I had a good rapport with the kids, though. I was an easy marker. If they earned a 30 on a test, I'd give them an 80. I let them pass. I had been a football player, I thought that's how the system worked.

It didn't take me long to realize teaching was not

to be my lifelong profession. But I did try. I really did. I thought I might enjoy it more if I had some involvement with sports, so I began helping my Uncle Nick coach his high school football team. I wasn't any better on the field than I was in the classroom. I'd spend fifteen minutes lecturing on the fine points of a cross-body block, and when I finished, one of the kids would look up at me through a helmet four sizes too big and ask, "Mr. Luciano, what's a cross-body block?"

However, by persevering, I was able to communicate successfully to these high school players all that I had learned during my professional career.

In other words, we lost every game.

I knew I couldn't continue teaching. I tried playing semipro football for a team in Herkimer, New York, hoping some pro scout might see me, but not a lot of scouts landed at Herkimer International Airport. That experience finally convinced me my playing days were over for good.

I decided to try to get back into pro football as a coach. In 1962 I called Spike Briggs and asked him for a job on the Lions' coaching staff. He said, "Ronnie, you cost me two years' salary without ever playing a game. You were a lousy player and you'd make a lousy coach. Why in the world would I want to hire you?"

I suggested he might admire my courage for calling him.

Actually, the time I'd spent hanging around the front office paid off. I was well liked and Mr. Briggs agreed to try to find something for me in the organization. A few weeks later he called back and offered me a college scouting job. I turned him down. How good an evaluator of talent could I be if I thought *I* could play? He couldn't believe my audacity, but I knew I'd go insane sitting in a thousand press boxes. I could almost hear him shaking his head in disbelief, but he promised to try to find something else for me.

An entire season passed while I waited to hear from him. I was still teaching and hating it. The big controversy in school was whether jeans were suitable student attire. I couldn't understand what difference it made. The Lions were playing the Chicago Bears for second place and I was mediating a dispute about dungarees. I began having fittings for a straitjacket.

Spike Briggs called back in the winter of 1963 and asked me if I knew anything about baseball.

The only thing I knew about baseball was that I couldn't hit a curveball. "Baseball!" I shouted enthusiastically. "I know even more about baseball than I do about football."

There was a deadly silence on the other end of the phone. "Come on, Ron," he finally said nervously, "stop kidding around. How'd you like to be general manager of the Tigers' minor league team in Lakeland, Florida?"

I had no idea what the general manager of a baseball team did, but I knew it had to be better than worrying about blue jeans. "Great," I said. "Sounds terrific. What do I do?"

"You're the liason between the town and the players. You try to get the town to come see the ballplayers, and you try to keep the ballplayers from destroying the town." To this day that remains the most accurate description I've ever heard of a general manager's job. A cross between a policeman and a negotiator. Perfect for me.

My resignation was gleefully accepted by the school board at the end of the semester, and I decided to go to Florida six weeks before the Tigers began spring training, to try to learn something about my

new job. I didn't know much more about baseball than
I did about woodshop. I had no idea how a minor
league system worked or exactly what was expected of
me. But I was back in the Detroit organization, which
had been good to me, and I was back in professional
sports, so I was happy.

A few days after I arrived in Florida, I found out a
baseball school was about to start in Daytona Beach.
Hey, I thought, this is perfect. I'll take a general manager's course and when the season starts I'll be ready. I
soon found the baseball school was Al Somers' Umpire
Instructional Course, which had nothing to do with
general managers. But I had six weeks, and since I
knew very little about baseball, I decided to take the
course. At least I'd know the rules when the season
started.

As soon as I arrived in Daytona Beach, the instructors looked at me and said I'd make an excellent
umpire. They said, "You got good size." In football,
coaches look for agility and strength. In baseball, managers wanted speed, a good throwing arm and hitting
power. In basketball, it's speed, ball handling and
shooting ability. Good size! That should have told me
something right there.

Right from the beginning I loved the job. We were
out in the sun all day and got to yell as loud as we
wanted and the instructors kept telling us that we
were virtually dictators on the field, that whatever
we said was final, that the players and managers
had to listen to us and respect our decisions. That
sounded pretty good to me.

The aspect I liked best, though, from the very
beginning, was that I could be back on the playing field
and I didn't have to worry about getting hurt or listening to coaches scream at me. I could be part of the

game—yet I didn't have to be concerned with winning and losing. While playing football, I had been taught that winning every game is all that matters. We practiced six days a week and played on the seventh. If we lost, the previous six days were considered wasted. In baseball, I found out, losing was not the end of the world. If a team wins a hundred games a season, they still lose sixty-two. Sixty-two losses! That's seven years of losses for a bad football team. That's at least four or five head coaches' jobs. Baseball people accepted losing, because there was always another game the next day.

The school was six weeks long, and by the end of the fourth week I knew I'd found a profession. So I called Spike Briggs and told him to find another general manager for Lakeland.

"Good," he said. "You probably would have done a rotten job anyway. But what are you going to do?"

I told him I was going to be an umpire.

"Ah, Ron, that's wonderful. I'm really happy for you," he said, then paused and asked, "What's an umpire?"

I know it seems improbable but it is absolutely true. This man owned a baseball team and didn't know what an umpire was. He always referred to them as "the officials." I explained that umpires were the officials on the field.

"You mean, you're the guys we call up and complain about all the time?"

"That's right, we're the bad guys."

He hesitated. "Do I hire you?"

"No, the league hires me."

"But I don't own a league, Ronnie."

"I know you don't own a league."

"Then why are you calling me?"

"To tell you I'm not going to be in Lakeland and ask you to do me a favor. I've got a job lined up with the Florida State League, but I need some experience. I want you to hire me for spring training."

"But I don't *own* a league," he insisted.

"I *know* you don't own a league. All you have to do is hire me to come to camp."

He silently considered this request for a moment, then said, "You mean, we hire the officials? And they treat us like that?"

"Now, wait a minute," I objected. "You haven't even hired me. . . ."

Finally Briggs agreed to bring me to the Tigers spring training camp in Lakeland, then asked, "Who pays you?"

"The league pays me."

He sighed in frustration. "But, Ronnie, I don't own a league. . . ."

Umpiring, I had discovered at Al Somers' school, could be a lot of fun. I was surrounded by nice people, all wearing the same conservative blue suits, all working together. We learned how to correctly position ourselves on the field to get the best view of each play, how to work behind the plate, how to deal with unhappy managers and players, and how to handle rulebook disputes. Until I reported to the Tiger camp, everything was fine. Then the problems started: they allowed players on the field.

The first time I worked behind home plate was during an intrasquad game. Frank Lary was pitching for the side in the field. Before allowing the game to begin I checked to see that all the players were in position, as we had been taught, then signaled Lary to pitch. I bent my knees slightly, leaned forward over the catcher and watched his motion carefully, keeping my eyes on the ball. I created an imaginary strike zone between the batter's knees and shoulders the width of the plate. I was ready. Lary threw his first pitch.

He was nearing the end of a fine career, but he could still bring it. The ball wiggled through the air, then smashed into the catcher's glove. I'd worked behind the plate with high school kids on the mound, but I'd never seen a major league fastball before. And this wasn't even a regular-season major league fastball. I was so impressed I forget to call anything. The catcher—I don't remember who it was—twisted around and looked up at me. I knew he wanted me to say something.

"Did you see that?" I said. "Wasn't that terrific?"

It went on like that for three innings. I forgot my job. I was in a dream world. My uniform was brand new and the players had never seen me before, so they probably figured I was just some guy who came out of the stands to fill in until the regular umpire arrived. Besides, I weighed 235 muscular pounds at that time and was in good shape. I had good size.

Finally, about the third inning, I got into the rhythm of the game. I called everything loud and clear, but I was trying so hard to be perfect that I couldn't get anything right. In the bottom of the fourth there was a close play at home plate. The runner made such a beautiful slide I figured anybody who can do that has to be safe, so that's the way I called it.

The catcher turned around and glared at me. "You don't need any more spring training," he snarled. "You're bad enough for the regular season already."

That passed as my graduation ceremony. I had become an umpire.

2

DOWN IN
THE MINORS
OR You Can't Play
Baseball Without the Bases

Around the turn of the century a rule stated that if a ball thrown by a fielder attempting to throw out a baserunner hit an umpire, the runner was automatically out. It didn't take long before clever infielders were using the umpires as moving targets and the league eliminated the rule—but only after prolonged and heated debate.

In football, officials are always treated with respect. Throughout my entire career, high school, college and pro, I never once raised my voice to an official. If I were penalized for holding, I was thankful they'd only caught me that one time and not the three times before. When they made a bad call, I gritted my teeth and maybe muttered under my breath and accepted their stupidity as part of the game. So when I started umpiring, I expected the players to treat me with the same amount of respect.

It didn't take me long to learn the facts of baseball life. For the first few games of my minor league career, as the pregame meeting at home plate broke up, I said happily to the opposing managers, "Good luck, gentlemen." Some of the managers looked at me as if I'd just been released from the rubber room and others challenged me to repeat what I'd said. Finally my partner for the Florida State League season, Danny McDevitt, who had spent parts of six years as a pitcher in the major leagues and was trying to make it back as an umpire, told me I was embarrassing him. In my innocence, I asked him why. He shook his head in disgust and said, as if telling me I had a fatal disease, "Don't you understand, Ronnie? You're an umpire!"

I wasn't really, not yet. It took me a year of arguments and yelling and cursing to get used to the idea that my blue suit set me apart from human beings—in fact, I never did fully accept it, to the frustration of American League President Lee MacPhail and numerous other baseball officials.

My first season in the Florida State League was a long one, although it only lasted a few months. I had graduated from umpires' school, but I really had no idea what I was doing on the field. Every day, every inning, every play, was a learning experience. In the fourth inning of one of the first night games I ever worked, for example, the home-team manager came up to me at home plate and said, "It's getting pretty dark, don't you think?"

I thought he was just trying to be friendly and I appreciated it. Since I've always been pretty good at telling the difference between day and night, I could see he was right, it was getting dark. "It sure is," I agreed.

Two innings later he came back and said a bit more firmly, "It's really getting dark now."

I nodded. "Sure is."

He was back an inning later, and said, "Don't you think we need the lights?"

"Boy, I'll say," I agreed. "I can hardly see out there."

"Well?"

"What?"

"Why don't you turn them on?"

"You mean, I'm supposed to turn the lights on?" Nobody had ever told me that. Well, once I found out, I got real good at it. Two o'clock in the afternoon, let's have the lights. Power companies all over the league got to love me.

My real problem that first season was overhustling. I was so worried about getting into the right position to call the play that the moment the ball was hit I'd put my head down and start running. Usually I had no idea where I was going, but at least I was hustling to get there. There were occasions that year that I ended up so far out of position I couldn't have made a correct call with radar.

Even when I managed to get to the right position, I would look in the wrong place. To make calls at first base, for example, you've got to watch the runner and listen for the sound of the ball hitting the mitt. Instead I'd watch the ball until it was caught, then try to pick up the runner, and never even bother checking to make sure the first baseman had his foot on the bag.

At first, because I had good size, the players and managers were reluctant to argue with me. But once they started, they didn't stop for fifteen years. I think I can most accurately describe my career as an umpire as "noisy."

A manager named Pinky May has the distinction of being the first man I ever threw out of a game. In spring training at Lakeland I'd gotten used to major league pitchers being around the plate with their pitches. They made it easy. But in the low minors the pitchers lacked that pinpoint control. They'd throw fastballs over my head, change-ups that bounced twenty feet in front of the plate, curves that broke into the next county, even spitballs that could end a drought. They were tough for me. One afternoon I was having a particularly bad game. One pitch would be too high, the next would be too low, and I'd call them both balls. But the third one would be right down the heart of the plate and I'd call that a ball, too. In the third or fourth inning I called a hitter out on a pitch that bounced on the plate and Pinky May started cursing at me. I got terribly upset. He didn't even know me and he was swearing at me. I didn't need him to embarrass me in front of the fans. I was doing a pretty good job of it myself. So I threw him out of the game.

Just that simply, the problem was resolved. He continued screaming at me for a few more minutes, but suddenly he was gone and it was quiet and peaceful and beautiful on the field once again. I immediately realized I was onto something good.

My partner McDevitt never had the problems I did because he had the perfect excuse. Every time he had a controversial call he'd let the manager or player yell for a while, then tell him, "That never would have happened in the majors," and walk away. That was the end of the argument. A pitcher would walk three men in a row and start screaming at Danny, and he'd yell right back, "In the majors they never walk three men in a row."

That was no help to me. If I caused a problem and needed help, I'd turn to him and he'd shake his head and tell me, "Gee, Ron, I don't know. That never would have happened in the majors."

Single-A ball was a wonderful place to learn how to umpire because there wasn't the same emphasis on winning as existed on higher levels. The players were there to learn fundamentals, and an umpire could get away with almost anything as long as he was consistent. That saved me. I might not have been good, but I was consistent.

I never regretted my decision to become an umpire rather than a general manager. I hated being yelled at, but I loved being back in the middle of the action. I was beginning to appreciate the world of baseball. Football is full of characters—linemen who eat light bulbs or throw halfbacks out of windows—but as I found out that year, baseball has its own brand of very special people. Among them was the legendary George Sosniak, perhaps the only umpire in baseball history to call for a do-over.

It took place in the Pioneer League sometime in the 1950s. A runner was on third base with less than two out and the batter hit a fly ball to medium-left field. The runner tagged up after the catch and raced home. The outfielder made a good throw and there was a very close play at the plate. When the dust had cleared George was standing there with his hands on his knees. Everybody looked at him, waiting for his decision. "I don't know," he admitted. "It was too close to call."

Everybody in the park was stunned. The umpire has to make a call, otherwise there can't be an argument. No one knew what to do, so after some discussion, George suggested they run the play again. It was such a startling idea that the managers agreed to it. The runner went back to third base and the left fielder was given the baseball. When George gave the signal the runner took off and the outfielder uncorked a perfect throw. This time George was right on top of the play at home and called the runner out. There was no argument.

George Sosniak might not have been the greatest umpire, but he was a very talented India-ink artist. To supplement his income he'd draw beautiful color pictures on baseballs and sell them for ten dollars if the customer supplied the ball or twenty dollars if he had to steal it from the game supply. He was always pushing those baseballs. He'd throw a manager or player out of the game, then, before the man could leave, he'd try to sell him a souvenir of the argument. He was always inventing reasons to do balls. First home run in organized baseball. Fiftieth slide in the Florida State League. Third rainout of the year. Shark scare.

It was a good gimmick and it was necessary, because minor league umpires were very poorly paid. I was making five hundred dollars a month, including expense money, and was constantly calling home to tell my mother to put some of my football savings into the checking account. Another minor league umpire supplemented his salary by writing a book about his experiences in baseball. Two hours before each game he'd set up a table outside the ballpark and sell copies to the fans. Then, inevitably, sometime during the game, he'd make an outrageous call against the home team and the fans would end up throwing his own book at him. He was thrilled; he'd simply pick them up and sell them again in the next town.

In trying to come up with a means of supplementing my own salary I learned the true value of a baseball that year. A professional baseball might well be the best item of barter in the free world. Normally frugal people would trade me twenty dollars' worth of goods or services for a baseball they could buy themselves for four dollars. But the fact that it was an official professional baseball and had scuff marks to prove it had been used in an official professional baseball game (or at least been bounced on the cement floor of an official professional umpires' locker room) gave it an intangible value far greater than its actual worth. I dined on baseballs, had my car washed on baseballs, and did my laundry on baseballs. Women were not that impressed, however.

The five-month season lasted about eight years, but by the time it ended I had learned how to get into position to call a play, I had some idea where I was supposed to look before making a call, and I could say, sympathetically, "Jeez, that never would have happened in the big leagues," almost as well as McDevitt. With the help of Spike Briggs I was hired by the Double-A Eastern League for the 1965 season. I was on my way to the major leagues.

It was early in that season that I first heard the two words that were to haunt me for the rest of my career: Earl Weaver.

Earl Weaver has become one of the greatest managers in the history of baseball. When he retires, he'll go directly from the Baltimore Orioles dugout into the Hall of Fame. He is a genius at motivating ballplayers and manipulating his team on the field. While some managers are thinking ahead two or three innings, Earl is already in the middle of the next week. It's impossible not to admire him, but it's pretty hard for me to like him.

Earl Weaver is the worst enemy umpires ever had. He'll come screaming out of the dugout at the drop of the temperature. He'll scream and yell and make life miserable for everyone around him. Except for a few months at the end of the 1968 season when he went up to the Orioles to replace Hank Bauer and I stayed in Triple-A, we were together from 1965 until I retired at the end of the 1979 season. We got along slightly worse than Hugh Hefner and the Moral Majority. Eventually our relationship got so bad that Weaver's players would establish a betting pool before the game trying to guess what inning I'd throw him out. So I might dump him in the fifth and look into the Oriole dugout and Mark Belanger or Jim Palmer or Don Buford would be jumping up and down and cheering, "Fifth inning, that's me!" It finally reached the point that the American League office transferred me when my crew went into Baltimore.

It all started in June 1965, in Reading, Pennsylvania. Weaver's Elmira Pioneers came into town for a four-game series. I'd heard other umpires talk about him, but I'd never had him for a game and firmly believed I could handle him. In retrospect, I handled Big Daddy Lipscomb better, and he only tore my arm out of its socket. We got off to a bad start at the pregame meeting at home plate. He politely introduced himself. I was aggressively unimpressed. Then I told him who I was, and he seemed less impressed than I was, which immediately turned me off.

By this time I was getting very good at throwing people out of games. I'd only gotten eleven my entire first season, but by June of my second year I'd already broken my record. Two umpires usually work a game in the low minors, one calling balls and strikes and the other handling plays in the field. That first night I was out in the field and there was a close play at second base in a late inning. It was a sliding tag play and I was pretty sure I got it right, but Weaver came out of the dugout like a cannon shot. He was screaming and telling me I was a rotten umpire and I'd never last in baseball, and finally I gave him the thumb. Had I known what was to follow, I would've had George Sosniak commemorate the occasion with a painted baseball.

The second night I was behind the plate and Earl started with the very first pitch of the game. I'd call, "High, ball one," and I'd hear this squeaky voice yelling from Elmira's dugout, "Ball's not high." He'd complain on every pitch that went against him. "Where was that one?" "He didn't swing." "You missed it again!" I'd never had anyone do that to me before and it really started irritating me. Every pitch. "Bounced in the dirt." "Worst call yet." Finally, in the middle of the third inning, I walked over to his dugout and told him he couldn't continue yelling at me. He said he'd keep yelling at me as long as I was wrong. Then I asked him how loud he could yell. "Why?" he asked.

" 'Cause you're gonna be doing it from the clubhouse!" It wasn't a great exit line—but after all, it was only the minors.

I didn't want to throw him out the third night. I was already in trouble with the league office for being too quick on the trigger and I'd gotten him two nights in a row. But I couldn't help myself. I was in the field again, and again there was a close play at second. By this time Weaver had me so intimidated I probably did miss it. He came barreling out of the dugout like an overdue express train and I had him out of the game before he reached the pitcher's mound.

Now I was three for three. I did not want to make it a four-game sweep. Before the game I sat by myself and tried to relax. I told myself not to pay any attention to his antics. I was determined to remain calm and keep my temper in check.

He lasted twenty seconds. When he came up to the plate to exchange starting lineups with the other manager he looked up at me—Earl is about 5'5" and I'm 6'4"—and cracked, "How 'bout it, Luciano, you gonna be as bad tonight as you've been the first three games?"

I gave him the only possible answer. "Earl," I said, "you're never gonna find out." I got him four for four, at least tying a record, and our relationship went downhill from there.

Admittedly, many of the problems I had with Weaver, and everyone else that year, were my own fault. In 140 games I had twenty-six ejections, far too many. My problem was that I had gotten pretty good on technique, but I hadn't learned anything about politics. I was trying to run the game with the charm of a South American dictator. It took me a long time to realize that umpiring is best described as the profession of standing between two seven year olds with one ice cream cone. No matter how good an umpire you are, your entire career is going to be spent making fifty percent of all the players and managers unhappy. Every call is going to anger half the people. The key to getting away with it is learning how to deal with other people's anger and frustration, and all I knew was how to give them the thumb.

The first time a player or manager raised his voice to me he was gone. No exceptions. I believe I hold the dubious distinction of being the only umpire in minor league or major league baseball to have run Baltimore Oriole shortstop Mark Belanger out of a game. Mark Belanger! That's like throwing Bambi out of the forest. Even in 1966, when he was at Elmira, he was a pleasure to watch. He was such a beautiful fielder, as well as being a soft-spoken gentleman.

I got him good, though. I called him out on a third strike to end an inning, then walked toward the dugout to pick up a new supply of baseballs. Halfway there I felt something brush my arm. As I turned around I almost tripped over Belanger's batting helmet. He was gone. Weaver was standing on my shadow a second later explaining that the bat boy had simply been throwing the helmet into the dugout, which was undoubtedly true, but by then it was too late. After all, I was trying to run a country.

It seemed to me that I was in the center of a controversy every game, and I wasn't enjoying it at all. Big guys need to be loved, too. But as much as I tried to control it, I couldn't. The abuse I was taking was get-

ting to me, and I began to think about quitting. At least
the kids in school didn't yell at me. In July, Barney
Deary, a minor league supervisor of umpires, came to
watch me work. I was on my best behavior while he
was there and only got two players. Both times they
were arguing with my partner and I barged in to break
up the argument.

Later, Deary told me what should have been obvious. I was trying too hard to run the whole show.
"Let the other umpire handle his own problems," he
said. "I've watched you work, you've got enough of
your own." We talked for a long time and he turned me
around. "Baseball's a great game," he said, "but you're
not enjoying it at all. Just relax, have fun out there." I
took his advice and began easing up a bit. But it was a
year later that I really began having fun.

At that time I was spending my winters avoiding
blind dates set up for me by my mother by working in
the Instructional League in Florida. This league was
made up of young prospects there for extra work under
major league supervision and veteran players trying to
get into shape after an injury or extended period on the
bench. Everybody worked hard, but only one man really
cared about winning. He was a minor league manager in the Detroit organization who was trying to
impress the major leaguers. This guy was a real Weav-
er-in-training. He thought everything I did was wrong
and felt compelled to tell me about it in a shrill voice.
Normally I'd have run him quick and enjoyed a quiet
afternoon in the Florida sunshine. But I remembered
Deary's advice and tried to figure out how to calm him
down. One bright afternoon he came bursting out of
the dugout to enlighten me about something. "You
stupid $#%_#," he bellowed. "How the $#%$*@!!!

can you make such a %$#%$#%! call? You no good
. . ."

I let him blow off steam for a few seconds, then
asked in a relatively peaceful voice, "Lemme ask you,
you think your second baseman is going to make it?"

"What?" He looked out at the second baseman,
who was standing there minding his own business.
Then he looked at me strangely.

"That second baseman you got," I said, "Whaddaya think about him?"

He shrugged. "He's all right. Doesn't go to his
right too good."

"That's what I think, too. What about . . ." I mentioned another player.

"Yeah, he's gonna be a good one. He can play the
game." It took him awhile to realize I was serious, but
eventually we started going over his lineup. By the
time he returned to his dugout he'd forgotten why he'd
come out in the first place. Of course, I was feeling
great. I'd kept control of the situation without resort-
ing to the gun. That was the beginning for me. I spent
the rest of the winter season discussing players with
that manager. With other managers or players I picked
different subjects, but my intention was always to get
them talking about anything except what they wanted
to scream about. Restaurants, children, grounds keepers, what a jerk the other manager was—I'd grab anything that seemed appropriate. And worked. It worked.

In 1966 my contract was purchased by the Triple-
A International League. The AAA is one step below
the major leagues and an entire staircase above the rest
of the minor leagues. In A Ball most of the ballparks
were so old and badly lighted that the players needed
flashlights to find second base—even when I remem-

bered to turn on the lights. In Triple-A everything was
better. Rochester had a beautiful ballpark. Columbus
was terrific. Jacksonville was almost major league. Instead of driving from town to town and being reim-
bursed seven cents a mile, we flew first class.

Even I was better. Once I stopped trying to be King
Kong on the field, I was free to start managing and
coaching. I was finally learning how the game of baseball should be played, and once I figured it out I wanted
to share my knowledge with everyone. I started talking
to the players between innings and during time-outs,
then began talking to them in the field between pitches,
and finally just started talking to them whenever I had
something important to say, which turned out to be all
the time. It might have been the bottom of the ninth
inning with the winning run on second base and a full
count on the batter. He'd be digging his spikes into the
dirt, the pitcher would be glaring in, no one in the
stands would be breathing, and I'd ask the batter what
he thought of a recently opened restaurant. Instead of
driving myself crazy, I was doing it to other people. It
was good to be in the driver's seat.

I was also feeling relaxed enough to allow my
enthusiasm to show on the field. Off the field I'm
actually a very shy person, but once I stepped between
the foul lines all my inhibitions disappeared. I started
screaming my calls and leaping in the air, making an
attraction out of myself. The fans loved it. Naturally
the league officials hated it. I'd constantly be getting
small reminders from the office that the fans had not
paid their way into the ballpark to see Ron Luciano
umpire.

The way the fans responded to me made that difficult to accept. I had begun to develop a real rapport
with them. Not satisfied simply to be disturbing the
players, between innings I'd wander over to the stands

and ask the fans what they thought of a call I'd made or their opinion of a certain player. They'd yell at me; I was still an umpire, true, but it was all in fun. It gave them a special contact with the field, and made it difficult for them to get on me later in the game. Suddenly I was their official representative. I was doing exactly what they would do if they had the opportunity. Quite often someone would buy me a hot dog or a soda and I'd forget I was working and end up having to run back to my position with half a frank in my mouth and soda splashing all over me.

In the minor leagues we'd have a few thousand fans for a game rather than the large major league crowds and as I got around the league I began to recognize some of the regular fans. I'd walk out onto the field and look up into the stands and instead of seeing a faceless mass I'd see people I knew, and I'd say hello to them by name.

That made the game more fun for me, too. I'd be in Rochester and call a Red Wing player out on strikes and the fans would start screaming at me, so I'd turn around and shout, "Whaddaya screaming at me for? He's the one that struck out!"

Some of them actually became good friends. They'd pick up the umpires at the airport or even invite them home for dinner. But no matter how close we became, they never forgot their essential job as fans was to criticize the umpire. Once, when I was working in Syracuse, I made a call at first base against the Chiefs. This was the same town in which I'd been an all-American football player, and I thought the fans would remember that. Instead they really gave it to me. "Hey, don't you remember me?" I shouted between innings. "You used to cheer for me up at the university."

They didn't remember me. "Ah, go hang yourself

with a wet noodle." "Once you put on that blue suit you died." But they were laughing as they screamed at me.

After a few months of this type of behavior I really believed I had discovered a magic potion. Things were just going great. But there was one woman in Buffalo who refused to be charmed by me. She weighed about 250 pounds (so we should have had something in common) and had a voice that would shatter plastic. She would get on anybody for anything. Grounds keepers, peanut vendors, ticket sellers, she yelled at everybody, but she yelled loudest at the umpires. Finally Dick Stello, who is presently a National League umpire, decided to get even. We found out she worked as a waitress in a suburban diner, and one afternoon we went there for lunch. And we gave it to her. "You call this a hamburger!" "Water!" "My napkin's soiled!" "More water!" We were thumbed out of the place before dessert, but we'd made our point. She came to the park that night and apologized to us. She never yelled at the umpires again.

Eventually, because I did such strange things on the field, I began to attract a lot of attention. Local newspapers began writing about me and radio stations requested interviews. I loved it, and never passed up an opportunity for publicity. If the home team needed an umpire for a cow-milking contest I'd put on a pair of farm overalls. If they needed somebody to umpire the ladies' softball game, I was available. Even my so-called feud with Weaver attracted a lot of attention. He was managing Rochester that year and we weren't getting along any better than we had in a lower classification. I'd be interviewed on radio before a Red Wing game and they'd ask me how Earl and I were going to get along that night. I'd tell them, "Like every other night. We're gonna yell and scream at each other and

I'm gonna be around for nine innings. I'm not so sure
about Earl, though."

If the press didn't come to me, I wasn't adverse
about going to them. Johnny Bench was playing in
Buffalo that year and you didn't have to know too
much about baseball to recognize that he was going to
be a superstar someday. So when I was in Buffalo I'd
make sure to stay near him before the game and, sure
enough, his picture would be on the sports page the
next day and Luciano would be waving over his
shoulder.

The more publicity I got, the more confident I
became on the field. I allowed myself to react spon-
taneously to the game, applauding great plays, shaking
hands with home-run hitters, congratulating players
after a good game. Umpires weren't supposed to do
this, though—they were supposed to be heard and not
seen—and I began to hear rumors that my showboating
was hurting my chances of making the major leagues.

It hadn't taken me long to realize that Triple-A is
as much a testing ground for umpires as it is for players. Everyone in the league is either trying to get up to
the bigs for the first time, or earn their way back after a
demotion. That includes managers, coaches, even
general managers, as well as umpires and players. So
there is probably as much pressure to excel on that
level as there is in the majors. This makes it very
tough for an umpire, and a lot of them quit the game
on this level.

While I was working in the Florida State League
I'd heard about an umpire who went into the locker
room at the end of the third inning and returned to the
field dressed in civilian clothes. He piled all his equipment on top of home plate, doused it with lighter fluid,
then set it on fire. It took me till Triple-A to see how
that could happen.

My first partner, Danny McDevitt, quit while working Triple-A. He had worked the plate in Syracuse and after the game was going to fly with the club on a charter to Toledo. Coincidentally the Chiefs' pitcher that night had been McDevitt's roommate in the majors. The pitcher had had a tough night. When Danny got on the team bus for the drive to the airport, the pitcher really opened up on him, screaming, yelling, cursing.

McDevitt couldn't believe it. This was a man who had been his friend. They had shared everything. Suddenly, because of a few questionable calls, the pitcher was enraged. McDevitt had finally had enough. When the bus reached the airport he got on a different plane and flew home.

McDevitt was only one of many former major league players who try to make it back to the bigs as umpires. A few actually make it, most don't. The transition from player to umpire is only slightly less difficult than that from warden to prisoner. One of them who couldn't do it was Dale Long. Long gained fame by hitting eight home runs in eight consecutive games while playing for the Pittsburgh Pirates. He'd had a fine career and would have made an excellent umpire, but in his heart he was still a player. He'd go out to the park early and take batting practice with the teams, and during the game try to instruct the hitters. A batter would step up to the plate and Dale would say, "Remember what I showed you, keep that elbow in tight." And then if he struck out, as he was walking away Dale would yell after him, "See, didn't I tell you . . ."

Bill Kunkel was a mediocre major league pitcher who made himself a good major league umpire, but he had his problems making the separation, too. One day I asked him about a pitch that looked outside from my position at second base that he had called a strike. It might have been outside, he explained, but he had called it a strike because he knew that was exactly the spot the pitcher was trying to throw to.

Perhaps the greatest minor league umpire I've ever known was the immortal, one and only, famous Mr. Angelo Guglielmo. Gugie was only about 5'3", but what he lacked in height he more than made up for in authority. He set ejection records wherever he umpired. In 1952, his only year in the major leagues, he became the first umpire to throw Jackie Robinson out of a game.

I met him my first year in the International League. He was in his mid-fifties and was getting ready to retire. Of course, as I later found out, he was often getting ready to retire. Because he was such an institution in the league, every time he announced his retirement one of the teams would honor him with a special day. He would be so moved by this show of support that he would then decide not to retire.

Part of his charm was his willingness to say whatever was on his mind. When they honored him with a "day" in Toledo, the glass-making capital of the world, the city gave him a beautiful glass key. He held it up so everyone in the park could see, then asked over the loudspeaker if it was plastic. In another city he was given a transistor radio and complained because there were no batteries in it. Finally the players in the league got together and gave him a cash gift, with the stipulation that if he came back the next season he'd have to return it.

Among his numerous claims to fame, Gugie is the only umpire in the history of baseball to change a ball-strike call. The hitter was Syracuse's Steve Bilko, one of the greatest minor league sluggers of all time. Bilko had been playing minor league ball almost as long as Gugie had been umpiring, so they knew each other very well. He was batting with a one-ball, one-strike count and took a pitch. "Strike two!" Gugie bellowed.

Bilko stepped out of the batter's box and asked pleasantly, "Gugie, how long you been umpiring?"

Gugie looked at him suspiciously. He didn't like questions that he couldn't answer with "Get back in the box or get outta here." Finally he decided it wasn't a trick question. "Twenty-six years," he snarled. "How come you wanna know that?"

Bilko took an easy practice swing. " 'Cause I've been watching you work for fifteen of them," he said as he stepped back into the batter's box, "and in all that time that's the only pitch you've ever missed."

"TIME!" Gugie screamed, throwing both hands into the air to stop play. Then he turned around and looked up at the official scorer sitting in the press box. "That's ball two," he shouted. He stood on the side waiting until the count had been changed on the scoreboard, then moved back into position behind the catcher. Finally, when Bilko got ready to hit again, Gugie announced loudly, "Now, I'm perfect."

Things always used to happen when Gugie was working. Once I saw him reach over a railing after a game and slug a fan who had been screaming at him the entire game. When we got to the locker room I tried to explain to him that it seemed unprofessional for an umpire to punch out a spectator. He casually dismissed my complaint, saying, "It's okay, kid. That guy's an old friend of mine."

Weaver didn't get along with Gugie any better than he got along with me, which made me feel better because I knew I wasn't alone. In mid-summer 1966 my crew went into Rochester while Earl's Red Wings were in the middle of a losing streak. We knew we were going to have a rough time, because he believes he can motivate a team by stirring things up. In the third inning of the first game of the series there was a close play at third base. I was right on top of it and called the Rochester player out. Weaver was coaching third and started screaming, but I held my temper. Finally he told me that if the play had been any closer I would have had to run him, because then he really would have had something to argue about.

Between innings I repeated this to Gugie and his face lit up like a pinball machine hitting a million. "Don't worry about it, kid," he said confidently. "I'll get him." So Weaver was looking for me, Gugie was looking for Weaver, and I was looking for a place to hide. I knew the eruption couldn't be more than a few innings away.

Three, to be exact. Rochester had the bases loaded with two outs and Steve Demeter was the batter. Gugie called the first pitch a strike and Weaver came running down the third base line as if he were on the long end of a stretched rubber band. I started moving toward home plate to help Gugie, but he waved me away. Weaver was going nose-to-nose with Gugie, which he can't do with too many other umpires, so I knew it was going to be a long argument. Earl was putting on quite a show, throwing his hat, kicking dirt, waving his arms, picking up his hat and throwing it down again. The fans were loving it. Finally, Gugie accommodated Weaver. With a grand flourish he threw him out of the game. That's when Weaver really got mad.

He refused to leave the field. The fight raged for a few more minutes. Gugie threw him out of the game a second time, but Weaver still refused to leave. He'd done similar things before—once he'd lain down on the pitcher's mound and faked a heart attack. The umpire had told him that if he were alive he was out of the game. But this time he looked pretty serious. He wouldn't get off the playing field.

Ten minutes passed and they were still screaming at each other. Even the players were getting bored by this time. The left fielder had gone over to his team's bullpen to sit down. The center fielder came in to talk to the second baseman. The shortstop was sitting on second base with the baserunner. The third baseman had gone into the dugout. I kept edging toward the plate, but every time I got close enough to hear them, Gugie stopped arguing and waved me away. The third member of our crew, Don Denkinger, was smart enough to stay out of it—he was standing near the pitcher's mound among a group of players.

After another few minutes Gugie tried to get the stadium cops to haul Weaver off the field, but Earl owned the city and no cop was going to come near him. Finally Gugie decided the only way to get rid of Weaver was to start the game again. He ordered the pitcher to throw the ball and warned Weaver that every pitch was going to be called a strike until he left.

The pitcher was just as confused as everyone else, so he just stood on the pitching rubber and lobbed the ball toward the plate. Demeter realized what was going on and leaped back into the batter's box. I saw what was about to happen and started retreating. Denkinger headed for first base. Demeter smashed a line drive into left field and the ball rattled off the wall. Everybody was running in different directions. One run scored. Weaver dived into his dugout. The second runner scored. Gugie was standing behind home plate waving his arms. I had no idea what he was trying to signal. By the time the ball was retrieved three runs had scored and Demeter was perched on third base.

Weaver was sitting placidly in the runway behind the dugout with his arms crossed.

Larry Shepard, the manager of the other team, strolled out of his own dugout to discuss the situation with Gugie. He was not a happy man. Eventually he officially protested the game because Weaver had refused to leave the field. He was right, of course, but that was no grounds for a protest. He should have protested that there were not enough players on the field when play began, and then he might have been upheld.

Rochester won the game and went on a twelve-game winning streak. The protest was disallowed. Gugie announced his next retirement.

Weaver and I spent the 1967 season in Triple-A, and our relationship continued to develop. That was the year he stole second base on me, another managerial first. I made a call at second that got him so mad he ran onto the field, picked up second base, and took it with him back into the dugout. He refused to give it back to me. I asked the grounds keeper for a replacement but he told me he was all out of second bases.

"C'mon, Earl," I said. "You gotta give me back the base. We can't play baseball without the bases." That logic didn't move him, so I warned him if he didn't give it back to me I'd forfeit the game.

"Ronnie," he told me, "you'll never forfeit a game in the minors because if you do you'll never make it to the majors. If they see you can't handle games down here, they'll never bring you up."

I was livid. He had discovered my weak point. Nothing infuriated me more than hearing Earl Weaver make sense. Eventually I negotiated a loan of his second base and we finished the game.

By the end of two seasons with Weaver in the

International League I felt ready for the major leagues. The fact that I had been umpiring only four years, and no one had ever made it to the bigs in that short a span, didn't bother me. I had been eating well the past few years and had even better size and I knew what I was doing. That fall the American League purchased the contracts of Larry Barnett and Bill Kunkel, two good umpires, but overlooked me and Denkinger, who'd been working in the minors nine years. I was happy for Barnett and Kunkel but angry that I hadn't been bought. I was ready to quit and find a profession where my work would be appreciated, if I could find one. I went to the supervisor of minor league umpires, Ed Daugherty, and told him how I felt, and he asked me to reconsider. The American League was planning to expand in 1969, he said, and would be hiring some new umpires. He couldn't guarantee me that I'd be one of them, but he'd seen the reports on my work and they had been generally positive. And, he offered, if I didn't get brought up, Barney Deary was going to need an assistant and I could have that job.

I agreed to give it one more season. In fact, I really did need the additional year. I had my fundamentals down, and got along well with most of the players, but like a fine wine, I needed some more aging.

The following July, Barney Deary called me in Jacksonville. "I've got some good news and some bad news for you," he said softly. "The good news is that the American League has just bought your contract, but you can't tell anybody yet. The bad news is that you've got to wait until next year to go up." Then he asked to speak to Don.

I was beaming as I handed him the phone, so he guessed the good news. Deary told him, "I've got some good news and some bad news for you." Denkinger's chin dropped. "The good news is that Ron's contract was purchased by the American League. The bad news is so was yours!" We celebrated.

It was difficult keeping the news secret, but we managed to do so. When Weaver went up to manage the Orioles a few weeks later I had an incredible desire to tell him, but then I decided it would be a nicer surprise. Why ruin his happiness?

Knowing I was going to be in the major leagues the following season made me feel much better, and I tried to conduct myself as a major leaguer. I walked taller. I yelled louder. I wore shirts only three times before sending them to the cleaners. But I still got into too many rhubarbs.

The crowning insult of my minor league career took place in Buffalo. During my three years in the International League I'd gotten to know many people in the city, among them a young boy suffering from cerebral palsy who was confined to a wheelchair. He was a knowledgeable, loyal baseball fan and each time I got to Buffalo I'd spend time with him before the game discussing strategy and International League players.

His hero, I discovered, was Johnny Bench, and one afternoon I surprised him with a baseball personally autographed to him by Bench. He held onto that baseball with both hands, as if it were made of solid gold. Just looking at the smile on his face made me really appreciate the impact that the game of baseball had on so many people's lives, and made me feel very proud to be even a small part of it.

We had a close game that day and in a later inning I called a Buffalo player out when he tried to score the tying run on a sacrifice fly. I don't remember who the player was, but he went crazy. He was screaming at me at the top of his lungs, calling me everything horrible he could think of. His manager was pushing him out of the way so he could get at me. The coach had come down from third base and he was yelling at me. The Buffalo fans were threatening to tear up the ballpark.

Suddenly, out of the corner of my eye, something caught my attention. Dribbling slowly across the grass, came the autographed baseball.

I knew I was ready for the big leagues.

3

UP INTO
THE MAJORS
OR My Wife is Fine
and Keep Your Mouth Shut

When the American League announced the purchase of my contract many of the players and managers I'd worked with for three years in the International League told me they really thought I'd earned it. Naturally I told them I'd miss them, but somehow they'd just have to get along without me. They told me not to worry—*they* had earned it.

To my mother my promotion meant something entirely different. When I explained to her that the American League had expanded into Seattle and Kansas City and I was going up to the majors, tears welled in her eyes and she said, with deep emotion in her voice, "I'm so happy, Ronnie. Finally you'll be able to find Nina, Fonda and Mary."

Nina, Fonda and Mary were my three lost cousins. Years earlier their mother had moved the family to Seattle and they were never heard from again. Rumors reached us that one of the girls had married and the entire family had moved with her to Dallas, but it was never confirmed. My mother had been trying to find them for years. It shouldn't have been difficult—it's hard to lose a Luciano in Seattle—but they'd disappeared. My mother wasn't quite sure what an umpire did—she'd seen me work in Syracuse and couldn't understand why the fans were booing me and

cheering the players—but as long as the job sent me to
Seattle it couldn't be bad. She made me promise to
send out a search party on my first trip west.

I was so elated I would have promised to deliver a
herd of Lucianos to her front door. I was finally going
to have my career in major league sports. It wasn't
football—but I wasn't going to get hurt, either. About
the only person who might have been unhappy about
my promotion was Earl Weaver. No one could have
blamed him if he developed a healthy persecution
complex. I'm sure he thought he'd left his problem
behind. But here I was. Having me come up to the
majors so soon after he got there was something like
having the dog eat your birthday cake before you got to
blow out the candles.

I spent the entire winter preparing for my rookie
season. I watched my diet and only gained fifteen
pounds. I spent a lot of time exercising my legs and my
mouth. I had my blue suit cleaned. In spring training I
was assigned to Jim Honochick's crew, along with
Frank Umont and Bill Haller. It was a good mix of
established veterans and aggressive rookies. Honochick was the senior umpire in the league and would
undoubtedly be a good influence on me.

Even Weaver was nice to me in spring training. He
was as happy to be in the bigs as I was, and we got
along very well. Of course, that was before the season
opened.

To make my major league debut perfect, our crew
was scheduled to work the season opener in Washington, D.C. The President of the United States, Richard
Nixon, was going to attend. I wondered how good his
memory was.

I could barely sleep the night before. I got up early
and took a long walk. As the junior umpire, I was
scheduled to work third base and I was ready. I had

worked hard for five years preparing for this day. I thought I had anticipated every possible problem. I didn't think anything could go wrong.

It was as I was packing my bag to go to the ballpark that I realized I had no uniform. Somehow, somewhere, my blue umpire's suit had been lost. Honochick made an emergency call to Cleveland and Hank Soar flew in to take my place. As a senior umpire, Soar was put at first base. I was devastated. I wear a size fifty extra-long suit, and you can't buy them off the rack, so I couldn't buy a new one. I didn't know what to do. Luckily, I had my black suit with me. No one had died recently so it was still clean. I put it on and went to the ballpark.

Honochick finally relented and allowed me to work the right-field foul line. I had never worked in the outfield before but I didn't care; I was on the field that day and that was all that mattered. The fans barely noticed me—and those who did must have assumed I was simply a wayward FBI man. The game was decided on two very close calls at first base. Soar got them both right, but each of them led to an argument. After the game he told me he would never, ever work for me again.

My suit turned up the next day and in the next two games I worked my way around the bases. I got my first plate job in Cleveland. The first game behind the plate is a milestone for an umpire. It couldn't have gone any better. It was a 2–1 game and I had no controversial calls. Every strike was right down the middle, every ball was two feet outside. More important, to an umpire, the game only lasted two hours and five minutes. After some of my four-hour minor league marathons, that was almost a vacation. At the end of the game the Indians' catcher, Duke Sims, gave me the game ball, a nice baseball tradition. Hey, I thought happily, this is easy. I can do this with my eyes closed (which I was later accused of doing). I said something like that to Honochick. Jim looked at me and smiled knowingly.

Actually, because Honochick and Umont were so good, my first few weeks went smoothly. Everything about the major leagues was better than I had hoped. I didn't have to worry about anything except my job, and I was working with three men who were capable of doing it for me. I didn't even have to turn on the lights. So, because everything was going so well, I began to get cocky. I started shouting my calls with the same exuberance I'd shown in the minors. I didn't just call a runner out, I called him outoutoutoutoutoutout, maybe fifteen times. I leaped in the air to call him out. I mean, he knew he was out.

The first time that Oakland A's third baseman Sal Bando saw me leap into the air to make a call, he went into shock. He was only in his third year in the majors but he expected umpires to know their place. After watching me perform he asked a teammate how long I'd been in the league. When he was told I was a rookie he just shook his head and said nothing. That said it all.

I couldn't help myself. I was enjoying myself on the field. I was finally in the major leagues and I was excited about it. I let my enthusiasm show. At first I had been a bit reticent about talking to the players, but I got over that by the time the National Anthem ended in Washington.

I needed to talk to the players, the coaches, the managers, the grounds keepers, ball boys, anybody who would listen to me. I get lonely if there are fewer than four people in an elevator. It would have been impossible for me to stand out there for nine innings without talking to somebody. It didn't matter if they answered or not. I had long, fascinating conversations with the Twins' Tony Oliva for four years before Rod Carew told me he didn't speak English. Whatever I said, Oliva would reply, "Pretty good, Ronnie," which usually made great sense to me.

The players and managers, except Weaver, had never seen, or heard, an umpire like me. It was as if everyone was surprised that umpires were bright enough to watch the game *and* talk at the same time. Later I proved that umpires could watch, talk, and enjoy a soft drink or throw paper airplanes all at the same time. But since I didn't act like an umpire, many people did not know how to deal with me. Some of them enjoyed the way I worked, others despised it. Some of the players wouldn't talk to me; the managers had no choice.

When Rick Burleson was with the Red Sox he would get livid if I bothered him, so naturally I kept after him. Once, when he came to bat, he told me that if I said one more word, he didn't care how much bigger than him I was, he was going to pound me into the ground. Of course, I wanted to discuss his attitude with him.

On the other hand, my questions never bothered Rodney Carew. Carew is the finest pure hitter I've ever seen, and he doesn't allow anything to break his concentration. One night in Minnesota, just as the pitcher began his windup, I asked Rod how they'd been pitching him lately. As he began striding into the pitch, he said, "Curveballs on the outside but"—the pitch began breaking and he started his swing—"I'm going to left with it." Which he did.

Most players were like Carl Yastrzemski; when they were going good they didn't mind my chatter, or at least ignored it, but when they were going bad they didn't want me fooling around with them. I remember

Yaz coming to bat in a gamer situation in Boston in 1976. 33,536 Fenway Park fans were screaming at him, but he didn't hear them. Before I could say a word, he looked at me and said, "Listen, Ronnie, my kid is hitting .300, my wife is fine, I haven't heard any new jokes, I don't want to know about Polish restaurants, I'm nothing for fifteen and I want you to keep your mouth shut."

What could I say?

On the second pitch he hit a home run. As he crossed home plate he looked at me and nodded. "Okay," he said, "you can talk now."

My talking drove managers crazy, and they couldn't even hear me. But they were convinced I was bothering their players. The only one who ever did anything about it was Cleveland's Frank Robinson.

I always liked working Indian games because they were usually out of the pennant race by the end of April and there was never too much pressure on the umpires. Although Robinson and I had never gotten along, I liked a lot of his players. One night during my first trip into Cleveland in 1975 I was out at second base and their shortstop, Frank Duffy, trotted by. I'd known Duffy since he came over to the American League from the Giants and we'd always gotten along. "Hey, Frank," I said, sidling over towards him. "How's it going with Robinson?"

He lowered his head and looked at the ground, kicked a few imaginary pebbles on the infield, and said, "Don't talk to me, Ron, 'cause it's gonna cost me two hundred bucks if you do."

Obviously I had to find out what was going on, so I strolled over toward my best friend on the team, third baseman Buddy Bell. "Hey, Mr. All-Star," I shouted at him. I'd given him that nickname the first time I saw him play because it was clear he was going to be a very good player. Instead of answering, he ignored me. "What's the matter?" I asked loudly. "You don't want to talk to me?"

"I can't talk to you," he answered in a loud whisper. Then he explained that Robinson had imposed a two-hundred-dollar fine for talking to Ron Luciano.

That made games in Cleveland last longer than ever. Not only couldn't I talk to the home team, there were rarely any fans in the stands, so I was real lonely out there. It forced me to concentrate on the job.

Usually, when the players wouldn't talk to me, or had nothing interesting to say, I'd talk to the fans. In the majors, just like in the minors, I got along very well with the fans in just about every city. Between innings I'd go over to the stands and we'd discuss a particular play, or players, a trade, strategy, just general baseball talk. We had a lot in common. They thought I was terrific and I thought I was terrific.

The toughest fans in baseball are in Arlington, Texas. No contest. Winning is all that matters to them. In most other cities if an opposing player does something worthwhile he is applauded. In Texas he's lucky to get out of town. But I even managed to win them over. The hated New York Yankees were in town and I called Lou Piniella safe on a close play at first base. Now, Piniella is the only baserunner in history to have gotten thrown out at every base in one game, but on this play he was safe. The Rangers' fans really let me have it. They called me some of the most creative names I'd ever heard. I ignored them for a while, but finally couldn't take it anymore. I turned to the stands and held out my hands in a gesture of helplessness. "Listen," I yelled, "whaddaya expect me to do? I'm from New York, you expect me to call him out?"

They couldn't believe I would actually say that. They called me a cheater, among other things.

I nodded vigorously. "Of course I cheat," I agreed. "Who do you think pays me, huh? I'll tell you who. The Yankees, that's who. So what can I do?"

The following winter the Texas Ranger Fan Club gave me their Umpire of the Year Award. They thought I was the only honest umpire.

From my very first year in the majors baseball's management tried to convince me to keep my voice down. I'm sure I caused a lot of headaches for Joe Cronin, the American League president when I was hired, and his successor, Lee MacPhail. In numerous ways both men tried to teach me how an umpire should perform on the field. And I tried to explain to them that if they forced me to be quiet they would be left with a 6'4" quiet umpire. Somehow that prospect did not seem to disturb them. Deep inside, though, I really believed that MacPhail enjoyed my flamboyance and appreciated the fact that the fans were entertained by it. In all probability, deep inside Lee MacPhail thought I was nuts.

The closest I ever came to getting in real trouble because of my loquaciousness was during the 1974 World Series between Oakland and the Dodgers in Los Angeles. It was my first Series and I worked the right-field foul line for the opener. Except for my first major league game I'd never worked the foul line because it isn't covered during the regular season. I got out there and started looking around for someone to bother, and there wasn't anybody within hearing distance. I started whistling and talking to myself but that didn't work. I already knew what I was going to say. Then I noticed former Red Sox manager Eddie Kasko sitting in the field boxes not far from me, so between innings I wandered over to talk to him. It was a dull game and this helped me get through it.

After the game Johnny Johnson, Baseball Commissioner Bowie Kuhn's assistant, came into the umpires' dressing room and told me the commissioner was livid and did not want to see me talking to no one, nohow, never. "You're an umpire," Johnny reminded me, "not a social director."

I could hardly wait until the second game so I could tell Kasko about that!

I worked the left field foul line that game and spent the time between innings meeting the Dodger fans. Overall I would say they were a very clean group. Some of them had seen me on television, but most of them didn't know me and couldn't believe an umpire was actually talking to them during the game.

The commissioner couldn't believe it, either. Johnson was waiting for me at the end of the game. "I'm telling you right now," he warned, "that if you talk on the field during the next game, I will personally come down and pull you off the field. You will not talk on the field."

I could see he was angry, and serious, and I agreed to keep my mouth shut. I decided that, for that game at least, I wasn't going to talk to anyone for any reason. I liked my job and the boss is the boss.

We traveled to Oakland for the third game. Before the game NBC approached me and asked if I would wear a microphone during the game. They *wanted* me to talk. Eventually they went to the commissioner and he agreed. They told me I could talk on the field. Naturally, I couldn't think of anything to say.

I did talk too much on the field. No question about it. If I had kept quiet and concentrated on my job, I would have been a better umpire. But I wouldn't have enjoyed myself as much. When I came up I knew the rules of the game, but I really didn't know baseball. I didn't understand the subtle movements of the game, the strategy that goes into every pitch, and who better to learn it from than the players? Then I got to know them as individuals, which made it even better. I could share their victories and sympathize with their defeats. I was an umpire, but beneath my chest protector beat the heart of a fan.

The only time I ever regretted my behavior was when it interfered with my job or it got other people in trouble. First baseman Jim Spencer was with the Rangers in 1974 when he successfully pulled off the hidden-ball trick. The runner wandered off base while Spencer was holding the ball and Jim tagged him. It's a tough play to pull off and a fielder has to be lucky to manage it even once a season. Unfortunately I was in the middle of an important conversation with the first base coach at the time and missed it completely. So I managed to get the coach in trouble with his manager and Spencer infuriated. "Jeez," I told Jim later, "next time you're going to do that you've got to warn me."

The Chicago White Sox' fine center fielder Chet Lemon was another player I got into trouble with my big mouth, although he didn't know it was me at the time. We were playing in California and Lemon was on first base. A young umpire named Mike Reilly was behind the plate and I was working second. I don't remember the batter, but he had a full count on him. Lemon took off from first with the pitch, running with his head down. From my position behind second base the pitch looked off the plate. Now, in reality, I can't see home plate from second, much less call balls and strikes. However, I did not let a little thing like that stop me. "Ball four," I yelled, at just about the same time Reilly's right hand shot up and he called strike three. Lemon did not see Reilly, but he heard me. Assuming the batter had walked, forcing him to second, he stopped running and started walking.

Brian Downing, the Angels' catcher, made a perfect throw to shortstop Bert Campaneris.

I closed my eyes.

I had to call Lemon out, and he walked off the field without an argument. It was entirely my fault. I was feeling just awful. Here was a nice kid trying to play ball and I was screwing him up. I didn't know what to do about it.

At the end of the half inning, as he was trotting out to his position, he came up to me. Here it comes, I thought. "Hey, Ron," he said, "who shouted that? I know I shouldn't have listened and should've slid but . . ."

I was nodding vigorously as he told me this. "Yeah, you really should've," I agreed, but finally I knew I had to tell him the truth. "Campaneris said it," I admitted, then quickly walked away.

In a career filled with as many highlights as mine, it's extremely difficult to select the single most embarrassing moment. But the day I picked Harmon Killebrew off second base would rate very high. The Killer was one of the most feared sluggers in baseball history, but he was also one of the nicest people ever to play the game. He was one of the few players who would go out of his way to compliment umpires on a good job, even if their calls went against him. I'd call a tough strike on him and he would turn around and say approvingly, "Good call." He was the same way in the field. And he never did this to get help on close plays, as some players do. The man hit 573 major league home runs and no umpire ever swung a bat for him.

Running was the weakest part of his game, however. He was not fleet of foot. He was, in all honesty, slow. And as he got older, and a bit heavier, he got even slower. By the time he reached the end of his twenty-two-season career he was so slow I would have gladly raced him for money.

He played his last season, as a Kansas City Royal, in 1975. One night he smashed a four-hundred-foot line drive off the outfield wall. He managed to get to second base, but he was huffing and puffing by the time he got there. "Nice shot, Killer," I said enthusiastically. "Looks like you're really stroking the ball the way you used to."

Unfortunately I was standing behind second base when I spoke to him. Harmon was so polite that he turned around to face me. "What?" he asked, stepping off the base and walking a few steps toward me.

"I said you're really stroking the ball well now."

"Yeah," he agreed, "but I'm getting too old to get it around anymore."

I told him that wasn't true and he said it was true and I asked him who would know better and he started considering that, and meanwhile the pitcher tossed the ball to the shortstop, who was walking toward Harmon.

I saw it all happening in front of me and realized there was absolutely nothing I could do about it. I wanted to shout a warning to him. I wanted to call time out. Instead, I bit down on the inside of my cheeks as hard as I could and made a horrible face.

At that instant Killer must have realized what was going on. He grimaced. "Ron," he asked softly, "they're picking me off second, aren't they?"

"Yeah, Killer," I practically whispered. "I'm really sorry, but you're out."

He nodded understandingly. "I gotta tell you, I don't want to go back to the dugout. How'm I going to explain this one?"

For the first time since I'd stepped on a major league diamond, I was speechless.

"If Herzog fines me," he asked, "will you pay half?"

Finally I had something to say. "No," I said.

I didn't always talk just to find out what was on my mind; there were occasions when I felt it was necessary. In 1973 I worked home plate for the first game pitched by an eighteen-year-old Houston phenom named David Clyde. The Rangers signed him out of high school and gave him his first start two weeks later. Naturally the stadium was jammed with Texas fans anxious to see the kid make the jump from high school to the majors.

Clyde was understandably nervous and his first two pitches sailed a foot over the batter's head. His third pitch was at eye level, but I didn't hesitate. "Strike one," I bellowed. I called that a life-and-limb strike because if I had called it ball three the fans would've come over the fence. The batter told me later he knew it was a ball but didn't argue because he was afraid he might've accidentally gotten hurt when they pushed him out of the way to get to me. After the game the other umpires in my crew asked me what I was doing. "Saving your lives," I told them.

Clyde had a decent fastball but no composure at all, and it was obvious after a few pitches he shouldn't have been pitching in the major leagues. But I knew I had to do something or he wasn't going to last. So between innings I'd go out to the pitcher's mound and try to settle him down. "Don't worry about all these people," I told him. "They're here to see me work, not you."

My attempts failed; he lasted only a few innings.

Once I spent an entire ballgame standing in center field trying to talk Detroit Tigers centerfielder Mickey

Stanley out of retiring. Mickey was an absolute sweetheart. If the bases were loaded and I struck him out on a pitch that bounced in front of the plate he'd just turn around and go back to the dugout. Umpires simply can't afford to let players like that get out of the game. So I decided to talk him into playing another year.

I was working second and Al Clark was at third. At the beginning of the game I told Al what I had in mind and he agreed to cover for me. Nothing of any consequence happened during the game and I was unable to talk Mickey out of quitting. Ralph Houk was the Tigers' new manager and Stanley didn't think he'd be playing too much, and a kid named Ron LeFlore had come along. So my mission failed.

The telephone was ringing in the locker room when I walked in after the game. Dick Butler, American League Supervisor of Umpires, had heard from Detroit general manager Jim Campbell that I had umpired the entire game from center field. He wanted to know what I was doing there.

It was a fair question, requiring a good lie. "I'm testing a new theory," I explained. "You know, one of the toughest plays for an umpire is the trap play in the outfield. Sometimes you just can't tell if the fielder caught the ball on the fly or short-hopped it. I figure that with nobody on base one ump can go out there." As I began telling this to Butler, it started making a good deal of sense.

Butler was silent for a long moment. "Ron," he asked softly, "please tell me, what were you doing in center field?"

By this time I had convinced myself. "Working on my trap play," I insisted. Clark was listening to my end of the conversation and was breaking up. Butler finally realized I wasn't going to tell him the truth, and emphatically informed me that my experiment was officially a failure. He warned me to stay in my proper position from that game on. I agreed to do so.

It wasn't just my talking that got managers and league officials mad at me; I did other things, too. One of my favorite time-killers was picking up the paper airplanes fans would aim at me and sail them back into the seats. On a windy day I could make the second deck in Yankee Stadium. But during the 1972 season I was in Anaheim, California, for a three-game set between the Angels and Dick Williams's Oakland club. The A's came in carrying a five-game losing streak and I knew Williams would be ready to bust. Every close call in the game went against them. Every one. Finally, in a late inning, I called out Reggie Jackson on a bang-bang play at first. But just before the pitch, I had picked up a paper airplane and was holding it while making my call. As soon as the play ended, I faced the stands and let it fly.

Then, out of the corner of my eye, I noticed Williams stalking me. His shoulders were hunched and steam was coming out of both ears. A four-alarmer was blazing in his eyes. The man was upset.

I was standing there looking ever so dainty with my thumb and forefinger extended in midair and the tip of my tongue protruding from my lips as I tried to body-English the plane into the seats. Williams stood watching me for a full thirty seconds, letting his anger reach the boiling point. But finally he got so angry he couldn't even speak. He just shook his head in disbelief, turned around and went back into the dugout. At a banquet that winter he told me he had probably been angrier at that moment than at any other time in his entire career.

Lee MacPhail's office warned me about my behavior on several occasions, but I didn't get fined until the foul bat incident in 1972. I was at first base in Boston and a bat slipped out of the hands of the Yankees' Bobby Murcer and came spinning down the first base line toward me. I was on top of it in a flash and as soon as it twirled into foul territory I gave it one of my foulfoulfoulfoulfoul calls. The television cameras caught me and compounded my crime by showing the replay twice during the game and again on the local news. Officially I was fined two hundred dollars for "conduct unbecoming an umpire," but I never paid it and they never pressed me on it. The best thing that came out of it was that nobody argued about the call.

Again, I was just having fun on the field. I only felt bad when my fooling around hurt the quality of my work. I missed a play at second base in Anaheim, for example, because someone had made a nifty paper airplane from a page in the game program and sailed it onto the infield. I picked it up and was just about to launch it when an article about the Angels' Carny Lansford caught my eye. I was reading it when the runner on first tried to steal second and I was out of position to make the call. I called him out, figuring I had a 50-50 chance of being right. No one argued so I guess I got it right. I did find out, however, what Carny Lansford likes to do in his spare time.

A photograph of me reading the program appeared in newspapers all over the country. Unfortunately it showed my wrong side. The front. The only complaint I received, except from the league office, was from my mother, who wanted to know why I was reading at work when I never read at home.

On another occasion I was working third base in Toronto. It was a delightful November evening, the air was fresh and clean and there was a chill in the air. However, this was in the middle of May. Between innings the club supplied the umpires with hot coffee, and I was drinking a fourth cup when the batter hit a shot into the right-center-field gap. In that situation the second base umpire has to go into the outfield and the third base umpire, me, moves up to cover second base. I chugged down to second with my coffee in my right hand and got into position. The throw came in from the outfield and there was a play at second. Deftly, I switched the coffee cup to my left hand, without spilling a drop, and called the runner out. Had he been safe, a two-handed call, I would have lost my entire cup of coffee.

I did lose a full cup of soda at a play at third one night. It wasn't actually lost; it was right there on the front of George Brett's uniform.

I was always looking for ways of keeping myself occupied on the field when the game wasn't keeping me interested. Sometimes I'd try to count the entire crowd, which in September, in some cities, took me until the end of the first inning. Or I'd try to pick out the prettiest woman in the park. Or plot methods of tossing Earl Weaver out of games. Or search the sky for constellations. Sometimes I'd try to play private mind games but, as numerous players reminded me, I was playing with a handicap.

From my very first game in the major leagues I knew some people were going to object to the way I acted on the playing field. My behavior was certainly a break with established baseball tradition. But what those people never understood is that I wasn't acting. I wasn't pretending to be anything at all. Even if I had wanted to, I couldn't have planned some of the things that happened to me and my reaction to them. I was simply having a good time and I wasn't afraid to show it. I was on the field during a major league baseball game and being paid to be there! I was working with Reggie Jackson and Fred Lynn and Rod Carew and

Nolan Ryan and Jim Palmer and even Earl Weaver. I
was in a World Series and an All-Star Game. How
could any sane person resist jumping up and down? I
was in baseball. Umpiring was often a difficult, thank-
less job, but it was always a pleasure. It's those baseball people who treat the game as a job who should be
suspect. I always made it quite clear I was having a
good time.

The fans always appreciated my work. As I've
said, I was their man on the field. And after the games
I'd often end up signing autographs and talking baseball for a half hour or more. I enjoyed that part of it,
too. Until that time the only people who'd seem interested in my autograph were my bank manager and
the power company.

As might have been expected, my harshest critic
was Earl Weaver. Baseball is Earl's religion and he
thought I was being sacrilegious. He saw the ballpark
as a beautiful chapel, but when I was around there was
a problem with bats in the belfry. I think the incident
that finally convinced him I was beyond redemption
occurred in Chicago my second year in the league. I
was working the plate in the seventh inning of a close
game. Tommy John was pitching for the White Sox
and Don Buford was the Oriole batter. As John began
winding up, the ball squirted out of his hand and dribbled a few feet behind the pitcher's mound. Tommy
continued his follow-through because he didn't want
to risk straining his arm by stopping abruptly. Naturally I couldn't resist the opportunity. I threw up my right
arm. "Strike one."

The fans went crazy. Buford stepped out of the
batter's box and glared at me. "What the hell are you
doing?"

"It caught the inside corner," I said.

Ed Herrmann, the White Sox catcher, agreed with me. "It was a good pitch, Don."

Weaver was on me in an instant, screaming about my making a mockery of the game. I told him it was just a joke, he said I was just a joke, and I changed the call.

But Tommy John couldn't stop laughing. He walked Buford. Then he walked the next batter. Then he gave up a double, a single and another walk. Then he took a walk himself. But as he was leaving the field, he cocked his head a bit and looked at me. And winked.

Dick Williams was another manager who thought I was showboating, and one afternoon in Baltimore he made me pay for it. It was the only time in my eleven-year major league career that I had to change a serious call. It was in 1975. I was at third base, Bill Haller was at first, and Armando Rodriguez was behind the plate. Armando was a veteran Mexican League umpire who had been hired because the president of Mexico convinced our government that it would be a popular goodwill gesture. Armando was an excellent umpire, unfortunately he spoke no English. "Steak and potatoes" were the only words he knew, which made it difficult for players to argue with him, unless they were arguing over a menu.

California's Tommy Harper hit a long fly ball down the left-field foul 'line. From the moment it left his bat it was either a home run or foul ball. It was my call all the way. I started running down the line, trying to follow the ball, but it was very difficult. The sun was glinting off Memorial Stadium's football press boxes and eventually I lost the ball in the glare. I had no idea where it landed.

The first thing taught in umpires' school is make a

call. Right or wrong, make a call. In this situation my only option was to try to fake it. I had a fifty percent chance of being right. I looked at the Orioles' left fielder, Don Baylor, and he was looking into the seats. I listened to the Baltimore crowd. The fans were quiet, as if something terrible had happened to their team. I figured it had to be a home run.

But, since I wasn't positive, and I knew it was a close call, I decided to give it the full Luciano special. I was going to sell it so hard no one could possibly doubt I knew what I was doing. I leaped high into the air. I twirled my hand. I spun around. I shouted at the top of my lungs. I blew up a small sandstorm.

I was about seven feet off the ground when I first realized I'd made the wrong call. Don Baylor was racing toward me. The Oriole relief pitchers in the bullpen didn't even bother opening the gate. They came right over the fence at me. I turned around and Brooks Robinson, who had never argued with an umpire in his life, was breathing fire. The fans were screaming at me. I was surrounded.

Then I saw Weaver leading the rest of the team out of the dugout. There was no doubt in my mind I had made a mistake. So before Earl could say a word, I shouted, "Don't get yourself thrown out of the game, I'm gonna get help."

He was so shocked he barely screamed at me. He pushed everybody out of the way so I'd have a clear path. I walked past him toward home plate to get help. Suddenly I looked up. Grinning happily at me from behind the plate was Armando Rodriguez. "#$!'— *!&," I thought, and veered off toward Bill Haller at first base.

When I reached him, I said, "I blew it, huh?"

He shrugged. "Oh, I don't know. What's forty or

fifty feet? Hey, Ron, when you started jumping around like that, I didn't know what you were trying to do."

"I gotta change it, right?"

He agreed.

"But if I do Williams is gonna go nuts and I'm gonna have to run him out, right?"

He agreed.

I had no choice. As I walked slowly past the Angels dugout I shouted to Harper, "Foul ball, you're still up," and kept walking. I was sort of hoping I could sneak this one by Dick Williams. In fact, he was waiting for me at third. He had already started the argument by the time I got there. "First you call it fair then you call it foul and you don't know what you're doing and you're making a mockery of the game the way you jump up and down and you know you're going to have to run me 'cause I can't stand to stay here and see you doing things like that and . . ."

I really couldn't argue with him. He had a legitimate gripe. I pushed my face up close to him and screamed, "You know I'm gonna have to run you, right? So you wanna go now?"

"No, I don't wanna go now and when I do go I want you to throw me out of the game the same way you called that a fair ball. I want you to leap into the air and make funny circles with your hands and I want to hear you shouting. . . ."

"Now?"

"No, not now, I'll tell you when. Then I want you to start spinning around like a damn top and I want it all in one motion and I want you to yell so loud the people back in Oakland can hear what a rotten umpire you are. . . ."

Eventually he shouted himself out. "Now?" I asked.

"Now," he agreed.

I bent my knees slightly, then leaped as high as I could straight into the air and at the top of my jump thrust out my right arm and shouted at him as loud as possible. I hit the ground twirling and jumped again and screamed louder than before.

Williams jammed his hands into his back pockets and nodded approvingly. "That's all right," he said, and left the field.

My trademark on the playing field, the thing that attracted the most attention, was my habit of "shooting out" players. In school, umpires are taught the basics of the job—how to get into the correct position, how to make calls and how to run a ballgame—but with experience each man develops his own style. Some of them give it the short arm extended and a crisp call; others drawl it out. Me? I just pulled out my trusty index finger and let them have it.

It started accidentally in 1972. Famous Amos Otis was the victim. Amos and I had been friends since his International League days in Tidewater, Virginia. He's a complainer, but I've always enjoyed watching him play ball and liked him. But for some reason during his first years with the Kansas City Royals I couldn't do anything but call him out. I mean, every play. If he tried to steal second my hand would be in the air before the catcher released the throw. I don't know why it happened, but I had a mental block and always thought he was out. Safe or out, he was out. No way he was going to get a close call from me.

So before the 1972 season I consciously told myself I was going to change. I thought over and over, Amos Otis is safe, Amos Otis is safe. It worked better than I thought. For half a season I couldn't call him out. He'd hit a grounder to short and be walking back to the dugout and I'd call him safe. Everybody on the

Royals knew about the situation and kidded both of us about it. Even Amos was embarrassed about it. "I know you like me, Ron," he said, "but I can get on base without your help."

I had to try to reverse myself again. We went into Kansas City for a three-game series and I was determined not to help him or hinder him. I was simply going to get it right. His first time at bat he hit a routine one-hopper back to the pitcher. He was running full speed because he knew I was going to call him safe and he wanted to make it look good. I was thinking, I can't possibly call him safe on this one, I know I'm going to get it right. The pitcher tossed the ball to the first baseman and Otis was out by fifteen feet.

I was so pleased that I was finally going to get him that I pointed my index finger at him, cocked my thumb and started screaming, "I gotcha, gotcha, gotcha ..." Meanwhile the rest of the Royals are standing on the dugout steps screaming, "Shoot him, shoot him!" I had no idea what they were talking about until I realized I had my trigger finger pointing at him. And, it was loaded. So I shot him with it. Three times. And when I finished, I casually blew the smoke away from the barrel and put it back in its holster.

Then I shot the next guy. Got him by five feet. He was racing down the baseline and I was yelling, "Bang, you're out!" I mean, I was actually yelling that at the runner. Suddenly the mundane out call at first base became a lot of fun for me and the fans. It was different, it didn't hurt anyone, and made a routine moment entertaining.

My personal record is sixteen shots. Bill Haller counted them.

The only player who ever complained about it was the shortstop Freddie Patek, when he was with the Royals. He approached me before a game in which I was scheduled to work first base. "Look," he said, "I haven't had a hit in about twenty at bats, and I'm gonna be embarrassed if you shoot me out. So please give me a break this time." I agreed not to do it.

He struck out his first at bat and flied to the outfield his second, so I didn't get a chance at him. But his third time up he hit an easy ground ball to short. John Mayberry and Frank White were yelling at me from the Royal dugout, "Shoot him, shoot him!" But I had given him my word and I intended to honor it. So I pulled the pin out of a hand grenade and threw it at him.

Turned out I just wounded him. Got him in the pride. He was so upset that he refused to come out of the dugout at the start of the next inning. Bob Lemon, the Royals' manager, came out to me and said, "Ronnie, he's not going to come out onto the field unless you apologize to him for making him look bad."

Lemon was absolutely right, and I went over to the dugout and apologized to Patek.

There were several occasions when I considered trying to tone down my exuberance, but they passed quickly. Talking and joking around were my only real skills on the field. Greg Luzinski can hit home runs. Steve Carlton can throw strikes. Willie Wilson can run. I can talk. I graduated with honors from college and I know a lot of different words. For some words I even know two or more meanings. I figured that baseball had survived a hundred years, through four wars and a decade-long depression, so there wasn't too much I could do or say that was going to make much difference.

In fact, I knew for sure that I was accepted as a major league umpire when Al Kaline spoke to me. I first saw Kaline when I worked at the Tigers' Lakeland camp in the spring of 1964. By that time he was an established superstar and I stayed away from him. But as the years passed and I got more comfortable, he still kept his distance. In spring training he'd nod to acknowledge my presence and during the season he would ignore me. At first it bothered me, but then I realized he was a very shy man and I accepted it. This went on for ten years.

Finally, one evening in Detroit I was standing at second base and Kaline jogged past me on his way to right field and said, "Hiya, Ron, how's it going?"

I did a major league triple-take. I looked around to make sure I was the only Ron in hearing distance, then took off after him. After ten years of silence he'd finally spoken to me and I wanted to know why. When he reached his position he turned around and found me standing in his tracks. "Listen," I said. "You've been ignoring me for ten years. Now, suddenly, you talk to me. How come?"

The corners of his mouth curled into a warm smile. He shrugged. "I just wanted to make sure you were gonna stick around."

4

LIFE BEHIND THE PLATE

OR Language, Mr. Martin, Language...

As senior umpire of the world, Hall of Famer Bill Klem broke with tradition and assigned himself behind the plate exclusively for sixteen consecutive seasons. At one point during that period a reporter had the audacity to ask him about a controversial call. Klem looked at him incredulously, then said, "Young man, I never missed one in my heart."

Of course, on the field was an entirely different matter.

They never built any statues to the legendary Old Arbitrator—after sixteen seasons behind the plate they simply could have had him bronzed—but he certainly earned it. Plate jobs are the toughest of all assignments. An umpire working the plate has to make between 250 and 300 ball and strike calls every game, and many of those are so close a surgeon with a scalpel couldn't split the difference. He also has to keep the game moving, handle the lineup changes, argue with the pitcher, take care of the baseball supply, cover plays at home plate, argue with the catcher, check the bats and baseballs to make sure players aren't making illegal alterations, work with the official scorer, and argue with the batter.

Because I had a weight problem during my career—I couldn't wait to get to the table—I heard every possible plate joke. Once, for example, as Reggie Jackson came to bat, I cleaned off home plate for him. It was so clean he could actually see his reflection in it—which was good enough for him. So as I walked back to my position he said admiringly, "Gee, Ron, they're absolutely right, you really do clean your plate." (I said they were jokes, I said nothing about quality.)

I loved plate jobs. That's where the real action took place, and if there wasn't any, I had a knack for creating it. I got my first major league ejection while I was working the plate. Frank Howard was the victim. That's *Big* Frank Howard. *Huge* Frank Howard. At the time he was the tallest, and probably the strongest, man in the majors.

I had made it all the way to June without throwing anybody out of a game. Jim Honochick and Frank Umont were doing a fine job of protecting me—if someone came out to argue he had to get past them before he could reach me—so I was feeling pretty confident. Howard was with the Washington Senators and swung and missed the first pitch for strike one. The second pitch was up in his eyes, but I missed it. A construction worker with a sledgehammer could've split that difference. I called it strike two. Howard glared at me and started muttering, "Putting me in a $#"%$# hole, always putting me in a $#"%%$ hole, don't know their job . . ." This surprised me, because he had a well-earned reputation for rarely arguing with an umpire and for never cursing.

He swung at the third pitch and popped it up off the bat handle. The Oakland A's center fielder Rick Monday went back against the wall 395 feet away and caught it. Howard was almost at second base by the time the ball came down and as he cut across the infield to get back to his dugout he started screaming at me, "You $#'"%$, you put me in the %$#'&_%$ hole, you made me swing at that %$#'&'&' pitch. . . ."

I looked for Honochick and Umont, confident they were going to show that big galoot that even though he was the biggest and strongest man in the world he couldn't get away with yelling at me. Jim was busy searching the sky for unidentified flying objects and Frank was carefully cleaning dirt off the infield. So I wound up and gave Howard the boot. From a distance, of course. I believe that was the only time in his major league playing career that he was thrown out of a game. So no one can accuse me of lacking guts. Or having brains.

Although many fans believe an umpire's job begins when the managers bring their lineup cards to home plate to exchange them and go over the ground rules, plate jobs actually start hours before that in the locker room. Every baseball used in a major league game has been rubbed down with special mud from a special old coffee can taken from a special place in the Chesapeake Bay, Delaware. This special mud costs fifteen dollars a can and must be taken from the same secret spot. I've always thought it was interesting that those same people who pay fifteen dollars for a can of dried mud were the ones who thought I was strange.

One of the things you learn a lot about as an umpire is mud. As a former football lineman who played before the days of artificial turf, I had been on eating terms with the stuff, but it wasn't until I became an umpire that I really became a mud expert.

In the minor leagues we rubbed the shine off baseballs with free mud from the town in which we were playing. In Daytona Beach we used sand from right outside the dressing room that made the ball look as if it had jaundice. In Sarasota, balls were tinted red because we used red clay. It took two trips around any league to learn which balls were representative of what city. If the ball was red I knew I was in Sarasota.

But because every ball used in the major leagues was rubbed with Chesapeake Bay mud, it wasn't easy to know where you were—until the ball had been in play. Every major league infield is made of a different composition and balls became scuffed various colors. In Oakland, balls that bounced on the infield were red. In Minnesota they were black. In Seattle, where the turf is artificial, they were sort of a shiny gabardine.

It is in the umpires' dressing room hours before the game that baseball's most amazing magic act is performed. There, in the depths of the stadium, out of sight of home-team officials, baseballs disappear. To most fans a major league baseball is the object of a lasting affection. When a fan holds a baseball, memories of a lifetime of park fields and erupting stadiums spring to life. When a fan runs his fingers over the raised stitches, the sweet possibilities of childhood are remembered and, for a moment, relived.

For an umpire a baseball is legal tender. An autographed major league baseball is the perfect tip for the bartender, bellhop or maître d' who has everything—including a long waiting list for tables.

Once, in Oakland, we had just finished putting two dozen new baseballs into safekeeping—our travel bags—when A's owner Charlie Finley walked in. Charlie and I always got along well, and he had just stopped in to say hello. But while he was there he pleaded with us to leave his baseballs alone, claiming he was paying more for baseballs than he was for players.

Knowing him, that might well have been true.

We protested our innocence, but he didn't believe us. Pointing directly to the pile of recently emptied ball boxes, he said, "I'll bet if I looked through that pile right now I'd find a dozen empty boxes."

"A dozen!" I said, finding an opening to squeeze the truth through. "I'll guarantee you that's not true." He waved his hand in disgust and walked out.

George Sosnak was the best I ever saw at getting balls out of the park. He started his career using the outside balloon protector, but eventually switched to the inside protector because he could slip balls in underneath and no one would know.

In the minors we were given only two dozen balls before a game as opposed to the five dozen we got in the majors. Once George started a game by throwing a ball out to the pitcher. The batter fouled off the first pitch, so he threw the second ball into play. The batter fouled that one off, too, and George told the ball boy to get him some more balls. The ballboy looked in the bag and found it empty. George had gotten twenty-two balls before the game began, an all-time record.

The umpire's day on the field begins with the pregame meeting in which the managers exchange lineups and review ground rules. Some managers take this seriously, others treat it as a formality. Ralph Houk, for example, wouldn't care if the opposing manager listed Miss Piggy as his starting pitcher, while Gene Mauch would stand at home plate examining the other team's lineup as if he were trying to figure out the punch line. And if he discovered the slightest error on the card he'd try to smash the team bus through it.

Besides the original card there are three tear-off carbon copies. The distribution of these copies has always confused me. Each manager keeps his original card, plus a copy of the opposition's. That's two. The home-plate umpire gets one. That's three. Then the official scorer gets one. That's right. Sometimes during these exchanges, when everybody was grabbing cards, I'd feel like I was in the middle of the long-forgotten Marx Brothers' classic, "A Week at Home Plate."

I've always felt discussing the ground rules was a waste of time. Fences don't move. Trees don't grow in the outfield. After you've worked in a ballpark dozens of times you know all its peculiarities. Some managers agree with me. Once in Anaheim I asked the managers if they wanted to go over the ground rules. The Angels' manager, Jim Fregosi, looked at me and laughed. "What's the use," he asked. "You're just gonna make 'em up as we go along anyway."

I agreed with him. "Don't worry about it. If something unexpected comes up, I'll think of something."

"Yeah, you sure will," he said, "and it'll be a beaut, too."

A few managers will use this meeting to socialize or try to ingratiate themselves with the umpires, hoping they'll get some close calls during the game. More bad jokes are told at home plate than at a meeting of the Future Lounge Acts of America. I had one manager tell me he'd walked into a grocery store and asked the grocer what he had that was fresh. The grocer replied, "A sixteen-year-old daughter." Now, did that manager really expect to get a close call from me with a joke like that? Even Reggie Jackson is funnier.

Only twice in my career did I actually throw a manager out of the game before it started. Once I got Earl Weaver in the minor leagues. The second time I got Earl Weaver in the major leagues.

The afternoon I ejected him in the major leagues marked a personal high for me. We were playing a doubleheader in Baltimore and I got him both games. I was at first base for the first game. He came out in a late inning to argue a call and I started laughing, because I knew I was going to get him. "That's the trouble with you," he started screaming at me. "You don't take anything seriously, all you care about is throwing your arms in the air and jumping around." As he yelled that, he threw his arms in the air in an extremely poor Luciano imitation.

"You can't throw your arms in the air," I screamed right back at him. "You're not an umpire." Then I gave him the thumb.

Before the second game began he came quietly up to home plate with his lineup. Earl is one of the managers who take this exchange seriously. Earl took the Three Stooges seriously. "Now, Ron," he said calmly, "I want you to take this game seriously. I want you to call balls and strikes the way they're supposed to be called."

I grimaced and shook my head sadly. "Earl," I told him, "I don't know how to tell you this, but it doesn't matter what you think, 'cause you're not going to be here to see it!" Then I threw both my arms up in the air and gave him the heave-ho.

Naturally he was upset. He refused to hand over his lineup card. "You're not serious about this game and I'm not going to let you umpire."

"Oh, yeah?" I grabbed the lineup right out of his hand, holding out one copy to the ball boy who was supposed to take it to the official scorer. "Don't take it," Weaver snapped.

"Hey," I said to Earl, "you can't tell him that 'cause you're not here. You're out of the game." The poor ball boy didn't know what to do, but eventually I got the starting lineups to the scorer. Weaver left the field, and managed the Orioles to a victory from the runway leading from the dugout to the clubhouse.

I had a good game behind the plate. Not an argument. In the newspapers the following day Weaver was quoted as saying he was pleased with my performance, and claimed to have motivated me to take my job seriously. He was partially right—I was so glad he wasn't around I had a good time.

Billy Martin almost made an exit before the first pitch once, but that was really my fault. Billy and I are good friends now, and I've always admired his ability to inspire a team, but there was a time we didn't get along at all. Both of us have typical Italian temperaments, so we would get into arguments over things like which one of us could better control his temper.

In 1975 he was managing the Texas Rangers and I came in for a series against Boston. I was in a rotten mood. Everything had gone wrong the previous week. Every play I had was an eyelash decision and decided a ballgame. It was either a hundred degrees or pouring rain every day. All of my clothes had suddenly started shrinking, and getting tight around my stomach.

I was working first base and there was a simple bouncer to second baseman Lennie Randle. First baseman Jim Spencer stretched for Randle's throw and dragged his foot about ten inches off the base. It wasn't close enough for me to give him the call, so I called the runner safe.

Spencer knew he'd blown the play and knew the Ranger fans were going to get on him for it, so he tried to protect himself. He raced up to me and screamed in my face, "I was off the bag!"

Unfortunately I was the only person in the entire ballpark who heard him. From the stands it looked like he was arguing with me, which immediately made me look guilty. Fans do not need too much encouragement to blame things on an umpire. Umpires are available to be responsible for anything that goes wrong: a player isn't hitting, the team is losing, a fan fights with his wife, the Cuban Missile Crisis. Blame everything on the umpire. That's what he's there for.

From the angle he had in the dugout Martin could not possibly have seen that Spencer's foot was off the bag, yet as soon as Spencer started arguing he raced out to tell me I was cheating his team. I just wasn't in any mood for an argument, particularly since I had gotten the play right. So just as Billy opened his mouth I started screaming at him, "Here the $#$"&$#% you are again you $#&%#$ and you're going to tell me I got it wrong and you don't even $#%"(&$% know what the $#&%$# happened and . . ."

"But . . ."

"You no-good $#" '&$%, you're trying to get the crowd off your $"#&$ back by blaming me and I got the $#%"& right and I'm out here sweating. . . ." I started moving toward him and he backed up.

"Wait a minute." He tried to interrupt so he could start his argument, but I was on a roll and I wasn't going to shut up for anyone. Although my vocabulary has been known to include some rather colorful language, I rarely curse on the field. This time I couldn't help myself. I unloaded on Martin. I spewed a week's worth of anger and frustration at him. Then I threw *him* out of the game.

He couldn't believe it. He hadn't raised his voice. "Whaddaya throwing me out for?" he demanded. "You're the one who's been swearing."

"You're $#$'$&% right," I agreed, "and I just don't think you should have to stand here and listen to that kind of language."

"I gotcha now," Martin warned. "You can't curse at me."

He was absolutely right. Who did I think I was, to curse on the field—a manager?

He went directly into his clubhouse and called Lee MacPhail to complain that I had cursed at him. By this time MacPhail was used to getting strange phone calls about my work. Once the general manager of Seattle called to protest that I had threatened to forfeit a game unless they turned down the air conditioning in the indoor ballpark, the Kingdome. "Ronnie," Lee had patiently explained on that occasion, "you can't call a game on account of air conditioning."

I asked him if that included drafts.

But MacPhail knew I rarely cursed on the field and told that to Martin. It was a bad night for Billy. Not only had he been cursed at, he couldn't get anybody to believe him. MacPhail agreed to speak to me.

His phone call was waiting for me after the game. "Did you swear at Martin?" he asked.

I had never lied to MacPhail, but I could see this was going to be a tricky one. "What constitutes swearing?" I asked.

Lee might have been president of the American League, but that didn't mean he wasn't smart. I heard a long sigh on the other end of the telephone. "Why, Ronnie," he asked, "tell me why." But before I could respond, he thought better of it. "No," he said firmly, "don't tell me why. Please, not now. Just don't do it again."

Martin was outraged that MacPhail had doubted him. So the next evening he marched out of his dugout for the pregame meeting at home plate dressed in his uniform, wearing a windbreaker—and carrying a cassette tape recorder with the microphone pinned to his jacket.

I almost threw him out of the game right there for what rookie umpire Joe Brinkman had once termed G.P., or general principles. But even then I couldn't resist a microphone. Instead, I laughed at him. A mistake. Billy Martin does not like to be laughed at. "Why don't you call me what you called me yesterday?" he challenged.

"And what might that have been, Mr. Martin?" I asked innocently.

He told me I had cursed at him and naturally I

denied it, loudly, and directly into his microphone.

"You son of a %#$@!!$#$ . . ." Martin started.

"Language, Mr. Martin, " I cautioned, "language."

Even Billy couldn't help laughing. Later, as he was walking away after handing over his lineup, he got in the last word. "Ah," he admitted, "I don't have any tape in there anyway."

After these formalities are concluded, the umpire throws out the first ball and the game begins. At that moment of expectation, as the leadoff hitter stepped into the immaculate batter's box, as the pitcher leaned forward to take the first sign from his catcher, as the roar of the crowd swelled into a crescendo, one thought used to race through my mind: only fifty-one outs to go. Fifty-four if the home team loses. There were only two things that bothered me throughout my career—making decisions and working long games. If I hadn't had to make decisions everything about umpiring would have been wonderful, except for the long games. No umpire really cares who wins or loses, as long as they do so quickly. Umpires have to stand on their feet the entire game, in the heat, in the cold, the rain, the snow in Toronto, the air-conditioning in Seattle, and want nothing more than a fast eight-and-a-half innings. If a team can win a game in two hours, why should they take three to accomplish exactly the same end?

If General Abner Doubleday was smart enough to lay out the bases ninety feet apart, so that every play at first would be close unless Lou Piniella was running, why did he also plan it so a team's best hitters would always come up to bat in the ninth inning of a close game? When a team is losing by six runs the three worst hitters in the history of the franchise will be due up, but if the game is on the line it's always Ruth, Williams and Mays.

I did my best to prevent ties. I tried. In close games I often asked batters not to hit a home run. Most of them were accommodating, but one night in Detroit Steve Kemp belted a three-run homer to tie the game after I'd specifically asked him not to. As he crossed the plate I smacked him in the arm and said, "I asked you not to do that."

"It was an accident," he claimed, but to this day I don't believe him.

The longest game I ever worked took place during my first season in the majors. The Minnesota Twins and California Angels crawled through seventeen innings in only four and a half hours. Four and a half hours! That's nine *Gilligan's Island*s!

It might not have been the worst night of my entire life. Or, it might well have been. It was absolutely miserable. I was hot and sticky and giant mosquitoes were feasting on us. To make the situation worse, I made a close call in the eighth inning that prevented the Angels from scoring and winning the game. If I were ever going to cheat, that should have been the game.

By the eleventh inning visions of cool drinks were filling my head.

In the fourteenth I closed my eyes and imagined myself floating in a cool swimming pool. A mosquito buzzed in my ear and I slapped the side of my head so hard I heard bells for two more innings.

I could see the players dragging as the game wore on, and I was afraid they would be so tired they would be incapable of scoring. I desperately tried to inspire them. "Use a lighter bat next time up," I suggested. Or "Have you given serious thought to bunting recently?"

The game ended after midnight, or just about the time every restaurant was closing. Frank Umont and I went to the first open bar we could find to get something cool to drink. We were really dragging. The bartender recognized us and immediately asked who had won the game.

Umont could barely keep his eyes open. He somehow managed to lift one bleary eyelid and whispered hoarsely, "I don't know, but it was damn close."

When American League umpires used the air-filled balloon protectors they had a wonderful way of moving games along. As it got into the later innings, particularly in a game that was out of reach, every time a player wasted time they'd open the air valve for a second. Soon as the player heard that sssssssss he'd jump into the box and get ready to swing. He knew it was going-home time.

I was rarely superstitious about anything except long games. If I held my hands a certain way and a batter made a quick out, I'd believe it was because my hands were in that position and keep them there. If I were standing in one spot when a batter made out, I wouldn't move unless I had to. And if a baseball were good to me . . .

Fielders have loving relationships with their gloves. They treat them gently, minister to their wounds, even talk to them. Some players, like the great fielding third baseman Aurelio Rodriguez, use the same beaten-up glove throughout their entire career. Graig Nettles went into a fielding slump when his favorite glove disappeared at an All-Star Game.

Hitters have passionate affairs with their bats. Some of them believe that each bat has a limited number of hits in it and, after wringing most of them out of the bat, put it in a safe place until a key situation arises.

The only thing an umpire has is the baseball. Fielders can have their gloves and hitters can keep their bats. It's my ball. If I don't want to put it in play, there's no game. After fifteen years of umpiring I can state unequivocally that baseballs are different from one another. There are good balls and bad balls. But there are only a few great balls.

I had a chance encounter with one of the truly great balls one night in Chicago in 1976. The White Sox were playing Oakland. It started out as an ordinary game, and there was no reason to suspect something special was about to happen.

The game dragged into the sixth inning with the Sox leading 5–4. At the beginning of the inning I reached into my pocket and put a new baseball into play. It seemed no different from all the other balls at the time. But on the first pitch the batter hit a ground ball to short and was thrown out. The second hitter popped up to the infield on the first pitch to him. The third batter took a strike down the heart of the plate, then bounced back to the pitcher. Four pitches, maybe three minutes, three outs.

I was beginning to suspect I had something special there.

The bottom half of the inning went almost as quickly. Every strike was either swung at and missed or was over the middle of the plate; every ball was well out of the strike zone. The balls that were hit resulted in routine plays, so my partners in the field had no problems.

After the first two men in the bottom of the sixth were out, the third batter asked me to check the ball to make sure it was okay. Darn right it was okay. It was beautiful. That ball was getting me quick outs. Its cover could have been coming off and I wouldn't have taken it out of play.

The leadoff hitter in the top of the seventh inning fouled it straight back against the protective screen, and the ball boy caught it when it rolled down. They

have the oldest ball boys in the league in Chicago.
Actually, they're ball gentlemen. "Gimme my ball," I
shouted to him. "Gimme my ball." He glanced at the
baseball in his hand, shrugged and returned it to me. I
put it right back into play.

The hitter flied out to center field. The next batter
struck out swinging on four or five pitches. The third
batter made out. It was then I realized I was in the
presence of greatness. This was no ordinary ball, this
was the horsehide of legends.

In the bottom half of the seventh the first hitter
lined out. The second batter stepped in. Suddenly, disaster! He fouled it against the screen. I started waving
to the ball gentleman, but either he didn't notice me or
thought I was playing my usual games. He took my
ball with him back to the dugout.

I threw another ball into play, but it wasn't the
same. I needed to get my ball back. At the end of the
half inning I called the man out to the plate. "What'd
you do with my ball?" I asked.

He looked at me as if he wasn't hearing correctly.
"What?"

"My ball. The one that was fouled against the
screen. Where is it?"

"It's in the ball bag." The ball boy keeps two bags
of balls, one for new balls, the other for balls scuffed or
dirtied in play. My special ball was associating with a
bag of common baseballs.

"Get it back," I said.

At the next opportunity he brought me a scuffed-
up ball. I took one look at it and knew it wasn't my
ball. I don't know how I knew, exactly, but I knew.
"This isn't it," I told him, shaking my head. "Find it."
I didn't bother trying to describe it to him. What could
I say? It's white, it has red stitches and it's signed by
Lee MacPhail? How could I describe magic?

Between innings he returned with my ball in his hand. Instead of putting it in my ball pocket with other balls, I slipped it into my jacket pocket for safekeeping. I wanted it handy when I needed it most.

That turned out to be the bottom of the ninth inning. The score was tied and Rollie Fingers, one of the best relief pitchers in baseball, was on the mound for the A's. If the White Sox didn't score, we would play extra innings, and that meant at least another thirty minutes of standing.

It was time to go to my ball.

Fingers usually had splendid control. The year before he had walked only thirty-three men in 127 innings. With my ball he walked the leadoff hitter. The winning run was on base and I figured I at least had a shot. The next batter tried to bunt, but got under the pitch and fouled it off. Even before my ball hit the ground I had turned around and was jogging after it. The fans thought I was hustling. Sure I was, I wanted my ball. The ball boy beat me to it. "Gimme that sucker," I ordered, and he obediently handed it over.

I flipped it back to Fingers, who had no idea he was a player in a great drama. The ball was scuffed up pretty badly by this time and a pitcher with his talent could have made it do a rain dance, so he wasn't going to ask for a new ball.

The batter struck out. The runner remained at first base. Somehow I had to get him to second so he could score on a single.

Fingers threw a wild pitch with my ball. It bounced about five feet in front of home plate and skidded past catcher Gene Tenace. The runner went down to second.

The next hitter grounded out and the runner held second. The game was on the line—two outs and the winning run in scoring position. A hit would win it, an out meant extra innings. The thought of a foul ball into the stands, the death of my ball, didn't even occur to me. In extraordinary situations, the obvious is often overlooked.

On Fingers's first pitch the hitter lined a single to left-center field. The runner raced home with the winning run and the game was over. I'd never taken a ball with me from one game to the next, but I wanted this one. I wanted my ball.

But it was gone. The A's' outfielders had let it go when they realized they had no shot at the winning runner. Somebody had picked it up out there, perhaps a fan, a security guard, maybe even one of the bullpen pitchers. Maybe today it's being used by little kids on a sandlot somewhere, or it's sitting proudly on a trophy shelf. I'll never see it again. Perhaps that's the way it was meant to be.

Only umpires and some pitchers really understand baseballs. To most players, including catchers, every baseball is the same. How easily they're fooled by surface appearances. Every baseball is different. Pitchers know that. The laces might be higher than normal, or tighter, the cover may be too slick, it might even have a nick in it. Some years baseballs are different sizes than other years, no matter what the league office claims. Balls used in the 1976–77 seasons were bigger than balls used the previous year, for example.

When a pitcher asks the umpire for a new baseball, the man in blue usually inspects the old one and either tosses it out of play or slips it into his pocket, and gives the pitcher a new one. Depending on who the pitcher was, I often pretended to put the ball in my pocket, but in fact kept the same one in play. Among others, Dennis Eckersley accepted and pitched with the same ball he'd just rejected.

My second year in the minor leagues I had a pitcher reject five of the six balls I had in my pocket. When he turned down the fifth ball I walked out to the mound holding three baseballs in each hand. "I gave you five of these," I told him, "and you tossed them out. If you don't pick out the sixth one, you're outta the game." He refused to try it, but his manager came out and picked one for him. It was the wrong one—I ran both of them.

Jim Palmer was the only pitcher who consistently rejected the same baseballs. I tested him on a number of different occasions and he passed every test. He'd reject a ball and I'd put it in my pocket and give it to him again a few balls later and he'd reject it again. That is a man who knows his business. Unfortunately, he is also a man who thinks he knows my business, and has never been shy about telling me.

Hitters can also ask the umpire to look at a ball and throw it out if it's marked or scuffed. Theoretically every baseball could be rejected for some reason, so the umpire's decision usually depends on who is asking. Umpires did not like the much-traveled Alex Johnson when he was playing because he was a chronic complainer, and so they gave him nothing. If he asked me to look at a ball I'd glance at it. That ball could've been square and I wouldn't have taken it out of play. "Good ball," I'd decide, and toss it back to the pitcher. On the other hand, if Rod Carew asked me to check the ball, I didn't even glance at it. That ball was gone. If Rodney didn't like it, I didn't like it. That's one of the reasons we were such a good hitter.

Ball and strike calls cause the most arguments. A batter believes every pitch he does not swing at is a ball. A pitcher believes every pitch the batter does not swing at is a strike. World wars have been caused by less. But actually making the calls is not difficult. Once an umpire has leaned over the catcher's shoulder and made twenty or thirty thousand ball-strike calls he really knows what he's doing. He may not be doing it correctly, but at least he knows what he's doing. If the ball passes through a predetermined area at a certain height, his right arm is going to signal a strike without waiting for a judgment from his brain. If it misses that area, it's going to be a ball. Other than a ball or strike, there are no options.

Because umpires make so many ball and strike calls, they can't cheat. After countless repetitions the mind becomes so programed it's impossible not to react instinctively. I know, because I've tried.

Mickey Lolich was pitching for the Detroit Tigers and Bill Freehan was catching. Lolich was my kind of ballplayer. Overweight. He had one of the best curveballs in baseball, although it was difficult to call because it broke down so sharply. I was having a bad game behind the plate. Umpires do have bad games. Somehow that "window" through which a ball had to pass to be a strike was moving. Maybe I was calling pitches too quickly, or I was working too low or too high, or I was trying to call pitches from a slightly different angle than usual, or Freehan was blocking my vision or maybe the moon was in my eyes. Something was wrong and Lolich and his great curveball were making it even more difficult for me.

Freehan was on me the entire game. If I called a pitch a ball he'd hold his glove in the spot he'd caught it, as if to say, how could that possibly be a ball? Umpires hate being shown up like that. Then he would complain about every pitch, even the few I was getting right. So I was mad at myself for doing a poor job and I was mad at Freehan for reminding me I was doing a poor job, and I wanted to get even with somebody. Freehan in particular.

He came to bat in the sixth inning. He'd been telling me all day what a bad umpire I was, now I was going to prove it to him. Any pitch near the plate was going to be a strike. No way he was going to get anything from me. If it was within six feet of the strike zone my right arm was going to snap into the air.

The first pitch was right down the middle of the plate. A perfect pitch. He watched it slice the plate in half without taking his bat off his shoulder. I smiled. I knew I had him. "Ball one," I called.

The other team started yelling at me. They thought I was giving Freehan a break, when in fact I was actually screwing him, but doing it badly. So before the pitcher released the next pitch I made up my mind that I didn't care where it was, it was going to be a strike. It didn't even have to stay in the county.

As soon as the pitcher released the ball I had my right fist in the air and was calling it a strike. It bounced four feet in front of the plate. It was so ridiculous even Freehan didn't argue with me. I'm sure he figured anyone capable of making a call like that had enough problems already.

I gave up trying to get even after that second pitch. I realized that after spending so many years calling a certain pitch a strike and another a ball I couldn't consciously reverse it. My reactions had become instinctive and I couldn't change them.

Bill Klem might really have believed he didn't miss a pitch in his entire career; I knew I was lucky not to miss at least one an inning. But many times, when I did miss an occasional pitch or five, it wasn't really my fault. In all honesty, I have to blame it on the pitcher.

During a game an umpire gets into a groove with a pitcher. People like Catfish Hunter and Ron Guidry are always going to be around the plate, so an umpire gets into the habit of calling strikes. Even when they miss the plate, it's usually a situation pitch intended to set up the batter for the next pitch or entice him to swing at a pitch outside the strike zone that he can't hit solidly. The umpire becomes so used to calling strikes that it's difficult to call a ball. Strike one, strike two, foul ball, it's close to the plate, strike three.

Then there are pitchers like Ed Figueroa. He was all over the place. One pitch would be high, the next pitch would be in the dirt, the third pitch would be in the concession stand. He would throw three pitches outside the strike zone, then nip the corner of the plate by a quarter inch and expect the umpire to be ready to call it a strike.

The situation is exactly the same with hitters. Rod Carew is a perfect example. He'll have a three-ball, two-strike count on him and foul off six consecutive pitches. Then he'll finally let one go. Well, if he swung at six and didn't swing at that one, it's got to be ball four. The great hitters get treated that way because they've proven they know the strike zone. If Ted Williams didn't swing at a pitch, it was a ball, wherever it was.

The hitters who give the umpires the most trouble with balls and strikes are the bad-ball hitters. They'll swing at pitches over their head or on one bounce, so the umpire can't rely on them to help him. Yogi Berra was supposedly the best bad-ball hitter who ever played, but he would've had to swing at some mighty poor pitches to be better than Tony Oliva. One night in Boston I had Oliva on a full count. The payoff pitch was a low breaking ball and Red Sox catcher Russ Nixon dropped to his knees to block it. I called it ball four, but Oliva reached out and swatted it over the Green Monster, the wall in left field.

I once asked one of Oliva's Minnesota Twins teammates why Tony was such a good bad-ball hitter. The player thought about it for a moment, then decided, "Probably 'cause he doesn't speak English." I asked no more questions.

The hardest pitch for an umpire to call is the half-swing. Did he or didn't he? Only the slow-motion cameraman and every baseball fan in the world know for sure. Very often it looks as if the batter has checked, or stopped his swing, but the human eye really can't register something that happens so quickly. The slow-motion tape will show that he actually spun around twice, made a bank deposit and renewed his driver's license before drawing back his bat.

The rule states that to be a strike the batter must make an attempt to hit the ball. Until recently that was interpreted to mean that the batter had to break his wrists while swinging. Unfortunately men like Dave Kingman and Mike Schmidt can hit a ball out of the park without breaking their wrists, so that interpretation isn't sufficient.

I would always guess on the half-swing, figuring I had a fifty-fifty chance of getting it right. Most umpires refrain from calling a strike on the half-swing unless it's really obvious. Their theory is that every fielder will eventually become a hitter and will want the same break.

In 1975 the National League decided to make the umpires at first and third responsible for the call because they had the proper angle of vision. Their rule stated that the defensive team could only appeal if the umpire called a half-swing a ball. This was logical, because if he called it a strike he was obviously satisfied the batter had swung and he didn't need a second opinion. The American League immediately adopted a rule allowing either team to question both ball and strike calls. The logic of that escaped me. Eventually it was changed.

I would like to be the investment advisor to any batter who seriously believes the base umpire is going to reverse the decision of the home-plate umpire on a half-swing call. Chances of that happening are about the same as those that Earl Weaver will host a surprise birthday party for me. But batters continue to ask, and umpires continue to have their call confirmed.

One day in spring training veteran umpire Tom Gorman was behind the plate during an Orioles game and Emmett Ashford, major league baseball's first black umpire, was working first base. Emmett was just as quiet and soft-spoken as I was. He was a wonderful showman and the only umpire I've ever known capable of turning "ball" into a six-syllable word. Brooks Robinson was the batter and he started swinging at a low breaking pitch. As it bounced on the ground he changed his mind, and tried to stop his swing. Gorman's right hand shot into the air. "Strike one."

Brooks rarely argued, but this time he stepped out of the batter's box and insisted he had checked his swing. "Check with Ashford," he demanded, "check it."

Gorman sighed, and pointed to Ashford at first base. Emmett shot his right hand into the air. "There you are," Gorman said firmly to Robinson. "I hope you're satisfied. Now you've got it in black and white."

Baseball has experimented with a number of different machines in a continuing effort to find the perfect home-plate umpire. We tested an automatic umpire in spring training in Fort Lauderdale in 1970. It was a short, stubby thing that made strange sounds. Kind of reminded me of Earl Weaver. Two laser beams created a screen over home plate and could be adjusted to the strike zone of each batter. If a pitched ball went through the beam, a red light flashed on.

The machine had the soul of a pitcher. During the first test it called every pitch a strike. Thurman Munson was catching and couldn't stop laughing. "Jeez, Luciano," he yelled at me, "this machine is even blinder than you."

The inventors of the machine claimed that was an easily corrected problem. A day later they returned with the machine. "It's fine now," they said.

It did seem to be working. Its conception of the strike zone had improved, and the inventors decided to try it with a batter. The first hitter stepped into the box and, without thinking, tapped his bat on home plate. The machine called that a strike. The red light started flashing urgently.

The inventors of the machine claimed that was an easily corrected problem. Two days later they returned with the machine. "It's fine now," they said, but asked the players not to tap their bats on home plate.

It worked very well for the first two batters. Then someone took a half-swing. Lights! I was standing behind home plate checking the machine, and I thought the batter had checked his swing. "Hey, that thing's crazy," he said.

I shook my head sympathetically. "Don't tell me about it," I said. "I'm just the umpire. Tell the machine."

The inventors of the machine claimed that was an easily corrected problem. A few days later they returned. "It's fine now," they said, but asked the players not to tap their bats on home plate and warned that there might be a slight problem with half-swings.

They turned it on. Even before the batter stepped in, Munson accidentally stuck his glove in the laser beam. Red lights! As soon as Thurman realized he could trip the machine so easily, he began sticking his glove into the beam on every pitch.

The inventors . . .

We didn't see them again for a week, and when they returned they brought with them a dozen special baseballs. To prevent a bat or glove from triggering the machine, they had inserted a tiny metal chip inside these baseballs. This chip was the only thing that would influence the machine. Unfortunately the baseballs cost three hundred dollars each. I closed my eyes and tried to imagine Charlie Finley's face when the league told him the price of baseballs had inflated from four dollars to three hundred.

"It's fine now," the inventors said nervously. Batters could tap their bats on home plate and catchers could stick their gloves in the beam. There was just one word of caution. "Don't hit the ball," they pleaded. "It'll break."

That was the end of the experiment. I wasn't surprised, but I was disappointed. I was looking forward to seeing Earl Weaver trying to blow the machine's tubes.

One call with which umpires could use the help of a machine is the hit batsman. Surprisingly, it is one of the most difficult calls to make behind the plate. Once veteran umpire Ed Hurley refused to give a batter first base on a pitch that hit him so hard it broke his wrist. The call becomes a problem because the hitter will either turn into the ball as he tries to duck out of the way, shielding the umpire's view, or the ball will just barely brush him. The best thing for an umpire to do if he's not sure, besides praying, is nothing. This was a technique I was particularly good at. Sometimes the batter will simply step back into the batter's box and get ready to hit. Buddy Bell saved me once by doing this. Cleveland was playing the Yankees and a George

Medich fastball might just have nicked him, but I couldn't really tell. I could imagine Billy Martin poised on the steps of the Yankee dugout and Frank Robinson poised on the steps of the Indian dugout, just waiting until I made my call. I knew I was going to get a fight no matter what decision I made. But Bell stepped right back into the box and said, "Close one."

"Hey," I said, agreeing fully, "sure was."

Only once has a man hit by a pitch refused to take his base while I was umpiring. Don Mincher was with Oakland and there was a runner on third with less than two out. All Mincher had to do was get good wood on the ball and he had himself another run batted in. But the ball clipped his uniform shirt and I told him to take his base.

"No," he said, "it didn't hit me. It hit my bat."

"It hit you," I insisted.

"Say it hit my bat," he pleaded.

The catcher looked up at me. "What'd you call?" he asked, his way of telling me he wasn't going to argue if I let Mincher hit. Mincher struck out a lot and he'd just as soon take his chances with him as a hitter.

"Foul ball," I yelled. "Let's play."

If the batter claims he was hit by the pitch and the umpire isn't sure, he can refer to the Jones Rule. He looks for evidence of any kind that the ball and the hitter made contact. Blood, of course, is the most convincing, but short of that almost anything will suffice. In the tenth inning of the fourth game of the 1957 World Series, Milwaukee Braves pinch hitter Nippy Jones proved he had been hit by Yankee Bob Grim's pitch by showing that there was shoe polish on the baseball. The event sparked a game-winning rally, thus marking the first time in World Series history that a game had been won by neatness. Twelve years later the Mets' Cleon Jones turned the final game of the

1969 Series around by proving precisely the same way that he had been nicked by the Orioles' Dave McNally.

I had a problem with Jim Spencer on a close pitch. It either hit him in the foot or bounced in the dirt. How was I supposed to tell? So, because I was in doubt, I guessed. "It's a ball," I said firmly, as if I really knew what I was talking about.

"Check the ball, check the ball," Spencer insisted.

I looked at it, and there was not a smudge on it.

"Whaddaya talking about," I sneered, tactfully avoiding a direct answer. "C'mon, let's play ball."

Instead of getting back into the batter's box, Spencer limped into the Rangers' dugout and sat down. I saw the team trainer and some of the players huddled around him, but I couldn't see what was going on. Finally I started walking toward the dugout. Spencer hopped out—with black shoe polish covering his foot and leg from the bottom of his spikes to his knees.

I almost threw him out of the game for that. I never liked anyone being funnier on the field than I was.

Besides shoe polish on the baseball, umpires will accept a welt or blemish on the batter's body as evidence. In fact, umpires will also create evidence when necessary. There were occasions during my career when I made a mark to prevent the other team from arguing. If the catcher or manager questioned my hit-batsman call I'd grab the player by the wrist or forearm and squeeze hard with my thumb, pretending to be looking for a mark, but really creating admissible evidence. Then I'd point the blemish out, ending the argument.

That got me into difficulty one afternoon. The batter was Ted McCraw, a black first baseman then with the California Angels. I thought he was hit on the wrist by a close pitch so I pointed to first base, but

White Sox catcher Ed Herrmann protested. I didn't know for sure that McCraw had been hit, but once I made the call I had to justify it. I grabbed McCraw's arm and took a quick look. I couldn't find a mark, so I started squeezing his wrist with my thumb. I weighed nearly three hundred pounds at this time and could squeeze a wrist.

But I couldn't produce a mark.

"Lemme see the bruise," Herrmann was demanding, trying to look over my shoulder. I kept turning away from him so he couldn't see, dragging McCraw around in a little circle with me.

McCraw was grabbing my hand with his free hand, trying to pull it away. "C'mon, Ron," he was yelling, "that hurts, you're hurting me."

"I'm looking for the mark," I said, continuing to turn him around and squeezing his wrist as Herrmann tried to push his way in.

Finally, McCraw pulled away. There, on his wrist, was a welt just about the same size as my thumb. "There it is!" I pointed victoriously as I pushed McCraw toward first. "Go ahead, take your base."

"Where is it?" Herrmann demanded. "I don't see it."

McCraw started trotting toward first, shaking his wrist. "C'mon, let's go," I yelled in Herrmann's ear. "Let's play ball."

Umpires get hit behind the plate, too, but it's usually with foul balls. When a ball is fouled solidly off that steel mask, you really feel as if the Bell System has set up an office in your head. The phones ring for the next few hours.

Lou DiMuro once got hit by a bulldozer named Cliff Johnson, who was trying to score from third on a short fly ball. DiMuro was in position to make the call, but Johnson didn't slide. Instead, as he crossed the plate, he veered to the side—and crashed full force into DiMuro. It knocked Lou out cold, and kept him out for the rest of the season.

In the minor leagues I once hit a runner on the top of his head with my mask while he was trying to score from third, and I've been winged by numerous foul balls. Once in New York a disgruntled fan threw a soda bottle at me and didn't miss by too much. Almost as soon as it hit the ground the Yankees' Tommy John came running out of his dugout, a look of deep concern on his face. "You all right?"

I told him I was fine, the bottle had just missed me.

"Those fans," he said sadly. "They've got the worst aim in the world." Later he claimed the bottle had been thrown by a man who had seen me play pro football and was just trying to get even.

Perhaps the worst few minutes I've ever had behind the plate took place during the third game of the 1978 Playoffs between the Yankees and the Royals. We were at Yankee Stadium in the seventh inning of a 4–3 game, and Lou Piniella tried to score on a short sacrifice fly. As he slid across the plate his feet were up in the air and Royals' catcher Darrell Porter tagged him. Piniella had beaten the throw, but his feet did not touch the plate, so I had to call him out.

Piniella snapped. He got down on his hands and knees and started beating the ground. Chris Chambliss, who never spoke to me in anything but a whisper, started screaming at me. Graig Nettles was yelling. The fans were going crazy. If Billy Martin had still been the Yankee manager he would have come running after me and I would have thrown him out of the game. Piniella would have been out of the game, Chambliss would have been gone, Nettles would have been gone, Section 3 would have been gone, the parking lot attendants, cops on the beat, baby-sitters, I would have gotten everybody. But Martin was not the manager, Bob Lemon was, and he was a sweet, gentle, reasonable man respected by everyone in baseball.

He came out with his hands raised in the air. At first I thought he was surrendering, but he was just trying to slow me down. "Don't throw anybody out," he said quickly. "Don't lose your temper."

"ALL RIGHT," I yelled at him.

"Don't yell at me, just relax," he said calmly, and I did. The anger drained right out of me.

I could see we were going to have a civil discussion about the call, and I was going to explain that Piniella had had his feet in the air when he crossed the plate. "All right," I said as calmly as I could manage, "I'm not going to throw anybody out."

"Good," he said. "BUT HOW THE $#%$#(!!! COULD YOU BLOW A %$%#$#% CALL LIKE THAT, YOU %#$#$@¼%%?"

We really went at it, but I didn't change my decision. I was absolutely, totally, one hundred percent almost positive I'd made the right call. But, just to reinforce my own opinion, I asked Darrell Porter what he thought. We had a good rapport and I knew he would be honest with me. "Pretty close," he said, "pretty close."

Uh-oh. That was not the answer I had expected to hear. I began worrying. This was a League Championship game and my call was going to cost the Yankees the game. I was feeling awful. When the Yankees took the field in the top half of the eighth inning, Thurman Munson came out shaking his head in disbelief. "You really screwed up that time," he said as he began warming up the pitcher.

Munson and I fought a lot, but we respected each other. He was a fierce competitor and a man proud of his accomplishments, and a great clutch ballplayer. "Don't start," I warned him, " 'cause you won't finish."

"Well," he answered, throwing the ball back to the pitcher, "don't worry about it. I'm up next inning and I'll get you off the hook."

Get me off the hook? Who did he think he was talking to? Didn't he realize that he was the player and I was the umpire? I outranked him!

I admit I had mixed feelings when he came to bat in the bottom of the inning. I wanted to be off the hook, but I couldn't stand his arrogance. Just as he had predicted, he hit the 2–0 pitch into the bullpen in left-center field. It was an enormous shot, probably the longest ball he hit in his entire career. It traveled 435 feet. Unbelievable.

He crossed the plate wearing the broadest grin I'd ever seen. "You're welcome," he said as he passed me. I didn't know whether to kiss him or slug him. Instead I replied, "Lucky shot."

Probably the most dangerous play for the home plate umpire is the foul pop-up behind the plate. The first thing an umpire does when the ball is popped-up is to try and locate it, then pivot away from the ball to allow the catcher a clear path. Sometimes I didn't even look for the ball, I just watched the catcher. I figured the ball wasn't going to hit me, but the catcher might run through me.

The first thing a catcher does on a pop-play is take off his metal mask and hold it until he locates the ball. Then he flings it in the opposite direction so he won't trip over it going after the ball. He flings it hard, and far, because the wind could conceivably carry the baseball a good distance.

Some catchers, unfortunately, use this opportunity as a chance to get even with umpires. They try to hit the umpire with their mask. It always amazed me that the same catchers who could barely reach second base with their throws could whip that heavy mask with such accuracy. One catcher who didn't get along with Don Denkinger took every chance to try and hit him. Normally catchers flip it away—he was throwing it overhand. He'd throw it on foul tips.

The Tigers' Jim Price was the only man who got me, and it was accidentally. When I was young and reckless I used to try to catch the masks when they were thrown in my direction. One afternoon a batter hit a foul pop and I deftly pivoted away, looked for it, and looked down just in time to see this mask coming at me. With my great hands I got four fingers out in time—but my little finger was knocked out of joint. Price turned around to see me jumping up and down and he thought I was applauding his catch.

From that day on I used the rubber balloon protector as a shield. Catchers threw their mask at me—I'd stick up that big protector and try to deflect it right back at them.

Never got one though—those catchers are speedy little fellows.

5

PITCHERS
OR That Didn't
Sound Like a Strike

Major league pitchers are perhaps the most blessed people in the world. Not only are they born with super arms, able to throw a baseball harder and with some movement to the same location 85 to 110 times every four days, they are also born with super eyesight that enables them to see better from sixty feet six inches than an umpire can see from only three or four feet.

The relationship between pitchers and umpires is only slightly better than that between the Christians and the lions, with one difference. The lions never held grudges. For them, the battle in the ring was all in a day's meal. Pitchers, on the other hand, believe umpires exist solely to make their lives miserable. They have difficulty understanding that there is a difference between a pitch that crosses the plate between the batter's knees and uniform letters and one that is three feet over his head and a foot outside. The Cleveland Indians' great fastballer, Sudden Sam McDowell, would start complaining even before he released his pitch. "Ball?" he'd screech, then release it—"How can that be a ball?"

With the possible exception of catchers and clinical analysts, umpires understand pitchers better than anyone else in the world. Umpires see more pitchers than anyone else—including catchers—and there is no better place from which to really learn about pitching than behind the plate, because you can watch a man work an entire game—or until he loses his stuff, which usually comes first.

When Ted Williams was managing the Washington Senators he often came into the umpires' dressing room after games to talk about pitchers. Williams knew more about hitting than any man alive, but he knew who to talk to about pitching. He'd ask about specific pitches during the game—for example, was that a good pitch Mike Epstein struck out on in the third inning? We'd tell him as much as we remembered and make up the rest. He'd also ask our opinion about potential trades. I thought deals were good for baseball, so I'd always tell him to go ahead and make it. "Sure," I'd say, "he's great. Get him if you can."

"I don't know," Williams would say, shaking his head. "He was 0–22 last year with a 17.50 earned run average."

"Yeah," I'd agree, "but you know how statistics lie."

Once these conversations led to a potentially embarrassing moment. Every third word out of Williams's mouth was a swear word. These adjectives were an absolutely essential part of his baseball vocabulary. One night, in Washington, President Nixon used our locker room as his ballpark office because it was small, secure and had a separate entrance on the field right next to the President's box. They even installed a red phone in the room—and you can imagine my temptation.

After the game Nixon paused to talk baseball with us. I was my usual delightful self, being smart enough not to mention football, and was in the middle of a wonderful story about me when Williams rapped on the door.

The four umpires in the room became so quiet you could have heard a stolen baseball drop.

The Secret Service agents brought Williams into the room. I knew exactly what was coming and closed my eyes, although that did not affect my hearing. "Hey," Williams said after being introduced to the President of the United States, "How the $&#* are you?"

Nixon didn't hesitate. He looked at the four of us and said, "Oh, don't worry about that. I've met the $&#*#$ before."

Because umpires see so many pitchers, and pitches, we're the first to recognize that a pitcher is losing his edge. It took me several years, but I finally reached the point where I could tell from one pitch that the pitcher was finished. His fastball would come in at eighty-eight miles per hour rather than ninety-two, or his curveball would arc instead of dropping sharply, enabling the batter to follow it down, or his slider would just glide outside on the same plane rather than dropping. It's such a slight difference that normal human beings still wouldn't be able to touch the ball, but major league hitters will jump all over him. The hitters can't tell because they've only faced him two or three times at most. Besides, they never believe the pitcher is losing it; they think they've suddenly become better hitters.

My feelings about the pitcher suddenly getting tired depended completely on the situation. I was always rooting for a fast game. If the pitcher's team was already behind, I'd figure, ah, that's too bad, enjoy your shower. But if his team was ahead by one or two runs, I knew I was in serious trouble.

The Bird Fidrych was a perfect example of a pitcher who lacked the stamina, or experience, to pace himself through nine innings. He'd be fabulous for seven innings, then lose it. First his fastball was gone, then his curveball was gone, then he was gone.

A pitcher loses his concentration when he's tired. When a pitcher is throwing well he should release the ball from the same spot with the same arm speed in the ninth inning as he did in the first. But if he gets too tired he starts dropping his arm an inch, just enough to make the ball go over the center of the plate rather than the outside corner.

A few pitchers can take a deep breath and regain their stuff. They'll struggle for a few innings and if they're lucky enough to get away with it, then they'll come back refreshed. The Royals' Larry Gura is like that. He'll be sailing along, then start to lose it, survive on junk pitches for two innings, then finish strong. It's his ability to get through those two innings when he doesn't have his best stuff that has made him a major league winner.

During my career I saw every possible pitch: curveball, slider, knuckleball, hesitation pitch, palmball, greaseball, spitball, cut ball, change-up, forkball, sinker, screwball, tobacco ball and nothing ball. But it all begins and ends with the fastball. A pitcher can win ballgames with a good fastball and guts, but it's difficult to win with every other pitch if you don't have a fastball.

Any discussion of the fastball has to begin with Nolan Ryan, with Goose Gossage in relief. Those two, and perhaps J.R. Richard of the Astros before his illness, are in a faster league than everybody else.

When Ryan was throwing hard he was so fast he was absolutely unhittable. I'd always have fun behind the plate with him—when I wasn't terrified I was going to get hit. He'd throw his hundred-mile-an-hour fastball and I'd call, "Ball. Sounded low." The batter would nod and agree, "Yeah, that did sound low," although once when I called a strike on Mickey Rivers he stepped out of the batter's box and said, "You're crazy. Anyone could hear that was outside."

In the very first inning of one Ryan game the other team's first batter stepped in and got ready to hit. Ryan was fiddling around on the mound and finally got ready to pitch. As he was taking the sign from the catcher I called, "Strike one." The batter stepped out and looked at me as if I was crazy. "Hey," I said seriously, "he's *really* quick today."

Ryan was also a complainer and most umpires didn't like him. The first thing he did after setting a major league record by striking out nineteen batters was complain that he would've done better if the umpire hadn't been squeezing the strike zone on him. Nineteen strikeouts and he criticized the umpire! That's as unnecessary as a Rockefeller using coupons.

Ryan was the first man I ever saw capable of throwing an exploding fastball. Although we knew he was supposedly the fastest gun in the National League, I didn't hear him pitch until the Mets traded him to the California Angels in 1972. It wasn't until August that I had the plate with him on the mound. I was immediately impressed, but not overwhelmed—not until the fourth inning. In that inning he went into his fluid windup, reared back, and fired. Until the pitch reached home plate it looked like a very good, but normal, rising fastball. Then, suddenly, it exploded! A million specks of shiny white cover blinded me. I closed my eyes to protect myself. I waited for the roar of the crowd.

Nobody else noticed it.

I blinked, tried to shake the flash out of my eyes, and called it a strike. I didn't mention the fact that it had exploded. What could I have possibly said? Did you happen to notice that baseball explode? I may be dumb, but I'm not stupid. Jeff Torborg, the Angels' catcher, tossed the ball back to Ryan and the game continued.

Must have been my imagination, I thought, and put it out of my mind. But a few innings later, Bam!, the same thing happened. The baseball actually exploded. That's when I began to worry that there was something wrong with my eyesight. An umpire who sees exploding baseballs is about as useful as a claustrophobic astronaut.

After the game I went to the Angels' trainer, Freddie Frederico, and told him I was having trouble with my eyes. "Yeah," he said, "I've heard that about you."

"I'm serious," I told him. I tried to explain my problem to him and he listened gravely.

"Tell me, Ronnie," he asked. "You ever give any thought to another type of work?"

After that I didn't tell anyone else, not even another umpire. It didn't happen again, but I was still worried about it. I thought it might be a symptom of something serious. Brain tumor. Water on the knee. Overdrawn checking account. So when I was in New York City I made an appointment with a noted optometrist. For a minute I thought about making the appointment under an assumed name so no one would hear about it, but then I decided that was ridiculous. Besides, everyone would know I wasn't Cary Grant.

The doctor examined my eyes thoroughly, then explained that Ryan's exploding fastball was simply an optical illusion. Normally, when a pitcher releases the ball, it appears to be the size of a golf ball, but as it comes toward the plate it grows into a regular-sized baseball. A number of times each game Ryan threw the ball with such velocity that my eyes simply couldn't adjust fast enough, so it remained golf-ball size until it got to the plate, then popped, or exploded, into a full-sized baseball. That explained my problem. "So my eyes are okay?" I asked the doctor.

"For an umpire," he said noncommittally.

When Ryan has his sharp-breaking curveball to compliment his fastball, he is as close to unhittable as any pitcher who has ever lived. In Detroit, in 1973, he pitched the finest game I've ever umpired—my only no-hitter. The first pitch he threw that day was a sharp curve that broke down as if it had fallen off the edge of a cliff and bounced off catcher Art Kusnyer's shin guard. Uh oh, I thought, if that was his curveball, we're in trouble tonight.

He was so good that game that I couldn't have hit him even in my fantasies—and in my fantasies I'm a pretty good hitter. I'd call one of the Tiger batters out on strikes and he would turn around and say, "Thanks, Ron." Norm Cash came up to bat in the seventh inning carrying one of the great big balloon bats sold at the concession stand. "I can't hit him with a real bat," he told me, "so you might as well let me use this."

Another Tiger hitter complained loudly, as he walked away from the plate after being called out on strikes, "Why can't he just throw the damn spitball like everybody else?"

Going into the ninth inning I was rooting for him—but I was really rooting for myself. I didn't want any close calls. There's nothing worse for an umpire than to ruin a pitcher's no-hitter with a bad call. I know, because I've almost done it twice.

The first time was in Chicago. Stan Bahnsen was on the mound for the White Sox and hadn't given up a hit in five and two-thirds innings. I was working first base. A batter hit a ground ball deep into the shortstop hole and Bucky Dent made a great play to even reach the ball, but I couldn't believe he could throw him out. The play at first was close, but I called the runner safe.

The moment I made the signal I wanted to crawl under the base and hide. I had made the worst mistake possible: I had anticipated the play. The runner was out and I knew it, but I had just told fifteen thousand fans he was safe and I wasn't going to change my call. At the end of the inning I walked over to Haller looking for support. "Close one, wasn't it?"

"Nah," he said, shaking his head, "wasn't that close. You just blew it."

Bahnsen retired the side in the seventh and eighth innings, and went into the ninth with a one-hitter. My hit. I was reading the newspaper headlines in my mind: Umpire Robs Pitcher! Bahnsen saved me, though. He gave up some hits and three runs.

A similar thing happened to me with Bert Blyleven on the mound. This time I was behind the plate and I was having one of my really bad days. I was calling good pitches balls and making him throw extra pitches, but I couldn't help it. In the sixth or seventh he threw a gorgeous two-strike curveball, a perfect pitch, and I called it a ball. My immediate thought was that I had cost him a strikeout and the batter was going to take advantage of my mistake by getting the first and only hit of the game off Blyleven, and that I would have to live with the fact that I had cost him his no-hitter. But then I realized I was being unduly pessimistic, that there was no reason to be paranoid, that Blyleven was probably going to strike him out on the next pitch anyway. I felt much better.

The batter lined the next pitch to right field for the first hit of the game.

Blyleven went into the ninth with a one-hitter, the Luciano single, but, fortunately for my self-esteem, gave up two more hits and two unearned runs in that inning. I felt as if I had been given a reprieve.

Few major leaguers can throw a fastball like Ryan

or a curveball like Blyleven, but what they can do is put their pitches where they want them to go. There are a lot of minor league pitchers with major league fastballs and little league control. Even Ryan can't win when he doesn't get the ball over the plate.

Catfish Hunter had the finest control of any pitcher I've ever seen. He was so good he could pick the sprinkles off an ice cream cone from the pitcher's mound. On his first pitch he'd throw the ball over the outside black edge of the plate. If the umpire called it a strike he'd throw the next pitch another inch outside. If he got that one, he'd go out another five-eighths of an inch, always moving just a hair further outside until the umpire was leaning into the dugout and still calling them strikes. But as soon as the umpire called a ball, he'd move right back to the black.

Of course, he had a tendency to get lazy with his fastball on occasion and gave up some majestic home runs. Mammoth shots. Launchings that would have made a space-project director happy. And he didn't mind. Catfish was one of the few pitchers I've known who actually admired the long-distance shots hit off his pitches. Once, after a game, I mentioned to him that a home run he'd given up was one of the longest I'd ever seen.

He laughed disdainfully. "If you think that was a good one," he said, "you should've seen the shot Rice hit off me in Boston. Brought rain."

Catfish had such confidence in his ability to place the ball where he wanted to that he would position his fielders before the pitch, then induce the batter to hit the ball right at them. Sometimes. I remember one night in Yankee Stadium he moved the Yankees' left fielder, Roy White, about seven steps closer to the foul line. Then, after thinking about it, he moved him three steps back toward center.

Unfortunately the batter hit a tremendous home run—but it did go directly over Roy White's head.

Besides control, the main difference between major and minor league pitchers is the movement of the pitch. In eleven years behind the plate I never saw a pitch reach the catcher that didn't sail or drop or rise or sing a few bars of a popular aria to confuse the batter. The thing that has made Jim Palmer a Hall of Fame pitcher is the movement on his pitches. Sometimes his ball moved so much I'd swear it had to be a Wiffle Ball.

Palmer throws what I called a positive fastball. Every batter was positive he could hit it. But as soon as he started his swing that ball would jump, or dive, or zip outside. He was one of those pitchers against whom a batter would go hitless in four at bats and think they'd had a good game.

Palmer made his ball move naturally, but there are means to do it unnaturally. Which brings us to the subject of the spitball. There are certain truths that exist in the world we live in: Never use an accountant who drives a larger car than you do. Never take a waiter's suggestion after 10:00 P.M. Never go to a bald barber. And never believe anyone who tells you pitchers don't throw the spitball. Ball boys throw the spitball. Ushers throw it. In father-and-son games I've umpired I've had six-year-olds throw the spitball. I've seen so many spitballs thrown that I've wondered if baseball should replace umpires with weathermen.

Or carpenters. *Spitball* has become the generic term for any kind of doctored baseball. A deformity of any kind on the smooth surface of a baseball's cover will cause it to do strange, unpredictable things. If a weight is added to one side of a baseball and it is rolled along the ground, it'll clunk heavily to that side on each rotation. A doctored ball does precisely the same thing as it moves through the air. A cut or slice or dab of saliva or sweat or tobacco will create a resistance, and that ball will dance to some strange music.

I saw my first spitball in the Tigers' Lakeland camp in 1967. Steve Hamilton was pitching and he threw a pitch that started out as an ordinary fastball but instead of rising, as I anticipated, it fell straight down as if it had splattered against a brick wall. My jaw dropped open. "What was that thing?" I asked him later.

Hamilton put a fatherly hand on my shoulder. "Son," he said, "that there was one of the most beautiful spitballs you are ever likely to see."

It was certainly not the last.

If baseballs could talk, the first thing most of them would say is "ouch!" Pitchers have more means of cutting up baseballs than a hospitalful of diabolical surgeons. In fact, about the only thing they don't put on the ball is spit. Instead they sweat on it, rub every type of substance imaginable on it, cut it with a tiny piece of emery board or sandpaper or even a straight pin or thumbtack. It's been joked that even Whitey Ford used to carry an entire set of carving tools in his back pocket, and was so slick he could put his initials on a baseball without being caught.

Tommy John has often been accused of cutting balls, although he denies it with a smile. Asked by a New York sportswriter how he doctored baseballs, he replied, "Sandpaper, razors, coke bottle caps, the eyelets of my glove . . . The truth is that Steve Arlin, who used to pitch for San Diego and is now a dentist, made me a phony crown that's really a file."

Fashion has robbed the modern ballplayer of one of the historically popular methods. Pitchers and catchers used to sharpen the tongues of their belt buckles then drag the ball across them. But the double-knit uniforms worn today don't require belts, forcing pitchers to come up with new methods of cutting the ball. They have.

Rick Honeycutt, while with Seattle in 1980, was caught with a thumbtack sticking through a flesh-colored Band-Aid and was suspended for ten days for lack of creativity. The irony of the situation is that Bill Kunkel caught him, and allegedly Kunkel himself used to cheat. And everyone knows there's nothing worse than a reformed spitballer.

Very few pitchers actually use the spitball as their main pitch. More often it's a situation pitch, used to get out of difficult predicaments. For pitchers like Gaylord Perry and Don Sutton, the threat that they might throw it is as important as the actual pitch. Hitters go up to the plate looking for it, and are just not ready for the good fastball or slider. In fact, short of a national advertising campaign, Perry has done everything possible to convince people he throws, it, and then he publicly denies it. That's just something else he throws well.

Baseball has done just about everything possible to make pitchers stop doctoring the ball except enforce the rule against it. They've sent out some pretty strong memos. I don't know why organized baseball is against it. At first I thought it was because the concept of spitting on a baseball was considered dirty, but then a tube of Vaseline was found in Gaylord's jacket and what could be cleaner than that?

More likely, baseball is afraid of serious injury because it is a hard pitch to control.

Umpires are supposed to prevent pitchers from doctoring baseballs and eject them from the game if they're caught with a controlled substance or means to cut and scuff the ball in their hands, under their uniform or glued to the back of their baseball gloves. But it's a very difficult rule to enforce. The moment an umpire approaches the pitcher to warn him, the pitcher's manager and attorney are out there arguing. Most umpires just try to ignore the problem.

If I were behind the plate and the pitcher threw a good spitter, I'd make my call and mumble something like, "Hey, he's really got that sinker working today." I was always in enough trouble without starting something else.

If an opposing manager complained to me, I'd tell the catcher or the pitcher, "Gee, it looks like we've got another supply of defective baseballs because they all seem to be cut. I sure hope no more are like that." That usually eliminated the spitball for the rest of the game.

But if it persisted, and the manager or hitters kept complaining, I was supposed to go out to the mound and frisk the pitcher. Let's really be honest. Who wants to touch Gaylord Perry's sweaty body? Not me. I'd go out there and touch him gently and he'd start giggling as if I were tickling him. Or as soon as I got close enough he'd look at me seriously and say, "Now whatever you do, Ronnie, don't look on my *left shoulder*. Remember, my *left shoulder*." Naturally I never caught him. Wouldn't shake hands with him because I don't like to get my hands full of grease, but I never caught him. If the league wanted a detective out there they should've hired Dick Tracy.

Only once have I gotten in trouble with the spitball. In the minor leagues a manager asked me to check the baseball to make sure it wasn't loaded. Well, it was. I knew it, he knew it, even Nina, Fonda and Mary probably knew it, but I also knew I wasn't going to do anything about it. I called for the baseball. Instead of tossing it to the catcher and letting him rub it off before he handed it to me, the pitcher rolled it along the ground like a bowling ball. There was a spot on it, but I ignored it, then rolled it right back to him.

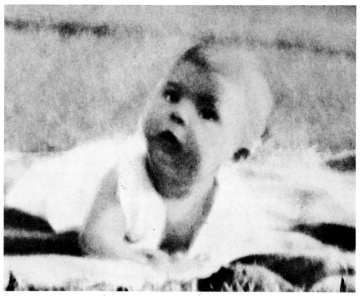

Great umpires are born, not made. Here's an early testimony to my love of being on the field...

...and here I'm seen demonstrating to my sister the alert pose and critical expression every umpire must master.

I had the 'safe' call down as early as 1959, at Syracuse University; but it was learning to wear protective pads that would serve me most in later life. SYRACUSE UNIVERSITY SPORTS INFORMATION OFFICE

Al Somers Umpires School, Class of 1965. I'm at the left of the front row in this photograph straight out of an Earl Weaver nightmare.

I chose to wear this stylish outfit from the House of Steinbrenner when my own equipment did not arrive by game time. The clothes fit perfectly; unfortunately, my body is rumpled. WIDE WORLD PHOTOS

The key to being a good umpire is timing and getting on top of the play. Here are two plays at second base where Bucky Dent has missed the tag.

Although I've often joked about my ability as an umpire—in fact, many people have joked about it—a 1974 polling of the Major League Players Association revealed that the players felt there were only two "excellent" umpires in the American League—and I was one of them.

The key to being a funny umpire is timing and exaggeration. Here I do a bird-dog imitation on a balk call against Tommy John which sent Amos Otis to second base. WIDE WORLD PHOTOS

And in this picture you can see I wasn't about to let Mickey Rivers miss home plate after tagging up on a Thurman Munson fly ball. The score had been tied in the bottom of the ninth inning and I was getting very hungry. WIDE WORLD PHOTOS

The follow-through is one of those baseball "fundamentals."
So I had fun following through. By the time I finished calling
Lou Piniella out at first on this play, the players had left the
field and the season had ended. . WIDE WORLD PHOTOS

Nothing better illustrates the real relationship between players and umpires than this picture from the 1974 World Series. Steve Yeager of the Dodgers, having assumed the classic pleading position, is about to stomp on my foot.

FRED KAPLAN/SPORTS ILLUSTRATED

After I established myself as one of baseball's most eloquent debaters, players, managers, and coaches often would wait in line to test their rhetorical skills against mine. Here, I rebut Cleveland manager Frank Robinson's interesting hypothesis while his coach, Tom McCraw, patiently awaits his turn. UPI PHOTO

Always eager to help young talent, I taped this argument with Mike Rojas, Barry Otis and Mickey Fitzmorris during a Father-Son game in Kansas City for later analysis. The immediate result of the argument was the same as it is for their dads: they lost.

Sometimes, though, they didn't wait in line. Gary Allenson, the Red Sox catcher, has already launched into his opening remarks without waiting for Bobby Murcer to collect his thoughts. I excoriated Mr. Allenson for his rudeness and terminated the debate, enabling Mr. Jackson (44) to take his turn at bat. WIDE WORLD PHOTOS

Of course, debating skill inside the ballpark is one thing, getting out of the ballpark another. Here I am during a spring training session devoted to sharpening one of the most important skills an umpire can master: the quick-exit leap. GRAHAM BEZANT/TORONTO STAR

I served two full terms as President of the Association of Major League Umpires, elected for my ability to remain calm and composed under duress. Here I lead our picket line outside Yankee Stadium during the 1979 strike through a chorus of "Look for the Union Label."

For twelve years I roamed the infields of the American League armed only with my trusty gun-hand. I transformed the 'out' call into a higher art form. Never satisfied to call a player "out!" when I could call him "outoutoutoutout!!!!!" the bang-bang play now had a new dimension. Bill Haller, my fellow umpire, tells me my record is a 16-shot out.

And for twelve years I worked hard to bring an older art form to the ballpark—ballet. Here I am seen in a performance of my very own La Ballet de l'Umpire *late in my career at the famed Stadium Yankeé.* LARRY C. MORRIS/NYT PICTURES

A face made for radio.

Here are my long-lost cousins Nina, Fonda, and Mary. If you see them, please write. They probably will not be wearing these bathing suits, however.

His manager came screaming out of the dugout that I was trying to show up his pitcher, thus earning a brief vacation. Then the pitcher started yelling and he went, too, proving you could throw the spitter when I was behind the plate, but you couldn't roll it.

Baseball outlawed the spitter in 1920, and umpires and pitchers have been playing out the charade since then. Supposedly Hall of Fame umpire Tom Connolly thought the great Lefty Gomez was throwing it and stormed out to the mound to find the evidence. Gomez was shocked. "I'm surprised at you," he supposedly said. "How can you accuse me of such a terrible thing? To imagine that a man with my talents would stoop to such a level. I'm embarrassed and hurt."

It was such a fine performance even Connolly began to believe him, and turned around to go back to the plate. As he did, Lefty shouted after him, "But jeez, Tom, wasn't that last one a honey?"

Then there was the sweltering afternoon the nameless umpire marched out to the mound and told the pitcher that what he was doing was illegal. The pitcher looked at him innocently and said, "What's illegal? Sweating?"

If baseball really wanted to stop it, they would give umpires the power to immediately throw out of the game any pitcher who appeared to be throwing it, guarantee their legal fees for the lawsuit that would undoubtedly follow, and make all pitchers step through a metal detector on their way to the mound. Then they could send out a whole new round of memos.

Personally I never minded the spitball. The pitch that did bother me was the knuckleball. Now, that's a pitch that should be made illegal. When I first came up to the major leagues Hoyt Wilhelm was still an active pitcher. Of course, he was forty-five years old then and had only four years left, but even then he threw like a man not a day over seventy. I hated to see him come in to relieve. It takes four or five years before an umpire learns how to call a knuckleball and I didn't have any idea what I was doing. I'd tried to follow it in, but that was impossible. It would go up, down, inside, up again, down, stop for a sandwich, up, down, then zip across the plate. "Strike," I'd call and immediately doubt myself. I always got arguments when he was on the mound and I couldn't understand that. Catchers used an oversized glove and still couldn't catch it, and batters couldn't hit it. How did they expect me to call it?

But by the time Wilber Wood reached his prime with the White Sox, I'd become a much better knuckleball umpire. When I made a call I *knew* I might be right. Actually, I liked to see Wilber on the mound because he made the game move right along. Everybody knew he was going to throw the knuckleball on every pitch, so there were no long pauses between pitches to plan strategy. And batters thought they could hit him because the knuckleball floated in so gently, so they would slash away at it like woodsmen going after a fly with an axe.

One of my fondest memories in baseball was being behind the plate the afternoon Wilbur Wood shook off the catcher's signal. Even the catcher started laughing. "We don't have any other signals," he told me.

The one pitch that almost every major leaguer has to throw is the purpose pitch. It's an inside fastball, high and tight, intended to push the batter away from home plate. To brush him off the plate. Its purpose is to remind the batter that a pitched baseball is a weapon, and if he digs in too close to the plate he's risking injury. Carlton Fisk explained it perfectly. "A pitcher can't let the batter have the entire plate," he said. "He has to make the batter aware that the outside corner belongs to the man with the baseball. The pitcher has to move the batter off the plate with an inside pitch just to prevent him from getting a good swing at the outside pitch."

The brushback is a legitimate part of the game. It's the beanball I detest. In my football career I saw a lot of blood, much of it my own. It didn't bother me. I saw bones snapped so badly they actually lifted up thigh pads. That didn't bother me. I was working second base the day Bobby Valentine smashed into an outfield fence and fractured his leg so badly the bone was sticking through his pants and I thought he'd never walk again. But the worst thing I've ever seen was Paul Blair getting hit in the head with a baseball.

Ken Tatum was pitching for the Angels and Blair was the Orioles' star center fielder. I was behind the plate. Tatum was an overpowering fastballer with erratic control, and Blair was crowding the plate. I don't believe Tatum tried to hit him, but his fastball got away and sailed toward Blair's head.

It happened so quickly it was impossible to do anything about it except watch helplessly. There wasn't even time to shout a warning. But every fraction of that second is frozen in my memory. Blair was wearing a metal helmet without an earflap and the ball hit him solidly just below the helmet. It made a "splat" sound, like someone slapping jello. It was the worst sound I've ever heard. He went down hard. Blood started trickling out of his nose and mouth and ears into the dirt. I thought he was dead.

Freddy Frederico got to him quickly and handled the situation perfectly. He kept everyone away and took emergency measures. I wasn't any help at all—for the first and only time in my life I got sick on a playing field. Blair was rushed to the hospital. Tatum was never the same pitcher after that. Blair was never the same hitter. And I was never the same umpire—after seeing Blair lying unconscious in the dirt I couldn't tolerate pitchers trying to hit a batter in the head.

One of the many things I've always respected about Weaver is that he will not allow his pitchers to throw at a batter. Umpires never have to warn Oriole pitchers about beanballs; Weaver's done it for them. I don't know if he instituted that rule after Blair was hit or has always felt that way, but the long list of twenty-game winners and Cy Young winners the Orioles have had is proof pitchers can win without the beanball.

Anyone who saw Blair get hit would agree with me. I've stopped batters from going out to the mound after being thrown at because that was my job, but I did it without enthusiasm, and on a few occasions I might have moved a little slowly. If a pitcher can go headhunting, I don't see anything wrong with the batter retaliating.

My strong feelings about this almost caused me to be fired in 1974. The problem started before a Brewer-Texas Ranger doubleheader in Milwaukee. The night before, the Brewers' eighteen-year-old rookie shortstop Robin Yount had gotten three or four hits to beat Billy Martin's Rangers. At the home-plate meeting before the first game Martin told Del Crandall, Milwaukee's manager, that Yount was going to be knocked down every time he came to bat. We all thought he was kidding. Billy once broke pitcher Jim Brewer's cheekbone with a single punch for throwing at him, so we all chuckled and shook our heads and thought, That's Billy, some character.

Yount led off the bottom half of the first inning. The first pitch to him was high, but definitely not a knockdown. He grounded out on the next pitch. The Brewers scored a bunch in that inning and he came to bat again in the second. This time the first pitch was right at his head and he went down. I didn't wait for a war to start. I went out and warned the pitcher, then I warned Martin.

By the time Yount came up again the Brewers had put the game out of reach. Martin had a relief pitcher on the mound, and before he pitched to Yount I went out and warned him against even thinking about throwing a beanball. His first pitch was a knockdown. I threw him out of the game. Then I threw Martin out of the game.

I was working third base the second game. In the top of the first inning a pitch to a Ranger batter was inside, but close enough to the plate to almost be a strike. Martin started screaming at me. "How come you don't throw him out? How come you let him throw at my hitters?" He wouldn't quiet down, so I threw him out for disturbing my peace.

Yount led off for the Brewers and got knocked down. I was absolutely livid. This was a player with a brilliant future ahead of him, and the Rangers were trying to hurt him because he'd done his job the night before. I couldn't understand it, and I didn't like it.

MacPhail suspended Martin for three days, but his report stated that Martin was being penalized for telling the opposing manager before the game that he would knock down Yount. That wasn't enough for me. I called MacPhail and told him that the three-day suspension was acceptable, but I wanted Martin to be told he was being penalized for defying the umpire. I had specifically warned him not to throw at the hitter, and the very next pitch was a beanball. I wanted the league to back me up.

MacPhail refused. If he wasn't going to support his umpires, I told him, then I would not work any more Ranger games. Later in my career the league took me off Baltimore games because of my difficult relationship with Weaver, but this was my own personal boycott. I meant it, too. My crew went to Texas to work a three-game series in July and I called in sick. Actually that was true. Martin, and the league, had caused me a great pain in my posterior.

I was assigned to another Texas series in September. I intended to skip that one, too, but the office put pressure on me. I was scheduled to work my first World Series and didn't want to miss that experience. Before the games in Texas, Dick Butler, American League supervisor of umpires, called and asked if I was going to be too sick to work the Series. I got the hint. They hit me right in the enthusiasm. I worked the Ranger games, and channeled my anger into working harder for the Umpires Association. It became obvious to me then that major changes had to be made in the relationship between the league and their umpires.

There are certain pitchers who are known as headhunters, there are other pitchers who won't throw at anybody, like Catfish, and then there are pitchers who can't throw at anybody, like Wilbur Wood.

Wilbur Wood wouldn't hurt a fly—Wilbur Wood *couldn't* hurt a fly. His knuckleball was so soft it would just bounce off. One day Wood hit Claudell Washington and Washington started to go after him. I stopped him that time. "He's not throwing at you," I yelled. "Who ever heard of knocking somebody down with a knuckleball?"

I never thought it was easy to be a pitcher. The pressure every fourth day for a starter or every day for a reliever is tremendous. The strain on a pitcher's arm is incredible and every pitcher realizes that he's always one pitch away from the end of his career. Danny McDevitt told me his first game in the major leagues was delayed because of rain. After the delay he didn't warm up quite enough and threw the first hitter he faced a curveball. That was his last good pitch in the major leagues. The list of pitchers whose careers were ended by arm injury could fill volumes. Tommy John was one of the few pitchers to really come back from the dreaded rotor cuff tear, but he had an unusual operation in which a leg tendon was grafted onto his arm. His body may be nearing forty years old, he tells anyone who asks his age, but his arm is only five.

Pitching, I believe, must put a strain on the head as well as the arm, because that's the only way to account for all the pitchers who are certified flakes. Relief pitcher Moe Drabowsky used to telephone the opposing team's bullpen from his own, for example, imitate their manager and order certain pitchers to warm up. On occasion he would also make long-distance calls from the bullpen phone—to Europe. Jim Kern, who briefly shared the Texas Ranger bullpen with Sparky Lyle, once lit a bonfire out there in the middle of a heat wave. When asked what he was burning, he replied, "Sparky Lyle's book." Lyle was no slouch in the flake department either, as anyone who has seen him sit on a cake can attest. Mark Fidrych first gained attention by talking to baseballs on the pitcher's mound, but that was no act. I once walked through the Tigers' locker room on my way to see their trainer and caught him talking to a bar of soap.

Relief pitcher Al "Mad Hungarian" Hrabosky puts on a great show. Before throwing a pitch he stands behind the pitcher's mound and psychs himself into a feverous state; then he takes the ball in his left hand and heaves it as hard as he can into his glove, stomps back onto the pitching rubber and goes to work.

I always like to watch this. But one day he came in to pitch in a critical situation and immediately went to the back of the mound. I could see his shoulders shaking with confidence. The muscles in his face tightened. I don't know what he was telling himself, but he was doing an incredible selling job. Finally he was ready. I mean, he was *ready*! He grabbed the ball in his left hand and flung it with all his might at his glove.

And missed. The ball bounced toward the second baseman.

I was working first base and I had to lean over and put my hands on my knees to prevent myself from falling over, I was laughing so hard. Hrabosky, however, did not think it was funny.

The Philadelphia Phillies' Tug McGraw has established himself as baseball's comic reliever. Tug was a protégé of Casey Stengel, which should explain something. He first caught Stengel's attention during the Mets' 1964 spring training camp with his ability to walk on his hands. Casey loved that. When a New York sportswriter asked him if he thought the Mets would improve in 1964, he replied, "Sure. Now we got a guy who can run around the bases on his hands!"

McGraw has the best philosophy of pitching I've ever heard. He calls it his "frozen ice-ball theory." "If I come in to pitch with the bases loaded and Willie Stargell at bat," he explains, "there's no rational reason I would want to throw the ball. As long as I hold onto it nothing bad can happen. But I'm aware that eventually I have to pitch. So what I do is remind myself that in approximately a billion years the sun is going to burn out and the earth will become a frozen ice-ball hurtling through space. And when that happens, nobody's going to care what Willie Stargell did with the bases loaded."

Once, the year after Tom Seaver won the National League's Cy Young Award, Mets manager Yogi Berra brought in McGraw to relieve Seaver. The game was on the line as he handed him the baseball and asked, "Think you can get 'em out?"

McGraw shook his head. "Jeez, Yog," he said, "you just took out the best pitcher in baseball. If he can't get them out, what do you expect from me?"

And people believe I'm a flake.

I've seen more than a thousand pitchers on the mound, and countless pitches, but there is one man who stands out above them all. The best pitcher I have ever seen is Dick Tidrow. Dick Tidrow! That doesn't mean he was the best pitcher in baseball, or that he threw better than Hunter in his prime, or Palmer, or Vida Blue or Guidry. It means that I saw him work for seven seasons, and in that entire time, I never saw him give up a run. Not one run. Umpires and players do have strange relationships like that. Whenever a certain umpire is on the field the player performs. On numerous occasions I'd be talking baseball to someone and they'd ask me about a certain player and I'd say, "Great hitter," and be told he was hitting .220. But whenever I saw him he hit .600.

Tidrow was my lucky pitcher. Or I was his lucky umpire. Whenever I was around he was nearly perfect. I remember one night at Yankee Stadium he came in to pitch against the Twins. The first hitter he faced tripled into right-center. There were no outs. Tidrow looked over to me standing behind first base, and smiled. He knew there was nothing to worry about. The Luciano charm was going to take care of him. Sure enough, he retired the side without giving up the run. As he walked back to the Yankee dugout he looked at me and said, "Thanks."

I appreciated that. But I couldn't have done it without him.

6
HITTERS
OR 4.2 Seconds to First Base, 3.9 Without Beads

Blink your eyes once. If, in the time it took you to do that, you were able to focus on a tiny white baseball coming directly at you from sixty feet six inches away at nearly ninety miles per hour, determine from the rotation of the laces what arc it was going to follow, judge if that arc would bring it across home plate somewhere between your knees and chest, then compute all that data and decide to swing or not, then begin a swing that will interrupt that arc, you might have the potential to be a major league hitter.

Now blink your eyes twice. If it takes you that long to accomplish exactly the same things, consider pitching.

Hitting a pitched baseball is the single most difficult feat in sports. It doesn't require the psychological preparation of hitting a golf ball, which simply lies there taunting you. Or involve the physical punishment inherent in football. Or demand the grace necessary to leap high into the air and make three complete turns and a somersault before slam-dunking a basketball. A batter doesn't need the stealth, cunning, and expensive equipment necessary to outsmart a two-pound trout. Hitting a baseball is a combination of instinct, coordination, endless practice and luck. If a batter starts to think about what he's trying to do with a pitch . . . too late, the ball is past him.

The difference between a good hitter and a poor hitter is about an eighth of an inch. The good hitter is consistently able to hit the ball solidly enough to drive it through the infield or into the outfield, while the poor hitter just misses getting solid wood on the ball and hits easy grounders or pop-ups. It only takes one additional hit every ten at bats, or every two-and-a-half games, to turn a .200 hitter into a .300 hitter.

Even the best hitters in baseball are going to make an out six or seven times every ten at bats. Players have all sorts of excuses for this, but they can be summed up as good pitching, good defense, bad luck and umpires. If it weren't for umpires, major league baseball would have more .500 hitters than a company softball team.

The key to hitting is good eyes. When I first got into the majors I spoke to great hitters like Tony Oliva and Yastrzemski and Carew and they all agreed the most important element of hitting is seeing the ball from the moment it leaves the pitcher's hand. Then Ted Williams, who was managing the Washington Senators at the time, went just a bit farther. He claimed he could actually see the ball hit the bat. He said he could see if the bat hit one seam, two seams or missed the seams entirely.

Williams was known to have exceptional vision, but I didn't believe him. I'd seen perhaps a hundred thousand pitches from behind the plate, I'd seen countless hits, and I had never seen the bat meeting the ball. I told him that was impossible. The human eye doesn't work that precisely. Doctors knew it. Scientists knew it. Umpires knew it.

Still, he insisted he could see the ball hitting the bat. In spring training, in 1972, he offered to prove it to me. Admittedly I was reluctant to go along with him. In his prime Williams had been one of the greatest hitters in baseball history, but at this time he was fifty-four years old. A hitter's reflexes usually start fading in his mid-thirties, and in Willian₁s's case that was two decades earlier. I didn't want to embarrass him by shattering one of his beliefs, but he insisted. With my head down, I followed him to a practice field. He covered the barrel of a bat with pine tar and stepped up to the plate. A hard-throwing rookie had been re-cruited to pitch to him. I took a deep breath, anticipat-ing what was going to be a very sad moment.

The young pitcher threw a bullet and Williams hit a rocket to center field. "One seam," he shouted con-fidently over his shoulder.

"Sure, Ted," I agreed. I was just glad he was still able to hit the ball. Someone retrieved it and brought it over to me. One seam was covered with pine tar.

He hit another pitch. "About a quarter inch above the $#%$%$% seam," he said.

That ball had a pine-tar scar just a quarter inch above the seam. He called five of seven perfectly, the most amazing display of hitting ability I've ever seen.

A few years later I overheard one of baseball's rising young stars—it might have been Fred Lynn or Rice or Brett, I don't really remember—talking about how well he could see the ball when it left the pitch-er's hand. "Oh, yeah?" I interrupted. "You think that's good? Well, Ted Williams can see the ball hit the bat!"

Very few hitters even dream of having that capa-bility. Rusty Staub was close. Most batters, when they disagreed with my call, would frown or curse or tell me it was "way outside," or suggest I should be insti-tutionalized. Only Staub would tell me precisely how far off the plate the pitch had been. "Jeez, Ron," he'd complain, "that pitch was at least a half-inch outside," or "How could you miss that one? It was an eighth of an inch too high." He wasn't complaining, he was just enlightening me.

Umpires are often accused of favoring the good hitters and robbing the weaker hitters. That's not true at all. Players and umpires who stay in the big leagues for any length of time get to know each other's strengths and weaknesses. Players learn which umpires have wide strike zones, or like high pitches, or know the good restaurants in town but can't call a knuckleball at all, and make adjustments for that. In my case they usually avoided restaurants I recommended and swung at any knuckleball that they could reach.

Umpires learn which hitters have a good concept of the strike zone, who the good guys are and who the complainers are. Inevitably the complainers get a reason to scream.

Over a period of seasons the good hitters have proven they know a strike when they see one. So when Carew doesn't swing at a pitch, I have to believe it's off the plate. If a future Hall of Famer like Yastrzemski doesn't think it's a strike, is Ron Luciano going to argue with him? So if it's close and the good hitters don't swing, it's going to be a ball.

That does not include the free-swingers or bad-ball hitters like "Old Gozzlehead," Mickey Rivers. Mickey will swing at anything inside the ballpark, so the rules are different for him. He's proven he's a fine hitter, and a great bunter, but he has absolutely no idea where the strike zone begins or ends. I have to believe that if someone asked him where the strike zone was he'd guess, "New York City?"

After good hitters, good guys do get a slight advantage. Umpires do not cheat. Umpires never cheat. Umpires never intentionally miss a call. But umpires do root. I've never rooted for or against a team, including Earl Weaver's Orioles, but it's impossible not to hope that players I liked did well. Darrell Porter, for example, never argued with me. So when he came to bat I was going to make sure a pitch was in the zone before I called it a strike.

The only problem I had in such a case was when a pitcher I liked was facing a hitter I liked. I had to root for a tie. I remember one night when Rodney Carew came to bat against Catfish Hunter at Yankee Stadium. It was an early inning of an ordinary midseason game, but I realized it was a special moment. Two sure Hall of Famers in their prime facing against each other, both of them absolute professionals with complete respect for their opponent. I didn't want to umpire, I just wanted to stand there and enjoy the confrontation.

Hunter started Carew off with a gorgeous fastball on the outside corner. Rodney realized he wouldn't have been able to do much with the pitch if he swung, so he took it for a called strike one.

The second pitch was a low curveball. He almost swung at it, but held back when it dropped out of the strike zone. One ball, one strike.

Hunter's next pitch was another breaking ball, but he got it up a little and Carew took a strong cut. He was just out in front of it, however, swinging too early, and he pulled it foul. Now he was down one ball, two strikes.

Hunter put a fastball an inch off the plate. A professional pitch. Carew watched it without moving his bat. A professional hitter. I followed it into Munson's glove and called it ball two. A professional call.

Throughout the series of pitches I had been trying to think along with Hunter. Trying to figure out what pitch he was going to throw next. Until that point I had been absolutely right on every pitch. So, with the count even at two balls, two strikes, I figured that last fastball had been used just to set up Carew for an off-speed breaking pitch. I guessed curveball on the outside. When Hunter released the pitch that's exactly what it looked like. I began anticipating the sharp break down into the strike zone, and when the pitch reached the plate I shot out my right hand and called strike three. I shouted it as loudly and clearly as I've ever made a third strike call, proud to be part of that moment, feeling as much the top professional as either Hunter or Carew.

The ball never broke down. Catfish hung that curve on a clothesline and it sailed across the plate neck high. I wanted to cut my hand off. If I could have changed my call without shaking baseball to its historic foundations, I would have. But of course that was impossible, so I had to stand there and pretend I'd made a good call. Rodney didn't say a word. He didn't even look at me. He just turned around and walked back to his dugout. I wanted to chase after him and apologize.

After the game I waited for him outside the Twins' locker room. "Rodney," I said, "I'm really sorry about that one I struck you out on. It was way too high."

"I know," he said pleasantly, "but did you see those other two strikes?"

"Damn right I did."

He shook his head at the memory. "Well, I missed two. You only missed one. So I guess I'm still one up on you." Now, the next time Carew came to bat, how could I not give him the benefit of the doubt on a very close pitch?

Contrary to published opinion, Richie Allen was another favorite of the umpires. He had his problems off the field, and with the press, but as far as umpires were concerned he could do no wrong. He never argued. Never. One night in 1972 stands out in my memory. He was with the White Sox and I was behind the plate. Mike Andrews, I believe, was the batter. He had two strikes on him and Rollie Fingers threw him a magnificent slider. It was the kind of pitch on which an umpire hates to strike out a batter because it was unhittable. Reggie Jackson couldn't have hit it in the seventh game of the World Series, that's how good it was. I called Andrews out and he snapped his head around and looked at me incredulously. "No way," he screamed angrily, "it can't be."

I took my mask off. I could see what was coming. But before we could get into it, Richie Allen got hold of Andrews and told him to relax. "That's the pitch they pay me a hundred thousand dollars to hit," he said. Andrews muttered something and stomped away. Allen looked at me and smiled. How could I not root for that man?

Then there are the complainers. Bill North believed any pitch he didn't swing at was a ball and any time he ran to a base he was safe. He would argue with umpires about anything, the time the sun came up, the outcome of World War II, absolutely anything. There was no way any umpire true to the blue was going to give him anything close. Alex Johnson was the same way, but potentially more dangerous. Johnson was a powerful man, and when things were not going his way he would throw things. A tantrum. A helmet. His bat. Section 3. Every time he got called out on strikes I'd look into his dugout and watch his teammates just sort of easing down to the far end of the bench. Nobody wanted to look as if he were running away, but the entire dugout did seem suddenly to be flowing downhill.

Lou Piniella only argues on days ending with the letter "y." He has such confidence in his ability he is stunned that any mortal pitcher is able to get him out. But he takes out his frustration on himself as much as he does on umpires and water coolers. When he was with Kansas City, he set fire to his bats and jumped off a two-story building. Supposedly he was in a batting cage one spring training throwing bats into the netting, waving his hands angrily and screaming at the pitching machine. A solid midseason-style eruption. When asked what he was doing, he answered, "Getting my arguing in shape." I can believe it.

Baseball lore is full of witty exchanges between batters and umpires about bad calls on balls and strikes. The old American League umpire George Moriarty once called a batter out on strikes and the astonished player demanded to know how he spelled his name. After Moriarty spelled it for him, slowly, the player nodded and said, "Just what I thought. One *i*." Players never said funny things like that to me. The players I knew would say wonderfully clever things like, "Where was it?" "That was a strike like your $%$'&#%$ is a %#$"&%$." Or my personal favorite, "Whaddaya, kidding me?" Naturally I always had a snappy comeback. "Just get in there and hit" was one of my big ones, as was "It was a good pitch." One night in Boston, Carl Yastrzemski swung and missed a pitch up around his eyes, then took the next one on the outside corner for a called strike. "It was outside," he screamed at me.

"No way," I shouted right back, confident I'd gotten it right. "And how can you tell that one was outside when you couldn't tell the first one was over your head?"

Reggie Jackson once got so angry at a call made by Bill Kunkel that he tried to hand him his bat, telling him, "If you think that was a strike, you'd better take this. You see if you can hit that pitch."

When Danny Cater was with Boston he tried the same thing with me. Unlike Kunkel, I took the bat. But before my enthusiasm overcame my good sense, I gave it back to him. "I don't want to show you up," I told him.

I can understand players fighting for every pitch. Baseball is a difficult game and hitting is the hardest aspect of it. Players will do absolutely anything to gain the slightest advantage. Some hitters get into the batter's box and wipe out the front line so they can cheat a few inches closer to the pitcher and maybe get the curveball before it breaks. Of course, other players get in the box and wipe out the rear line so they can gain an extra inch on the fastball. The things hitters do to bats would embarrass a highwayman. Reggie Jackson got caught using a bat with the barrel flattened to give him a wider hitting surface. Graig Nettles somehow found a bat with a steel rod implanted in the middle. Eventually the league cracked down and sent out memos and directives instructing umpires to examine all suspicious bats. Tell me, how do you define a suspicious bat? Does it come disguised as a glove? It took me twelve years to remember to turn the lights on and the league wants me to run a search party.

Few players would admit that they are superstitious, but when they come to bat some of them go through routines more intricate than those of an Olympic gymnast. The Texas Rangers' Mike Hargrove, for example, walks up the first-base line, no matter which dugout he's come out of, and takes exactly three practice swings. Then he returns to the plate and starts digging a hole in the back of the batter's box with his left foot, while keeping his right foot on the side line or out of the box so he can't be quick-pitched. When he's satisfied with the hole, he adjusts the batting glove he wears on his right hand and the "donut" (a piece of rubber protection) he wears on his left thumb. Then he wipes off the perspiration over his upper lip with the crook of his left elbow.

Meanwhile the concession stands are doing big business.

Once he's taken care of the perspiration on his upper lip he either tugs the right shoulder of his uniform with his left hand or the left shoulder with his right hand. Then, with the palm of his right hand, he pushes down on top of his batting helmet to make sure it stays on his head. Finally he reaches behind his back with his left hand and pulls up his pants from the center.

At last he's ready to hit.

While he's going through his routine, meanwhile, the pitcher is on the mound touching his cap, banging his spikes against the rubber, pulling up his pants and tapping his belt buckle twice.

If Hargrove is ready before the pitcher, or if the pitcher steps off the rubber, he repeats his entire routine, with the exception of the practice swings. I've always wondered how much sweat he can work up on his lip between pitches.

Many players make the sign of the cross before stepping in to hit. I remember once overhearing a catcher telling the batter it wouldn't make any difference, because the pitcher was devoutly religious and had been to church that morning. "I'm not asking for help for myself," the batter replied as he got ready to hit. "I figure Luciano needs all the help he can get."

How do you throw a player out of the game for praying for you?

National League umpires told me that Roberto Clemente was the most superstitious player in the league. He played no favorites, he believed in everything. He went through a batting routine similar to

Hargrove's; he carried charms, he wore bracelets. Supposedly he also consulted soothsayers and carried voodoo symbols. They used to say about him that he could run from home plate to first base in 4.2 seconds, 3.9 without beads.

The Great Scott, George Scott, also wore a strange necklace. When a writer asked what those things hanging from it were, he admitted, "The teeth of opposing pitchers."

Some players are so desperate for hitting help they will even ask the umpires for assistance. Jim Rice, for example, is constantly worried that he's either pulling up his head too soon or opening up—striding forward on his front foot—too quickly. He'll ask an umpire to watch him at bat and see what he's doing.

Although it must have become obvious from these pages that I do not like to brag about my somewhat limited accomplishments, I must admit I have given the benefit of my wisdom to a few favored players. One day in Oakland, Sal Bando came up to me and started talking about the slump he was in. "You've seen me enough," he said. "Whaddya think I'm doing wrong? I just can't seem to get my weight moving forward."

In all modesty I know as much about hitting as I do about Alaskan wines, but I was not about to admit that. "Yeah, I noticed that, too. Have you checked the films?" I asked, relying on my audio-visual experience.

He said he had, and hadn't seen anything unusual.

"Doesn't surprise me," I said knowingly. "Tell you what," I guessed. "I think maybe you're standing a little too far off the plate. You're seeing the inside pitch good, but you can't reach the outside pitch."

He was skeptical. "You think that's it?"

"Absolutely. That's probably definitely it. Try crowding the plate a bit."

I was working third base the next day. Bando came

out in the first inning and told me he'd checked the films and I might be right. "Watch me when I'm up. I'm gonna get up close and hit the ball out."

"Sure," I agreed, "just crowd the plate."

He came to bat in the second inning. Just as he had predicted, he hit the second pitch a ton. A tremendous shot over the left field wall. I don't know who was happier, me or Bando. As he rounded second base he was clapping his hands and whooping. I totally forgot where I was and ran toward him. As we came together he held out his palm and I slapped it hard, then slapped him on the behind as he trotted past me. I watched him swing around third base and . . . then I realized what I'd done. I'd broken every behavior code in the book. I'd actually congratulated a player on the field. What were the fans going to think? What was the opposing team going to think? Most importantly, what was Lee MacPhail going to think?

I lowered my head and began slinking back toward third base. As I got close, the third baseman was looking at me as if I was slightly out of my mind. But before he could say a word, I looked at him and said firmly, "It's okay. We're Italian."

I never heard another word about it.

Some teams actually prefer to rely on batting instructors and hypnotists rather than umpires. Chicago White Sox coach Charlie Lau, now in the Yankee organization but formerly with Kansas City, is currently considered the best hitting instructor in baseball. Players swear by his theories. Some say he knows more about hitting than anyone else who has ever lived.

In his eleven-year major league career as a second-string catcher, Charlie Lau compiled a .255 batting average. You figure it out.

In reality hitting instructors serve two important purposes. They can help individual players regain their confidence, and they take the blame off the manager when a team isn't hitting. But I don't believe they can teach anyone how to hit, since I don't believe hitting can be taught. If it were really a science Albert Einstein would be in the Hall of Fame. Obviously there are certain aspects of hitting that can be learned: a good hitter watches the ball from the moment it leaves the pitcher's hand; he extends his arms and swings level. A good hitter is selective, meaning he swings only at those pitches he knows he can handle, and doesn't swing at pitches out of the strike zone. A good hitter tries to hit the ball where it's pitched, taking the outside pitch to the opposite field and pulling the inside pitch. Finally, the good hitter always remembers to compliment the home plate umpire on a job well done.

A hitting instructor can teach these things, and detect flaws in technique. But there is no such thing as a right way or wrong way to hit. Stan Musial batted out of a stance more twisted than a neurotic's paper clip. Yaz stands straight up. Carew has a stance for every pitcher, reasoning that a hitter can't bat the same way against Bert Blyleven's curveball, Wilber Wood's knuckler and Goose Gossage's heater.

The key to hitting is confidence. Every player in the major leagues earned the right to be there by proving his ability in the minors. At one time every one of them—with the exception of pitchers—was potentially a good hitter. But sometimes they simply stop hitting; they go into a batting slump. At the heart of most batting slumps is a loss of confidence. Players forget what they were doing when they were doing it right. I didn't know what Bando was doing wrong. But Bando believed I did. So I did. Reggie Jackson suffered through a horrible slump in 1981. Even from my seat in the broadcast booth I could see he had totally lost his confidence. When Reggie is going good he can shoot

spit through his front teeth more than twenty feet—
against the wind. During his slump his spit just sort of
dribbled out his mouth down his chin. I knew he
hadn't lost his ability. I believed he was just one or two
bloop hits and a good twenty-footer away from snap-
ping out of it.

One of the amazing things about batting slumps is
that they can be ended by an accidental hit, a bad-
bounce single, even a successful bunt, anything that
convinces the player his slump has ended. Once he
believes it—it usually has.

In the past it was said that home run hitters drive
Cadillacs and singles hitters drive Fords. The huge
salaries players are now receiving have changed that.
Now the difference is that the sluggers' Mercedes are
chauffeur driven. Power hitters are the glamor boys of
baseball. The game breakers still get most of the attention. And none of them gets more attention than Mr.
October Jackson. Reggie and I have always gotten
along very well. We understand each other. When we
meet I tell him how good he is, then he tells me how
good I am. We've always appreciated each other's honesty.

Reggie has powered some of the longest home
runs ever seen. One night in Yankee Stadium he took a
close pitch with two strikes on him. The catcher complained and I told him it was an inch or so outside.
Jackson crushed the next pitch. I mean, he flattened it.
As he was circling the bases the catcher, who thought
he'd had Jackson struck out on the previous pitch, said
to me sarcastically, "I guess baseball's a game of inches,
huh?"

"Yeah," I told him, "and Reggie hit that one about
five thousand inches."

Everyone knows that Jackson is one of the great
pressure players of all time, but what is generally not

known is that it was Reggie Jackson who brought freedom of speech to the American ballplayer. My favorite silly rule prohibits rival players from talking to each other on the field before a game. I imagine some executive sometime believed the game's image would be forever soiled if fans saw opposing players actually talking to each other. So for an hour and a half before each game one umpire is supposed to sit in the stands writing down the names of players who dare fraternize. The fine for the first offense was twenty-five dollars. The second offense cost fifty dollars and it got progressively higher. No appeal was allowed.

In the year 1974 Reggie Jackson defied the baseball establishment and spoke to opposing players before the games. In full view of the fans! I'm sure a barrage of memos flew back and forth about this scandal, but somehow our nation's investigative reporters never picked it up. Umpires like Reggie and tried to warn him that he had embarked on a dangerous path, but he remained determined.

"Write me up," he'd say in his Patrick Henry voice, and we would. We wore out pencils writing him up. Finally, when I asked him why he persisted after repeated warnings and mounting fines, he explained that he wanted to learn as much about hitting as possible, and to do that he was going to talk to the best hitters in baseball whenever he had the opportunity.

Although, in light of my Bando success, I was a little hurt he hadn't come to me, I could understand. Who would be better to talk hitting with than Tony Oliva or Tommy Davis or Yaz?

I never learned what his fines amounted to, but they were rumored to be nearly five thousand dollars. That may not be a realistic figure. Supposedly Jackson wrote the league a letter refusing to pay because he was simply trying to do his job as well as possible. All of baseball held its collective breath waiting for the wrath of the American League to come down upon his shoulders. "Good-bye Reggie" parties were planned.

Nothing happened. One night in Cleveland I was in the stands with my little pen and pad and caught Duane Kuiper risking words with Chicago's Bill Melton. I got 'em good. Wrote their names down on my pad and sent it to the league office. A month later I caught up with Melton in Chicago and asked him if he had been fined. He shook his head and said he'd never heard from the league. It was the dawn of a new day.

From that day forth, give or take a few months, umpires stopped writing these tickets. So today, whenever opposing players stand shoulder to shoulder talking, they can thank Reggie Jackson for every free word.

Another baseball tradition started by Jackson: standing at home plate and admiring tape-measure home runs. All the big guys do it now. As football has its touchdown dance, baseball now has its home run pose. The key to a good pose is confidence, not cockiness, and pride. Points are deducted for any show of surprise.

Of course, when an umpire or reporter speaks to the sluggers about a grand shot after a game they are always self-effacing. A nice man like Andre Dawson calls himself lucky and claims he just got the flat part of the bat on the ball. I remember telling Reggie once that he'd gotten all of one fastball. He shook his head. "Nah, I got it down on the handle," he said. "If I'd gotten the bat out just a little quicker I would have really mashed it."

The man had hit the ball four hundred feet. It would take me three throws to reach that part of the ballpark, and I'd still be a few feet shy. "Would have really mashed it," he says.

Now, Reggie may hit the 'taters as far as anyone in baseball, but he is not the strongest player in the game today. My candidate for that honor is Jim Rice. I've seen numerous players break their bats in half when hitting the ball, but Jim Rice is the only man I've ever seen actually break his bat just by swinging it. At Fenway Park one night he missed a pitch, but snapped his wrists so violently he broke the bat in half. I looked across the diamond at Bill Haller, who just shook his head in amazement. Haller retrieved the pieces because he didn't believe it was possible to break a bat just by swinging it and wanted to examine it for flaws or cracks. We looked at it carefully after the game but found nothing unusual. We decided it had to have been cracked beforehand, but Rice told us he'd checked it, as he always checked his bats, and it was perfect.

Rice is a right-handed pull-hitter so when he gets up the third base area suddenly becomes the single most undesirable plot of real estate imaginable. Swamps are more attractive. Naturally, if I was working third base, I'd show the fans exactly how brave I am. I'd back up about sixty feet down the foul line and tap my temple, as if saying, I'm much too smart to get any closer than this when *he's* up. Then, if he hit a ball anywhere within ducking distance, I'd take out my white handkerchief and wave it in the air. The fans enjoyed this show. They thought I was kidding.

Dave Kingman might be Rice's only serious challenger. As with Nolan Ryan, American Leaguers had heard a lot about him when he was with the Giants, but when he came over I wasn't particularly impressed. He had good size and could power the ball, but he didn't make good contact that often. Then one night I saw a pitcher fool him with a change-up. Kingman was way out in front of the pitch, so he released his front hand and hit the ball out of the park with the other hand. He hit the ball 370 feet with one hand!

From the stands, and in the field, it is possible to tell how well a ball is hit from the crack of the bat. But the home plate umpire gets a completely different range of sound effects. I always thought football players made strange noises when they charged off their marks into an opposing player, but compared to baseball players they sound like the Mormon Tabernacle Choir. Hitters grunt and groan, they moan, sob, cry, curse, inhale, exhale and shriek. About the only thing I never heard around the plate was a good yodel. Rico Carty was the champion curser. He hit the ball and simultaneously let loose a torrent of nasty words and anyone within hearing distance would assume he'd popped up. Not him. Line drives up the alleys, good shots to the fence, hard grounders up the middle. I once asked him about a 350-foot line-drive double to left-center that had unleashed a stream of colorful language. "Oh, I missed that %$%#$#%," he said. "I shoulda hit it out of the park."

Personally, I don't think I would ever have been a productive major league hitter. When I was growing up I could always pound the fastball, but the day they started throwing breaking pitches was the day I began looking around for someone to tackle. There is, however, one thing I can still do better than most major league hitters—miss the pitch. As difficult as it is to hit the ball, missing it intentionally is almost as hard. And that just happens to be one of my better skills. I could stand at the plate missing pitches all day without anyone realizing I was doing it on purpose. From the stands it would look like I was simply overwhelmed by the pitcher.

The best major leaguers have difficulty doing this.

There are some situations in which a hitter wants to make an out. A baseball game doesn't count in the standings until the losing team has had five complete innings at bat. So when rain is threatening before five at bats have taken place the team in the lead may intentionally try to make out so the losing team can complete the necessary innings. It's not that easy. Just as it's difficult for an umpire to intentionally call a bad pitch a strike, hitters cannot easily overcome years of practice and concentration. Their pride prevents them from simply flailing helplessly at the ball, so they pretend they are really trying to hit it. The results would make Woody Allen proud. Some players, rather than strike out, take half-swings and try to hit routine grounders or playable pop-ups. Naturally they pop the ball just out of reach of an infielder or hit a ten-bouncer right between the shortstop and third baseman.

Complicating matters is the fact that the team that's losing when rain is threatening often doesn't want to come to bat again.

Perhaps the most embarrassing thing a player can do is get a hit when his team is leading by four or five runs and it's starting to rain. One Yankee outfielder did exactly that, and as his grounder bounced through the infield he started running toward first screaming, "Get it, get it, get it." Luckily he was tagged out on a bad throw by the catcher while trying to steal second. In other circumstances it might have been a good throw, but because it was raining and his team was four runs down in the fourth inning against Ron Guidry, it was a bad throw. And some people think nuclear physics is complicated.

The single person a team has to satisfy with their efforts when making intentional outs or stalling is the home plate umpire. Once the game has started, he is the one responsible for stopping play because of rain. It has been said that umpires don't know enough to come in out of the rain—which is often true if less than five innings have been completed. For me a five-inning game was the next best thing to a free meal at a fancy restaurant. I knew that if I could get five good innings in one day—without jeopardizing players on a wet field or cheating the fans by continuing in unplayable conditions—my crew or another crew wouldn't get stuck working a makeup doubleheader some future day. Why would anyone prefer to work two shifts rather than half a shift, even in the rain?

But if either team embarrassed me or baseball by making obvious outs, or stalling, I would do everything within reason to make sure they didn't get their way. If, as often happened, a manager started changing pitchers just to waste time while the field became a quagmire, we were going to play five innings if I had to learn to dog-paddle.

Before games are called off they are halted, and a tarpaulin is pulled over the dirt part of the infield, the home plate area and the pitcher's mound. Once that tarp is in place there's a fair chance play will not be resumed, so an umpire has to consider all factors before ordering the ground crew to cover the field.

I had the plate one Sunday afternoon for the Tigers-Brewers and the rain kept stopping and starting. I couldn't decide whether to put the tarp over the field and hope it stopped raining, or continue playing. The weather forecast didn't help me make my decision; it was for scattered showers into the night. There were forty-thousand people in Tiger Stadium at approximately five dollars apiece and if I called the game the Tigers might lose two hundred thousand dollars. I was also aware that this was Milwaukee's last scheduled trip to Detroit that season and if a makeup game became necessary they'd have to make a special one-day flight, an expensive and exhausting proposition. In addition, my crew had a 6:00 P.M. flight out of town and if we halted play for any length of time and then resumed we'd never make the flight; we'd have to catch an early bird the following morning. On the other hand the field was getting pretty muddy.

I didn't know what to do, so I asked Haller what he thought. "I wish I had an umbrella," he said.

Finally, in the bottom of the fourth, the Tigers' first baseman Norm Cash made the decision for me. He came to bat wearing glasses with tiny windshield wipers. I was reminded that the umpire's primary concern has to be for the safety of the players. We halted the game.

Other than rain situations and those few games each season that get so lopsided everybody wants to get it over with, the only time players will do anything to finish a game quickly is in spring training in Arizona. In the spring, Florida is the center of the baseball world. The majority of big league clubs train there. Club and league officials gather there. Most of the media attention is focused there. In fact, they have everything there—except fun. Fun is what they have in Arizona. Florida teams play to win in preparation for the season. In Arizona they play for exercise, training and tans. My kind of place.

In Florida, Earl Weaver once forfeited a game to Kansas City in the seventh inning because the home plate umpire refused to provide him with a written list of the Royals' numerous substitutions. "This game counts to me," he told the umps.

In Arizona, Dick Williams once replaced his best pitcher, Vida Blue, with rookie Glen Abbott with the bases loaded and a full count on the batter because Blue had thrown his scheduled forty pitches. Abbott's first pitch sailed over the catcher's head for ball four. When Reggie Jackson was with Oakland and training in Arizona he played forty minutes. Not three innings. Not three at bats. Forty minutes. He did not play overtime.

Until 1972 I had always been assigned to Florida for spring training. Although no one explained my change of assignment, I figured it was punishment for my outrageous behavior on the diamond. It took me about an hour to realize that Arizona was the place to be, and as soon as I did so, I started protesting loudly that I didn't want to be there. Strategy. I was afraid the league would send me back to Florida if they discovered how much I was enjoying myself in Arizona, so I did everything I could to get sent back, knowing that would assure me an assignment to Arizona. In the middle of the regular season I'd call the office and demand a transfer for the following spring and they would promise to consider it. When my contract arrived in the winter I'd warn the office I wasn't going to sign it until I was guaranteed I'd go to Florida. They promised to try to work it out; I signed the contract and made reservations for Arizona.

At the end of my tenth major league season, when I'd earned the right to select the place I wanted to spend spring training, I wrote on the proper form: Arizona! The league office must have figured I was trying to get even with myself.

Nobody wanted to play long games in Arizona. Not the players, not the American League umpires, not the fans. The Brewers train in Sun City, an absolutely beautiful retirement community. The fans come to the park in motorized golf carts and sit under frilled sun parasols. One sunny afternoon some rookie pitcher was meditating between each pitch, driving us sun-worshipers crazy. Finally, from the bleachers, a little old lady implored in a squeaky voice, "Please, Mr. Pitcher, hurry up. Some of us don't have that much time."

National League umpires took the games far more seriously than anyone else. They believed in getting prepared for the season. I did, too. When I got to New York in April I wanted to have a fantastic tan. The National Leaguers would even throw players out of the games and make them sit on the team bus without air conditioning. Talk about a tough league.

I remember a Brewers-Chicago Cubs game in Scottsdale. It was the worst possible situation in a spring game—a tie score in the bottom of the ninth with a National Leaguer behind the plate. If I had been working the plate we'd have been out of there in the space of a hit batsman and three balks, but not with the man from the Senior Circuit. Luckily Tom Murphy, a man who understood tanning, was pitching for the Brewers.

He had already pitched two strong innings and wanted the game to end as much as anyone, but he wasn't about to give it away. He began the inning with a good fastball. The National League umpire called it strike one.

Murphy took two steps toward the plate. "Looked a little low," he yelled.

The umpire stared at him. Murphy wound up and threw his second pitch. The umpire called it ball one.

"That's the way to go," Murphy agreed. He eventually walked the batter, who was sacrificed to second with a bunt and scored on a line single to right field. Some of Murphy's paler teammates patted him on the back as they left the field, but manager Del Crandall was furious. The man had obviously spent too many spring trainings in the Florida sun.

During the regular season, players would probably

find it much easier to make out intentionally, if doing so weren't included in their batting averages. Most players know their personal stats better than they know their bank balance. That makes sense, of course, since one usually determines the other. Sometimes, of course, they do get a bit carried away with meaningless statistics. On the final day of the 1969 season Haller called the A's' young outfielder Joe Rudi out on a close play at first base. Rudi had not yet established himself as a great clutch player, but even then was known to be a very quiet, pleasant man. But when Haller called him out he exploded. I didn't understand it. It was a meaningless play in a meaningless game. Afterward I asked Rudi what had set him off. "That would have been my twenty-fourth hit of the season," he said seriously.

"Oh," I said, as if I understood. At that time I had a lot to learn about the competitive nature of big league ballplayers.

Probably the worst thing that can happen to most hitters is that they eventually become baserunners. For some that is an extremely difficult transition. Baserunning is actually not as difficult as some players make it. There are only three bases and home plate, and they are only ninety feet apart, and there are two coaches whose sole function is to point out the next base. Yet there are some players who manage to make baserunning into a high adventure.

Without doubt the worst baserunner of all time is Lou Piniella. Piniella has successfully combined his hitting ability, his lack of speed and his fierce determination, to make himself into a truly terrible runner. When he was with Kansas City he did something unequaled in baseball history—he ran for the cycle. In a single game he managed to get himself thrown out at every base.

It started out as an ordinary evening. His first time at bat he belted a line drive into the left field corner, a routine double. But the ball bounced away from the outfielder and Lou kept going. By the time he reached third he was gasping for breath, but he didn't even pause as he rounded the base and headed home. Conservatively he was out by an hour. The catcher grew a beard waiting for him to get there.

His second time at bat he hit an easy hopper to second base and was thrown out at first. So far there was nothing unusual in his performance. But in the sixth inning he lined a single to right and was thrown out trying to stretch it into a double. It wasn't a bad gamble on his part; had he been a little faster he might have made it.

When he came to bat in the ninth inning everyone in the park was aware that baserunning history could be made. The crowd gave him a sitting ovation. He was still three bases short of immortality, however, and getting thrown out at third is probably the toughest out.

Lou made it happen, though. He sliced a line drive down the right field line. He rounded first base with his head down and steamed toward second. The right fielder retrieved the ball. Piniella hit second with his legs churning. The fans were on their feet screaming. The Royals were on the top of the dugout cheering him on. The outfielder unleashed ‧a fine three-bounce throw.

Lou never had a chance. No umpire with a sense of history would have given him a break on a close play, but he didn't need any help. He was out on his own ability. The fans cheered him off the field with a standing ovation.

True to his competitive nature, Piniella was furious. I don't think he realized the enormity of his achievement and, knowing him, I doubt he'll ever truly appreciate it. Years from now he'll probably be claiming the umpires were wrong on all four calls.

Too many fans underestimate the importance of baserunning. An extra base in a key situation often turns a game around. Charlie Finley understood this and in 1974 signed world-class sprinter Herb Washington as baseball's first designated runner. As often happened, Charlie had the last laugh. Washington appeared in ninety-one games that year without coming to bat. He scored twenty-nine runs, meaning he scored one of every three times he was put on base, a very good average. But the threat he created was often as valuable as the potential stolen base. He couldn't do anything but run, which is like saying Frank Sinatra can't do anything but sing, so when he went into the game he was running. Many pitchers paid too much attention to him and not enough to the hitters.

Unfortunately the highlight of the 1974 World Series was his appearance. It was the only series I worked and it was a dull one. Even my presence didn't make it exciting. Oakland beat the Dodgers in five games. In a tight situation Alvin Dark inserted Washington to pinch-run. Mike Marshall was on the mound. Everybody tensed for this confrontation. Washington took a short lead off first. Marshall looked over there.

And picked him off. End of confrontation.

The best baserunning feat I've ever seen was accomplished by Rodney Carew, of course, who actually stole home twice in the same inning. A steal of home is one of the most exciting, and one of the most difficult, plays in baseball. The runner literally has to outrun the ball. It's also a very difficult play for the home plate umpire; he has to watch the pitch to see if it's a ball or strike, make sure the batter doesn't interfere with the catcher, make sure the catcher doesn't jump out too soon and interfere with the hitter, and finally determine if the runner is safe or out— and do it all from the worst possible angle.

Carew was on third with one out. As the pitcher began winding up he made his break for home. But just as the play began, one of the infielders asked for time out. Carew didn't know it, the pitcher didn't know it and I didn't know it, so the play continued. Carew slid across the plate in a cloud of dust and I called him safe.

Then Haller told me he had called time out before the play was completed. I had to send Carew back to third. I was sorry to have to do it; it was a wonderful play, but there was no question it was the proper decision. "I guess you're gonna have to do it again," I said to Rodney.

So he did it again. Two pitches later. The batter squared to bunt, Carew came charging down the third base line, the pitch was high, and he barreled in before the catcher could bring it down.

As incredible as that was, perhaps even more amazing was John Mayberry's successful steal of home. Mayberry is the least likely runner ever to attempt a steal of home plate. He's so slow that you could take sequence photos of him with a Polaroid camera.

We were in Kansas City for a night game. Mayberry was on third and another runner was on first. The runner on first broke for second. The catcher played it correctly and faked a throw to second, then fired to third, hoping to catch Mayberry watching the play. It worked. Mayberry was caught off base and started running home. The third baseman threw it home and John started running the other way. The catcher made a high throw to third and Mayberry huffed home standing up and was credited with a steal of home. The entire Royals squad emptied out of the dugout to greet him. They carried him back to the dugout. Even the scoreboard operator recognized the significance of the moment, flashing the message "That was John Mayberry's first steal of home this season."

Actually I understood how Mayberry felt after he'd been picked off base. I've been caught in a run-down myself. This was in 1973, when I was still hustling. A California player got caught between first and second. I started moving back and forth with him so I could get a clear view of the play. We were dancing back and forth, four steps toward first, five toward second. A properly executed rundown shouldn't require more than two throws, but we had them so mixed up they'd made four throws and we were still alive. I was really into it, waiting for the opportunity to make a break for the base. But somehow, to this day I don't understand how, I got too close to the runner. I sort of tripped him. Not tripped, exactly. It was more like running into him. We both went down and I had no choice but to call both of us out. Neither of us argued.

My favorite runners to watch are the daredevils, the players who dive into bases, who smash into second basemen or shortstops to break up the double play. These are baseball's outpatients. Munson was one of the most aggressive runners I've ever seen. Pete Rose is in a cloud of dust by himself. But the very best I've ever seen at this is Don Baylor. No sane person gets in his way at second base.

Shortstops and second basemen let each other know who is going to cover the base on an attempted steal by flashing an open glove. Once, I remember, Baylor was on first and the shortstop showed the second baseman the open glove, meaning the second baseman was to take the play. The second baseman then showed the shortstop his open glove, meaning, don't you see who's on first? Are you crazy? The two of them stood out there angrily flashing open gloves at each other. I was laughing so hard I could barely control myself, and of course nobody had any idea what I was laughing about. Luckily the batter flied out before Baylor had a chance to run. My guess is either I or the center fielder would have had to take the throw, and I'm not so sure about me.

Only once did I ever try to help a baserunner and there was a very good reason I did so. Greed. Pure greed. In 1975 baseball was running a promotion around the one millionth run scored in the major leagues. Whichever teams were involved in the game in which the run was scored would receive engraved wristwatches. The magic word was *free*. Everybody in baseball was going for it.

I was working third base for the White Sox and A's on the fateful day. We were in the fourth inning, nobody out, Oakland runners on first and third, when the announcement was made that the 999,999th run had been scored. Man on third nobody out? I could hear that snazzy timepiece ticking on my wrist. I could feel the gold against my skin.

The batter lifted a short fly to right field. No way it was deep enough for the runner to tag up and score. No way at all. But I saw him bend into the running position, his back foot pushed against the base. "Don't go," I yelled pleadingly, "don't go!"

He went. White Sox catcher Ed Herrmann caught the throw from the outfield on a fly and stood at home plate with a sad, incredulous look on his face. He had no choice but to make the play, and he did. I couldn't believe the runner had taken my watch away from me.

We still had a shot, though. On the play at the

plate the runner on first had alertly tagged and gone to second. A base hit would score him with the one millionth run. And on the first pitch the batter smacked a line-drive single. The runner tore around third . . . and stopped. He just stopped and scampered back to third base. Again I was screaming. "Go! Go!" I was signaling with my hands. "Go!" I wanted to take him by the hand and drag him home.

It was probably too late anyway. As soon as that play ended the announcer informed the crowd that Houston's Bob Watson had scored the millionth run in major league history. So today some National League umpire is wearing my watch.

I remained an optimist, though. A few pitches later the runner scored on a long sacrifice fly. At the end of the inning, while the teams were changing sides, I stood on third base clapping my hands and urging them to hurry. "Come on, let's go," I shouted. "Only 999,999 more to go."

7

FIELDERS
OR The Glove is Quicker than the Eye

One label that could never accurately be applied to me, even during my childhood, was baseball's traditional scouting report, "good field, no hit." I couldn't field any better than I could hit. My fielding ability gave an entirely new meaning to the phrase "Watch out!"

But because I was one of the biggest kids in the neighborhood, as well as a close personal friend of the Barbaras, I was often picked to captain one team. To determine who had first pick of the players, one captain would toss a bat to the other, who would attempt to catch it as close to the knob at the end of the handle as possible. Then the two captains would grasp and regrasp the bat in turn, using either the entire hand or just the thumb and forefinger, until one of them was left holding it by the knob. Then he would either have to twirl it over his head three times or hold it while the other captain tried to kick it loose. If he held it he got first pick; if he dropped it the other captain had first pick. It was a very elaborate ceremony.

My problem was catching the bat.

In fact, I should have been a good fielder. My Uncle Nick taught me when I was very young that the most important aspect of fielding is to get your body in front of the ball. And I had more body than anyone else.

Finally, because of my great speed and range, they found the proper position for me. Catcher. It was while I was crouched behind home plate, ducking tipped Spaldings, that I first learned to appreciate catchers.

A catcher's accoutrements—his iron mask, shin guards and chest protector—are known as the "tools of ignorance." The reason for this is obvious. Any man who would willingly allow Nolan Ryan to throw a baseball at him is not outstandingly intelligent. Basically a catcher is a crouching target. Catchers are the most beat-up, bruised, broken, knurled players on the field. They are the only athletes I know who can stick their hands out straight and point behind them. And, unlike other fielders, who simply have to catch the ball when it is hit near them, catchers have to run the defense. They must select the pitch and its location and make sure every fielder is in the proper position. They have to keep everyone alert, and they have to psychologically lead the pitcher through the game as carefully as they would lead a Luciano through a china shop.

I firmly believe catchers are universally under-rated and underpaid. Most of them are great humani-tarians. Brave men who do a magnificent job under torturous conditions.

Of course, catchers are the only thing between the umpire and the pitched baseball.

The first lesson I learned in baseball was to be nice to catchers, for my own safety. Like most umpires I tended to think of catchers as brick walls, but often smarter.

Before Spike Briggs offered me a job I thought baseball was a relatively simple game in which a pitcher stood on the mound adjusting his uniform, then threw the ball at the catcher, while somebody stood in between them trying to hit it. If he did, he got so excited that he ran around the bases. Catchers quickly taught me the facts of baseball life. They taught me how the game is really played. Very few things happen on a major league diamond by chance. Every pitch, every swing of the bat, every throw, is made with specific intention. And at the center of everything that happens is the catcher.

The primary job of the catcher is to pit the strengths of his pitcher against the weaknesses of the batter. This involves knowing how each hitter bats and thinks, what the specific situation in the game calls for, and thoroughly understanding how to squeeze the most ability out of the pitcher.

Nobody was better at motivating a pitcher than the late Thurman Munson. He knew when to be gentle and when to come down hard. He personally made Ed Figueroa a big winner with the Yankees. Whenever Figgy threatened to lose his composure, and his curve-ball, Munson would waddle out to the mound and get him under control. Once I was behind the plate and Munson was taking too long on the mound with Figueroa so I went out to bring him back. As I got close, I heard the tail end of his pep talk. "All you have to do is throw that slider over the plate," he was saying, "and there's not one hitter in either league who can hit you. You hit my glove with it and they'll never touch you. Just throw it over the plate, that's what you gotta do. I know you can do it. I've seen you do it."

I didn't know what effect the talk had on Figueroa, but it had convinced me.

We started walking back to the plate together. "You really think all that's true?" I asked.

Munson chuckled, then said knowingly, "He won't last the inning." He didn't.

But with a pitcher like Rich Gossage, Munson was an entirely different man. Instead of being understanding and supportive, he was angry. He'd whip the ball back to Gossage and scream at him to bear down and call him names. Goose would get so mad at Munson he'd throw his next pitch even harder, if that were possible.

Munson also called an intelligent game. By the time a catcher reaches the big leagues the one thing he has learned to do is catch the ball, with some notable exceptions, of course. Like the Met immortal Greg Goossen, about whom Casey Stengel once said, "He's twenty now. In ten years he has a chance to be thirty." But catching the ball is only part of the game.

Baseball really became fun for me when I began to understand the strategy taking place right in front of me. I began to see each pitch as a mathematical problem to be solved. Good catchers think in multi-pitch sequences, using different pitches thrown at varying speeds to set up a hitter for a specific pitch, the "out" pitch. There are few things more satisfying to see in sports than a catcher setting up a hitter to do a certain thing—for example, to hit a ground ball to the right side, setting up a probable double play—and then seeing it properly executed. Unfortunately only the pitcher and catcher, the infielders, the batter and the umpire are privy to this part of the game. This is really baseball in the trenches.

I used to love trying to figure out what each catcher was going to do in a specific situation. I considered the same facts and decided what pitch and location I would call for, then compare the catcher's decision with my own. If he called for the same pitch I would have, and the results were positive, I'd feel that I had correctly solved the problem. If he called for a different pitch and the batter hit it, I'd feel even better. And if he called for a different pitch and the batter missed it, or made out, I'd feel he was lucky.

Some situations were obvious. With two balls, no strikes on the batter the pitch is usually going to be a fastball over the plate. If a good fastball hitter is at bat, a Fred Lynn or a George Brett, I'd know a power-against-power confrontation was about to take place, and relish the situation. Baseball, I learned, is more a game of anticipation than action.

It wasn't always the best-known catchers who called the best games. Jim Sundberg and Buck Martinez, for example, used to fool me all the time. I'd be expecting a fastball outside and Martinez would cross me up with a breaking pitch inside. "Now, what'd you do that for?" I'd ask.

"What were you looking for?"

"Fastball away."

"Right. So was he," he'd reply, indicating the hitter. "That's why I wanted the hook."

The batter would be standing there listening to this dissection and, on occasion, get involved. If I were to believe their claims, no catcher has ever outsmarted a batter. Never, in my entire career, did a single hitter agree with the catcher's thinking. "No way was I looking fastball," he might tell Martinez, "but I knew you were thinking that I was, so I was sitting on the curveball. I wanted it up, though, and he got it down."

"I knew it," I'd say, feeling vindicated.

Martinez or Sundberg or Fisk or Munson or Herrmann or Roseboro would simply laugh.

Sometimes, after a particularly effective sequence resulted in a strikeout, I'd lean over the catcher's shoulder and say, "They really should credit you with that strikeout." No one argued.

There are also catchers who call bad games. Some catchers have trouble handling certain pitches and will never call for them with runners on base, even if they might be effective in that situation. Stengel once complained that another Mets catcher, Chris Cannizzaro, called for the curveball too often because "He can't hit it so he doesn't think anyone else can, either."

The catchers I most enjoyed working with were those players who liked to talk. The White Sox' Carlton Fisk is a talker. He talks to the batters, the umpires, anyone who will listen to him. He talks too much, in fact. He talked so much he often made it difficult for me to hear myself talk. But he's also very smart. When he was with Boston we were in Fenway Park one night for a game against Cleveland. Luis Tiant was on the mound and in the seventh inning the Indians sent Charlie Spikes to the plate as a pinch hitter.

As Spikes dug himself into the batter's box Fisk started muttering, "You're right, Ronnie, all he wants to throw is that curveball."

"Huh?" I blinked my eyes to clear my ears. I hadn't said any such thing.

". . . Curve, curve, curve, you'd think that was the only pitch he can throw. I keep telling him they're gonna wrap it around his neck. . . ."

I could see the wheels spinning in Spikes's head. Curveball? Fastball? Fisk had him thinking. He was in serious trouble. Tiant threw a fastball down the middle of the plate. Spikes's bat never moved. Strike one.

Charlie stepped out of the box and knocked imaginary dirt clumps out of his cleats. When he started getting resettled in the box, Fisk mumbled, seemingly to himself, "All right, now Louie, com'on, lemme see that heater."

Fastball. Spikes tensed. Tiant threw a curveball, just a little outside. Ball one. Fisk exploded. "#$#$'|$%! I told him I wanted the fastball." He hopped up and trotted out to the mound. I could see him standing there bawling out Tiant. Luis was nod-

ding as if he understood. When Carlton came back to
the plate he shook his head disgustedly. "He says he
misunderstood the sign. We'll see."

Fisk hunkered down into his crouch and shook his
head. This was a signal to Tiant. He wanted Tiant to
shake his head, in turn, to make the batter think he
was rejecting Fisk's signal. Tiant shook his head.
"Dammit," Fisk screamed, "that damn curveball. No
way I'm gonna let him throw it again. No way." Tiant
broke off a sharp curveball for strike two.

"Son of a $#$%($%!" Fisk screamed, and stalked
out to the mound again. Even from behind the plate I
could hear him yelling at Tiant. Then he slammed the
ball into Louie's glove and stomped back. "Now, was
that a fastball, Ronnie? Huh? He's trying to tell me
that was his fastball."

"Well, I . . ." I started to reply.

He really wasn't interested in my opinion.
"Course it wasn't," he continued. "I know a
$#%$(&% curve when I see one. What's he trying to
tell me that was a heater? All right, one more chance."
He yelled to Tiant, "Fastball, Louie, throw the fastball."

It really made no difference what pitch he threw,
Spikes had no chance. Fisk knew it. I knew it. Even
Spikes knew it. He was trying so hard to outguess Fisk
that he had completely lost his concentration. He
moved up in the batter's box a few inches to jump on
the curve before it broke down. Tiant blew the good
fastball right past him. He struck out without a swing.
I credited that strikeout to Carlton Fisk. Evidently so
did Spikes. Without a word of warning he spun around,
grabbed Fisk and started punching him. I was laughing
so hard I could hardly break up the fight.

Surprisingly I usually got along very well with
Baltimore's catchers. I think I was sorry for them. Earl

Williams was not a great catcher, but he disliked Weaver more than I did, so with that in common we became good friends. The only thing we ever argued about was who Weaver yelled at more. "You think he yells at you?" Williams would complain. "You should hear what he yells at me."

"Well, I don't know about that," I replied. "The guy is on my back every pitch."

"Sure, but that's only during the game," he countered. "At least you don't have to listen to him in the clubhouse."

"That's true," I agreed, "but he doesn't talk about you in the newspapers."

"Weekly or daily?"

Elrod Hendricks, on the other hand, tried to serve as a buffer between me and Weaver. "Now, Ron, just relax," he'd caution when he felt Weaver was really getting to me. "You know Earl. He's not happy unless he's not happy."

Ellie had the nicest way of arguing of anyone in baseball. My first year in the league I had the plate for the Orioles with Dave McNally on the mound. He threw a sharp-breaking curveball that Hendricks caught just before it hit the ground, but it just might have caught the batter's knees as it crossed the plate. I called it a ball and Ellie didn't say a word. McNally's next pitch was a rising fastball that tailed up high, but just might have been at the letters when it crossed the plate. I called it ball two.

Hendricks stood up and tossed the ball back to McNally, then turned his head just enough so I could hear him clearly, then said calmly to me, "Hey, I'm not gonna argue with you, but you've either got to give me that low pitch or the high pitch or we're gonna be out here all night."

Those were the magic words. Threaten any

umpire with a long game and he'll listen to you. I liked being in the majors, but I didn't want to live in a ballpark. That was probably the best piece of advice any ballplayer ever gave me. An umpire has to give the pitcher either the high strike or the low strike, and he has to be consistent about it. Personally I favored the high strike. And, as I gained more weight, the higher strike. Bending down to call the low pitch was something I did not enjoy.

Over a period of time I learned to trust certain catchers so much that I actually let them umpire for me on the bad days. The bad days usually followed the good nights. Those were the days when I knew I was in trouble because I'd be seeing two baseballs and Nolan Ryan wasn't pitching. On those days there wasn't much I could do but take two aspirins and call as little as possible. If someone I trusted was catching, Hendricks, Ed Herrmann, Johnny Roseboro, I'd tell them, "Look, it's a bad day. You'd better take it for me. If it's a strike, hold your glove in place for an extra second. If it's a ball, throw it right back. And please, don't yell."

"What about tips?" one of my friends asked me.

"Nah," I said, "I'm not paying at all."

It would work just fine. If they held the ball I'd call it, softly, a strike, and if they threw it right back a ball. If the game was close in the later innings I'd take back control. No one I worked with ever took advantage of the situation, and no hitter ever figured out what I was doing. And only once, when Ed Herrmann was calling the pitches, did a pitcher ever complain about a call. I smiled; I laughed; but I didn't say a word. I was tempted, though, I was really tempted.

There are situations in which an umpire can depend on the catcher—if he knows he can trust him. With runners on base catchers often stand up as the pitch is delivered so they can get a quicker release on their throw to a base. That's fine for them, but it prevents the umpire from seeing the pitch. Unless I leaped into the air, the pitch might be a ball, a strike or it might completely disappear, and I would never know it. When someone I trusted was catching, I'd ask, "Was that a strike?" If they said it was I would call it.

This used to drive Herrmann crazy. "C'mon, stop doing that," he complained after I asked him about a pitch. "I've got enough trouble doing my job and the pitcher's job without doing yours, too."

"But somebody's got to do it," I explained. He didn't think that was funny.

Obviously I couldn't trust every catcher. I know it is hard to believe, but some of them will actually try to cheat. A lot of young catchers in particular try to "pull pitches," or quickly move their glove after catching the ball to make it appear to be a strike. Then they hold their glove in that spot and demand, "What was the matter with that one?"

It is their belief that the glove is quicker than the eye. It isn't. "You pulled it," I'd explain, "and don't do it again." This is something umpires really dislike. By pulling a few pitches a catcher can totally destroy an umpire's credibility with a club and guarantee he is going to have a long game. All the catcher has to do is hold his glove in a spot for a few seconds, as if showing the entire world it was a strike, and every player or coach on the field or in the dugout will believe the umpire is having a bad day. Then they will spend the rest of the day "helping" him.

Some catchers try to gain an advantage by creating dissension among umpires. Many times when I was behind the plate a catcher would say to me, "Hey, Ron, I'm glad you're working tonight. Lemme tell you, Bill had a rough game last night." Or, if this was the first game of a series, he might criticize the entire crew that worked his team's last games. "We couldn't wait to get away from them."

There are umpires who do not get along with each other. There are entire crews who are not particularly friendly. But umpires never reveal this to a player. If a player tried to create a rift between me and any other umpire, I'd take his leash and drag him down a one-way street. "You think so, huh?" I'd ask.

"Oh, yeah, absolutely. He's not like you at all. He was awful."

"I'm glad you told me that. I'll tell you what, I'll let him know you're not satisfied with his work. That'll make him bear down every time you're involved in a play."

Invariably a long, thoughtful silence would follow, then, "Uh, Ron, maybe you shouldn't say anything. . . ."

When umpires hear that players are complaining about them they'll often confront that player at the first opportunity. What I would do in that situation is go stand by the player between innings and discuss the problem with him calmly and rationally in an attempt to clear up matters. I would very politely say things like "You think I was bad last night, huh? You were nothing for five. You smelled up the whole ballpark."

Laughing out loud when the player fails at the plate or makes a bad play in the field can also be effective.

There was a time in my imaginary playing career when I thought that given the choice, and another body, I'd want to be an infielder. Infielders don't receive physical punishment like catchers and don't have to cover acres of outfield territory. They play so close together there is usually someone, or something, nearby to blame every bad play on. Outfielders can't blame a dropped fly ball on a bad bounce, for example.

So I decided I would be an infielder—until I made my major league debut.

Spring training, 1973. Tucson, Arizona. The Cleveland Indians were playing the California Angels in an exhibition game. Buddy Bell was at third base for Cleveland and having an awful day. I was umpiring at third and reminding him he was having an awful day. After he committed his second ridiculous error I did the natural thing—I laughed at him. He turned around and warned me, "Watch your step, Luciano. I blow one more, you're gonna have to play third and I'm gonna ump." An inning later a routine grounder skipped through his legs, setting up my major league career. Bell turned around and flipped his glove to me, and we exchanged hats.

In an instant I made the transition from umpire to player. Suddenly I was part of the team. Winning mattered. I was no longer neutral. We were the good guys and the Angels were the bad guys. I moved into Bell's spot on the front edge of the infield grass. I shifted my weight to my toes so I could charge in on a topped grounder or bunt, or dive to my right or left for a hard line smash. I bent down as low as possible and made sure the fingers of my glove were almost brushing the grass so nothing could get under it. I was ready. Then the batter, a right-handed hitter, stepped up to the plate and looked in my direction.

I knew then I was going to be killed. He was so close to me. And so big. And he was actually swinging a telephone pole. I'd never felt so vulnerable in my life. When I'd played football I'd worn protective padding. The only padding I had that day was hanging over my belt.

The batter took a few vicious practice swings. I could feel a slight breeze. I backed up a foot, thought about it, and backed up another few feet. Bell was standing behind me yelling at the pitcher to keep the game moving. I didn't know what his hurry was. I started yelling at the pitcher, too. "C'mon, babe," I screamed, "you can walk this guy." Ninety feet had never seemed like such a short distance before.

The pitcher started his windup. Everything was wrong. Bell's glove was too small for me. I needed spikes. I wondered if I should call time out to get some sunglasses in case the batter hit a pop-up, but decided against it, knowing I wouldn't catch the ball anyway and not wanting to deprive myself of a potential excuse.

The first pitch was high and outside. "Way to go," I screamed. "Keep it away from him."

"Come on, Luciano," Bell sneered, imitating a well-known umpire. "Bend down."

I glanced over my shoulder. "No talking to the players, huh."

The second pitch was low and inside, a perfect pitch to pull through my stomach. The batter stepped into it and began swinging. I began retreating. Luckily he missed it. "Good pitch, good pitch," I yelled, "way to go."

The batter hit the third pitch on a rope to right field. I knew enough to cover third base in case the runner from first tried to go to third. Unfortunately he did. Shortstop Frank Duffy went into the outfield to cut off the throw to prevent the hitter from going to second. The right fielder's throw came toward third on a low, hard line, but I could see it wasn't going to beat the runner. "Cut it," I screamed thankfully, "cut it."

Duffy ducked out of the way. Laughing.

I actually caught the ball without suffering any permanent injury. Self-defense. But the runner was safely on third. The batter, however, was racing toward second, testing my throwing arm. I wound up and threw a small-caliber bullet over second. Way over second. Eight feet over second. Jack Brohamer leaped into the air and somehow managed to come down with the ball. By that time, though, the batter was standing on the base dusting off his uniform. Brohamer tagged him anyway. Joe Brinkman called him out.

He couldn't believe it. He began screaming, but Brinkman cut him off in mid-yowl. "Who do you think threw it?" he asked, pointing toward third.

The runner turned and saw me standing next to the base with the glove on my hand, kicking the dirt and looking sort of sheepish. "Oh," he said softly, and trotted off the field. That ended my brief playing career. As soon as the league office heard about it I received a letter telling me never to play again—as if I needed a warning—and both clubs were reprimanded but not fined. I've never been invited back for Old Timers' Day, either. How quickly they forget.

In all modesty though, I was one of the best fielding umpires ever to call. So long as I wasn't too close to home plate I wasn't afraid to scoop up groundballs in my bare hands. Once, for example, I was well behind first base in Anaheim. There were two out and the Red Sox' Carl Yaztremski was at bat. He smashed a sizzling grounder down the first base line.

As soon as the ball was hit, Angels' pitcher Frank Tanana started running towards first to take the throw from first baseman Don Baylor and step on the base. The ball was foul by inches, but I was much too involved in the play to call it. Baylor dived for the ball and missed, but I was right there backing him up. I went down low and picked it up, and in one motion tossed it to Tanana who stepped on the base, just barely beating Yaz. Then, without hesitating, I called Yaz outoutoutout.

The play happened so fast neither team im-

mediately realized what I had done, and since it was the
third out, began changing sides.

Suddenly, reality struck. It was the only time in
my life I've ever seen an entire team do a double-take.
Second base umpire Ken Kaiser was laughing so hard
he was crying, and had to lean over to keep himself
from falling down. No one on either team complained
about that play, though. Shocked speechless, I
assumed.

Actually, I like most infielders. They're usually
quick, sure-handed, and smaller than me. The problem
I have with them is that the infield is not big enough
for the two of us—me and any fielder. Throughout my
career I've had my share of collisions with infielders.
Unfortunately, I've also had Bill Haller's share. And
Don Denkinger's share. And Jerry Neudecker's share.
I've had a bunch. Most of the time it was not my fault.
I would be in the middle of a very important conversation and everyone else would insist on continuing the
game.

Once the Red Sox were playing Minnesota and the
Twins had a runner on first with one out. That was all
very interesting, but I was trying to tell Boston second
baseman Doug Griffin about a great sale at Filene's
department store. Griffin was such a nice man. All he
wanted to do was be left alone to play baseball, but he
didn't want to hurt my feelings by telling me to be
quiet. So, as I was telling him about the sale, the
Twins' batter hit a grounder toward the middle of the
diamond, a sure double-play ball. Griffin started moving over to make the play. He took four long strides
and ran right into me, effectively stopping me in mid-
sentence. He bounced off and dived for the ball, but it
was too late. The ball ended up in center field. So,
instead of the Red Sox being out of the inning, the
Twins had runners on first and third with one out, and

Harmon Killebrew was at bat. Griffin never said a word to me, but manager Dick Williams said it for him. There was nothing I could do but accept the blame.

Killebrew saved me. Being the perfect gentleman, he hit a double-play ball to shortstop to end the inning. I was so happy I spent the rest of the game talking to Griffin about it.

There are some infielders who have left *me* speechless, however. There are simply no words sufficient to describe some of the plays I've seen made. By 1970 I had been in the American League for an entire year, so I thought I had seen everything. But one night I was behind the plate in Chicago and the visiting team's batter hit a hard grounder over second base. I'd seen numerous balls hit in about the same spot and every one had gone into center field for a base hit. This time, though, moving as gracefully as a young boy's fantasy, the Sox' shortstop Luis Aparicio outran the ball, reached out as far as possible and grabbed it. Then, in a single motion, he leaped into the air, twisted his body, and made a perfect throw to first base to beat the runner by a step. I wanted to call time out and go over to Aparicio and thank him for doing that for me and tell him it was the greatest play I had ever seen. "We can go home right now," I said to the Sox' catcher. "We're not gonna see anything like that again."

"Least not till tomorrow," catcher Duane Josephson agreed. "He doesn't usually make plays like that more than once a game."

Mark Belanger is the only shortstop I would rate in the same universe as Aparicio. When I was at first base one day I saw him go behind third base and make a play on a ground ball that was so fantastic I couldn't even call it. I just stood there with my mouth open.

The first base coach started yelling at me, "He's safe, he's safe, he beat the throw."

I looked at him scornfully. "How can you try to cheat him on a play like that?" I asked.

Graig Nettles plays third base as well as any human being has ever played it, but Brooks Robinson can't be described as merely human. He owned that position. They should name a vacuum cleaner after him.

The best double-play combination I've ever seen was the Royals' Freddie Patek and Cookie Rojas. Not only did they make the real double play as well as any shortstop and second baseman in the league, they turned an exceptional phantom double play. The phantom double play is a sophisticated version of the hidden-ball trick. On the hit-and-run play the baserunner takes off from first base as the pitcher releases the ball. Some players, particularly rookies, run with their heads down, watching the reaction of the infielders in front of them to determine what the hitter has done with the pitch. Sometimes the batter hits an easy pop-up or fly ball, but the infielders will pretend he has hit a playable ground ball, and execute a perfect fake double play. If the runner is fooled, he'll go barreling into second base to try to break up the double play, while the player who catches the ball tosses it to first base to complete a double play.

Patek and Rojas were so good at this they should have been forced to join Actors Equity. I remember seeing Patek actually pretend to bobble the baseball, conning the runner into a head-first dive into second, while Rojas made a perfect pivot on the base. I stood there with my hands at my side because I had no call to make. The runner, a rookie I never saw again, jumped out of the dust cloud screaming, "I beat the throw, I beat the throw." When he realized I wasn't making any call at all, he demanded, "What am I? What am I?"

I looked at him and shook my head. "Fooled," I said, and walked away.

Only once have I ever known an infielder to successfully talk a ball into going foul. Lenny Randle was playing third base for the Seattle Mariners when Amos Otis topped a ball down the third-base line. Randle had less chance throwing him out than I did making the Olympic hurdling team. Realizing that, he got down on his hands and knees and started screaming at the baseball. "Go foul," he yelled as loudly as possible, being careful not to touch the ball, "go foul." Sure enough, the ball rolled foul. Home plate umpire Richie Garcia called it foul, at first, but after a long argument from Royal manager Jim Frey gave Otis first base on the grounds that Randle had interfered with the rolling ball.

I communicated with outfielders mostly by gossip. Except in the Mickey Stanley situation I didn't get too near them in the field, so I never really got to spend any time talking with them. But I did learn that the two hardest things for an outfielder to do are catch a fly ball hit directly over his head and remember his sunglasses. Outfielders were always asking me to hold on to their flip-down sunglasses between clouds. Sunglasses are to a baseball player what shirts are to an umpire. There are shirts of mine waiting to be picked up at dry cleaners in every American League city. So today I own about fifty pairs of sunglasses and three shirts.

About the only time outfielders don't use sunglasses is when they most need them. One glaringly bright afternoon in Detroit, Champ Summers lost a routine fly ball in the sun. That can happen to anyone.

But in that same inning, that very same inning, he lost a second fly ball in the sun. That doesn't happen to anyone. After the second fly dropped a few feet behind him, he called time out and got his sunglasses from the dugout.

At the end of the inning I asked him why he hadn't gotten his glasses after his first error. "I was too embarrassed," he said honestly.

"But then why did you go and do it after the second fly ball?"

"I was stupid."

My favorite defensive plays to watch are great catches in the outfield. There are few things in sports as beautiful as watching a fleet outfielder running down a long fly ball. Time really does stand still. Fred Lynn made the greatest catch I've ever seen. I was working second base in Minnesota and the Twins' batter hit a drive to right-center. Lynn took off at the crack of the bat. I didn't think he had a chance to get it. When he reached the wall he leaped into the air as high as he could and flung his body over the fence. For a few seconds he was actually parallel to the ground, balanced on the fence like a see-saw. Then, slowly, he fell back onto the field and did a somersault. I was thrilled he had survived; it didn't even occur to me that he might have caught the ball. I thrust my hand in the air and started signaling home run.

Then Lynn held his glove up in the air triumphantly. The ball was in his webbing. I was so busy applauding I never bothered to call the batter out. When Lynn came in at the end of the inning I went out to meet him, and ran in with him partway, telling him that was the greatest play I'd ever seen.

"But I paid for it," he said, showing me his uniform sleeve. It was soaked with blood. He'd ripped off at least three layers of skin on the top of the fence and still held on to the ball. If he had made the play in an All-Star Game or World Series, baseball fans would talk about it forever; since it occurred in a regular-season game it just made the nightly news.

Great fielding plays don't happen by chance. Like every other aspect of baseball they are the result of preparation, skill and experience. Knowledgeable fielders know when to "cheat," or play a few steps out of position, for a certain hitter in a certain situation, enabling them to make extraordinary plays. But a fielder can think too much. In 1975 The Great Scott made one of his infrequent appearances at third base for the Milwaukee Brewers. George was a great fielding first baseman, but as a third baseman he was still a great first baseman. Late in the game the Brewers brought in a relief pitcher. Scott carefully watched him take his warm-up pitches, then just before play resumed ran into the dugout and emerged with a new glove.

I hadn't seen anything wrong with the glove he had been using, so I strolled over to him and asked about the switch. "Had to go to the bigger glove," he explained seriously. "This pitcher gives up a lot more hits."

I nodded and walked away. As an old third baseman myself, I understood.

8

MANAGERS
OR How Can You Yell at Me
When You Know He Touched
the Base with the Wrong Foot?

During the winter of 1977 I was invited to appear at a banquet in Nova Scotia with Jim Rice and Earl Weaver. Because my plane arrived late, I missed the afternoon press conference. With nothing to do until dinner, I wandered into the hotel bar. As my eyes focused in the dark room, I spotted Earl Weaver sitting by himself at the far end of the bar. This being the off-season, I figured we'd have nothing to argue about, so I decided to say hello to him and maybe even smooth out some of our differences. The empty glasses in front of him indicated he'd been sitting there for a long time. "Earl," I said, "you'd better take it easy. We've got a banquet to go to in a few hours."

He twisted his head and looked at me for the first time. "You'd drink, too," he said in the saddest voice, "if you had to sit on the dais with Ron Luciano."

Umpires and managers are not natural enemies. A really good feud like mine and Weaver's isn't just a matter of luck. It has to be developed and nurtured over a hundred afternoons on the diamond. The game of baseball positions umpires and managers on opposite sides of the foul lines. They have very different goals: the manager wants to win and keep his job; the umpire wants to get the game over with as quickly and quietly as possible. But umpires and managers can become friends. I know it can happen. I have actually seen it happen.

After years of battling each other through various minor leagues the inimitable Gugie Guglielmo and manager Frank Verdi had come to really like each other. Once, when I was in the International League, Gugie and I went into Syracuse to work a game for Verdi's Chiefs. I had learned to like going to Syracuse as an umpire because the fans were so brutal that it made me appreciate all the other cities. Before the game Verdi told us he was having a tough time because his team wasn't winning—the fans were booing his car in the parking lot—but through the first few innings he was very calm. Gugie would make an awful call and the crowd would threaten to destroy upstate New York but there wouldn't be a peep out of the Syracuse dugout. I thought, Gee, that Verdi must really like Gugie. But in the fifth inning he came storming out of the dugout to argue what appeared to be a pretty good strike call. He was furious. I couldn't believe he hadn't complained at all on some of the dubious earlier calls but was going to the well on this one, so I moved down the line to hear his complaint. "Those %#$&#$ fans are really on me tonight," he screamed at Gugie, "and I gotta do this to get them off my back."

"You go ahead and yell at me all you want," Gugie shouted right back at him, "and we'll show them they can't yell at you."

"You know what I'd like to do with them . . ." Verdi continued, throwing his hat, kicking up dirt, waving his arms like a Weaver.

Gugie held up his end, poking his hand in Verdi's chest and finally kicking him out of the game. Hatless, Verdi marched off the field to the appreciative cheers of the Syracuse fans.

Gugie never minded taking abuse from a crowd.

He was always willing to meet the entire crowd underneath the stands after the game.

One-time Kansas City Royals manager Jack McKeon and umpire Ken Kaiser were also friends, although I didn't know it the first time I went into Kansas City with Kaiser. Ken is a delightful man. He's one of the few men I know who wrestled professionally and still thinks that pro wrestling is for real. "The Hatchet," as he is known professionally, once mud wrestled the famed Gonzo Sisters—and claimed they were dirty fighters. (He won the bout, however.) I had home plate one night and he was working first when the visiting-team batter took a half-swing. I said he had checked his swing in time and called it a ball, figuring I had a fifty-fifty chance of being correct. The Royals' catcher asked me to check with Kaiser at first base and I did. He put his palms down, safe, meaning the batter had not swung. Suddenly McKeon came racing out of his dugout toward Kaiser, and those two really got into a good one.

I got very upset. That was my argument they were having. McKeon had no right to scream at Kaiser when he should have been screaming at me. I took off my mask and hustled down the line. "What's going on?" I demanded when I reached them.

"Get outta here," McKeon said to me. "Can't you see you're ruining a good argument?"

Kaiser agreed. "Leave us alone, Ron. We're doing a good job, we don't need any help."

I suddenly started feeling very lonely. They were having a wonderful argument and wouldn't let me have part of it. Dejected, and admittedly a bit confused, I turned around and went to home. After the game I learned that the single thing McKeon and Kaiser disagreed about was who was the better arguer, and were taking advantage of *my* questionable call to fight it out.

Unfortunately these friendships are rare. Much more common are personality clashes. There are simply some umpires who are not going to get along with some managers. Like myself and Weaver, for example. Or Bill Haller and Weaver. Or Marty Springstead and Weaver. Or Don Denkinger and Weaver. Throughout baseball history there have been classic umpire-manager confrontations. Like every other tradition, the situations are familiar, only the participants change.

The great National League umpire Tom Gorman did not get along with Leo "The Lip" Durocher any better than I got along with Weaver. In 1970, for example, Durocher was managing the Chicago Cubs and one of his players hit a slow infield roller. Gorman got down on one knee to call the play at first base and the runner plowed into him, knocking him out cold. As he came to, he heard a familiar voice demanding, "What was he? Safe or out?"

Gorman's answer should be etched in granite for all young umpires to memorize. Without opening his eyes he said, "If that's you, Leo, he's out!"

Feuds do not have to be permanent. Even Gorman and Durocher developed an understanding and, except for the occasional brawl, got along. In my career there was a time I didn't get along with Billy Martin. A long time. Years. We argued over everything. We argued over attendance figures. It just grew over a number of seasons, finally reaching the point where I almost lost control. It was the only time in my life in sports—college and professional football, minor and major league baseball—that I almost slugged somebody on the field.

Martin was managing the Texas Rangers in 1974 and my crew went into Arlington for the televised Saturday afternoon Game of the Week. The Rangers were playing the California Angels. Unfortunately one member of our crew got sick, so we had to work the game with three umpires, which meant I had to do a lot of running. Then, it was a typical Texas afternoon. Temperature a hundred degrees. Humidity a hundred percent. Chance of rain: zero. Early in the game I called a balk on the Angels' pitcher and California manager Bobby Winkles came out to yell at me. He accused me of giving the breaks to managers who complain all the time and yell the loudest. I considered that a direct attack on my integrity. No umpire wants to be told he can be intimidated by a manager who constantly screams at him.

I explained this to Winkles in my own calm way. I had a fit. I practically kicked him off the field.

I stayed angry through the rest of the game. And sweaty. I didn't need very much to set me off and, late in the game, I got enough.

In the seventh inning the Rangers had runners on first and second with less than two out. Because we were one umpire shy, I had to cover the whole right side of the infield. The batter hit a ground ball to the second baseman, a routine double-play ball, and I tried to watch the play at second while I was running toward first to make what I anticipated would be the close call.

The second baseman made a high throw to the shortstop covering the base; from my viewpoint I couldn't really tell if the shortstop was touching the base when he caught the ball. If we had been working with a full complement of umpires I would have been on top of the play. I still might not have gotten it right, but I would have had a good shot at it. But this time I had to guess, so I went with the odds and called the runner out at second.

Martin was watching the play from the dugout and had a better angle than I did, plus the advantage of the televised instant replay. The shortstop was evidently about a yard off the base when he caught the ball. Martin had a legitimate gripe and he was going to tell me all about it. In complete detail. Loudly.

I tried to hold my temper as I explained to him that I hadn't gotten a good look at the play because we were working with only three umpires.

"#$#%$#$('%&," he screamed. "Then why didn't you ask for help?"

"Yeah? Who was I gonna ask? You?"

"#$#%$&#$#," he continued, "#$'&$%#$#!"

Finally everything got to be too much. The heat got to me. I was still furious at Winkles. Martin being right. I could just feel the anger boiling up inside me. I could feel my body tensing. . . .

"Hey!" Martin yelled suddenly. "Don't hit me!"

His screaming demand shocked me into reality. My hand was cocked into a fist and drawn back. If Martin hadn't stopped me, I would have socked him.

I was so flustered I didn't even throw him out of the game. I mumbled a few words and walked away, staring at my offending hand as if it were a stranger. Billy knew enough not to follow me, and didn't raise his voice again that afternoon.

After the game I calmed down enough to put my actions into proper perspective. Once I figured out a way of blaming the entire incident on Billy I felt a lot better. Just because *I* had lost my temper was no reason to assume I was at fault.

A season passed. Martin was fired at Texas. I was

happy for the Rangers. But in midseason 1975 he was hired to replace Bill Virdon in New York. I was unhappy for me.

I didn't see him until September. The Yankees were playing at Shea Stadium in Queens, while up in The Bronx, Yankee Stadium was being renovated. During the three-game series we had a few words, but nothing to shout about.

When I left the dressing room after the third game I ran right into him leaving the Yankee clubhouse. I decided to be polite and ignore him completely. But he grabbed my arm and asked me to join him for a drink. We went into the stadium club and ordered a round. Then another round. Then more rounds than Muhammad Ali fought in his entire career.

Our conversation began very pleasantly. "I'm gonna tell you why I don't like you," Billy said.

"Oh, yeah? I'll tell *you* why you don't like me," I replied. "You don't like the way I jump around out there, that's why."

"No," Billy protested, "that's not it."

"I know why you don't like me," I continued confidently. "You don't like the way I shoot people out and . . ."

Martin shook his head.

"Well, then, you don't like the way I talk to the players during the game. . . ."

"Nah, I don't care about that. . . ."

I was beginning to get angry. I didn't want to give him the pleasure of telling me why he didn't like me. But other than the minor things I'd mentioned, I couldn't think of anything he could object to.

"I just think you hurt my ballclub by not bearing down all the time."

Then I told him what I thought of his antics on the field. And he told me how I should act during the games. And I told him that no umpire could get them all right. And he told me he was only protecting his players. And I told him he probably wasn't the worst manager I'd ever seen. And he told me that he had seen a few worse umpires in his career.

By the time we closed the club that morning we had vowed eternal friendship and promised to try to get along on the playing field. We toasted the beginning of our new relationship and we toasted the end of our combative relationship. Before we were through, we also toasted the Haitians who sew covers on baseballs, every American president, world peace and most television quiz show hosts.

Our truce lasted the entire winter—or until the first time I had Martin's Yankees in 1976. I blew a play at first base. I admit it. I was wrong. But I wasn't *that* wrong. It was a bang-bang play and I anticipated the throw arriving before it did and I called the runner out.

Martin came red-hot raging out of the dugout and started screaming at me.

I held up my hands. "Wait a second!" I shouted right back. "Don't you remember that night in Shea when I told you I wasn't going to get everything right?"

"Yeah, I remember that," he screamed, "but don't you remember that I told you I was gonna climb all over you when you weren't bearing down?"

"Yeah, right, but remember when I said that when you did that you didn't have to rant and rave and . . ."

"But I told you sometimes I couldn't help myself because your calls got me so angry . . ."

"But wait, then you said . . ."

So we stood there reminding each other as loudly as possible what we had agreed to that night in Shea Stadium, and Billy never bothered to argue about the play at first base. After that we had our share of disagreements—I was right on some and he was wrong on others—but we maintained a mutual respect. Billy may have had his problems with some owners, and some fans, and a few umpires, and a few reporters, but we never had a serious argument after that.

Umpire Richie Garcia and Cleveland Indian coach Rocky Colavito also had a long-time feud that included a lot of unpleasant words, bumping incidents and even a league hearing. But when Garcia and I were in Anaheim a few years ago the owner of a popular Mexican restaurant invited us for three-foot tacos. As we walked into the place we saw Indian broadcaster Herb Score and Colavito sitting at the owner's table waiting for us. Garcia and Colavito glared at each other, but as the evening progressed they began talking and by the time we'd finished the tacos and beer they had smoothed out many of their differences.

These incidents proved to me that an umpire and player or coach who constantly have problems with each other could reach an understanding if they simply sat down in a room and talked it out. However, just in case the discussion didn't work out, I would suggest the room have padded walls.

When an umpire finally reaches the major leagues he is usually going to stay there for a long time. Managers come and go. And come. And go. And come. And go. Billy Martin has managed Minnesota, Detroit, Texas, New York (twice) and Oakland. Ralph Houk has managed the Yankees, Tigers and Red Sox. Dick Williams has been in Boston, Oakland, California, Montreal and San Diego. Gene Mauch: Philadelphia, Montreal, Minnesota, and the Angels. Whitey Herzog: Kansas City and St. Louis. Sparky Anderson: Cincinnati and Detroit. Don Zimmer: San Diego, Boston and Texas. Yogi Berra: The Bronx and Queens. Bob Lemon was voted Manager of the Year at Chicago in 1977 and at New York in 1978. He was fired in 1978 and 1979.

Because one team's failure is usually another team's new manager, once a man is hired to manage a major league team he's usually somewhere to stay. So umpires and managers do get to know each other. Over a period of time the managers learn to appreciate the umpires and the umpires learn to tolerate the managers. Umpires also learn who the good guys are, the field generals, the bullies, the bad guys. Reputations are earned over many seasons and often with more than one club. And once earned, they stick. Don Zimmer had problems in Boston with the press and fans, but rarely with the umpires. When he came out of his dugout umpires knew he had a legitimate argument; they listened to him. Zimmer is so well liked he could probably lead a conga line across the infield without being booted.

Each manager has his own way of conducting a game. Weaver is a statistician. If he hadn't become a great manager he could have made the Bookkeeper's Hall of Fame. He has the record of every player in the league against every pitcher in every situation. If a redheaded, right-handed hitter with freckles once hit a home run off a 5'8" left-handed relief pitcher during a thunderstorm in a game played on a Thursday afternoon with the temperature less than fifty-eight degrees, Earl knows it. And the next time that situation arises he'll put his information to good use. The reason Earl gets so much more out of his players than other managers do is because he uses them in situations in which they're proven to be effective. He'll go against baseball's Golden Rule—Always use a right-hander against a left-hander—by pinch-hitting left-handed John Lowenstein against a left-handed pitcher because he has a card showing that Lowenstein had three hits in six at bats against that pitcher.

Ralph Houk is representative of the more traditional manager. He likes to put in left-handers against right-handers, in the later innings he plays for the win on the road or the tie at home, and he bunts the runner on first into scoring position when losing by one run.

Gene Mauch is still busy inventing baseball. He's the innovator; he does things no other manager would even think of, much less actually try. Mauch has a special fondness for unusual shifts, moving players out of their normal position when a certain hitter is at bat or a standard play is called for. In three different games I worked he brought an outfielder in to become a fifth infielder when the other team had the winning run on third base in the ninth inning with less than two out. It was a fascinating setup to see. It failed each time.

Alvin Dark is the best field manager I've ever seen, although he has difficulty handling players off the field. He's a master strategist, but sometimes he goes just a bit too far. I had the plate in Oakland one night in 1974 and Dark's A's were winning by four runs at the end of seven innings. Before the eighth began he came out to the plate to give me some lineup changes. "Let's move Tenace from first to catcher," he began, reading off a card, "Rudi from left to first. Washington goes to left. Haney's out. . . ."

"Wait a second," I said, "just wait." I looked at my lineup card and saw that he was managing a different game from the one I was umpiring. "You took Haney out of the game three innings ago. Rudi's been at first base for two innings. Washington pinch-hit in the fifth. . . ."

Dark checked his lineup card and smiled broadly. "Oh, I see what I did. I was giving you the changes I was going to make if we were behind in the eighth." Then he pulled an entirely different lineup card from his pocket and gave me the changes he wanted. I couldn't believe any manager would plot entire games inning by inning before they even started.

Personally I'm extremely pleased when I can remember what city I'm in.

Strategy obviously is important, but a manager's primary job is motivating his players. Houk's players like him so much they would build a brick wall for him, then run right through it. Weaver's players would try to figure out if they could dig under the wall, maybe climb over it, or rent a plane to fly above it.

Houk is one of the most popular managers in baseball. Everybody in the game likes him and considers him a winner. When Houk's Detroit team was in the midst of a nineteen-game losing streak, Kansas City was looking for a new manager. The Royals' general manager was asked what type of man he was looking for, and he said, "A winner, like Ralph Houk." The man was in the middle of the longest losing streak in his team's history and was described as a winner. That's not a manager, that's a hypnotist.

I have my own reason for being a Ralph Houk fan. He did the nicest thing for me that any manager has ever done. I had a lot of trouble with him my first few years in the league. We really went at it a few times, and he really knows how to go at it. He puts on a truly spectacular argument, complete with multiple hat-kicks, punting dirt for distance and rapid arm waving. Finally veteran umpire Larry Napp told me the secret of getting along with Ralph Houk. "Shut up," he said. "Houk is coming out either to protect a player or to get himself thrown out. If he comes out with his hat in his hand, he wants to go. So put him out. But if he comes out to protect his player don't argue with him. Just stand there, look at him and listen to him. When he's done, he'll turn around and walk away."

I took that advice and from that point on it was a cinch. If I was arguing with one of his players he'd come out screaming at me. "What the $#&%$$'s going on," he'd yell. "That's the worst $"##$'%$ call I've ever seen. How can you"—in the middle of this argument he'd pause, push away his player and tell him, "It's okay, you get outta here—I'll tell him how bad he is"; then he would turn back to me and continue screaming—"make a #"$'#&$# call like that?"

But if he came out holding his hat in his hand, I'd give him a quick thumb.

In 1974 I was working first base in Detroit in the seventh inning of a close game. The visiting team's batter hit a simple grounder to second base and I did the one thing an umpire should never do: I watched the ball going into Tiger first baseman Norm Cash's glove and then looked at the runner, rather than watching the runner touch the base and listening for the sound of the ball hitting the glove. Naturally, by the time I looked up, the runner had crossed the base. I figured he had to be safe.

That only turned out to be the worst call in the history of baseball. The second baseman started screaming, I threw him out. Cash exploded, he was gone. Houk put on a kicking display that would've earned him a job with the Radio City Music Hall Rockettes, he was gone. By the time things quieted down I had cleared out the right side of the Tiger infield and gotten their manager.

It got worse. The runner I put on first with my bad call eventually scored the tying run and we went into extra innings. I figured that was my punishment, but there was more to come. In the eleventh inning the replacement for the second baseman made an error allowing the visiting team to score the go-ahead run. Then in the bottom part of the inning the Tigers had the tying run on third with two out and Cash's substitute at bat. He struck out to end the game.

I lost that game for the Tigers. I put the tying run on base, kicked out two starting players and saw their replacements contribute to the loss. At the bottom of the official league standings there should have been an entry for "Luciano 0 wins, 1 loss." I was really feeling dejected. I've often kidded about my umpiring career, but I was proud of my ability and hated making a mistake. This mistake was a big one.

By the time I had taken a shower and cleaned up, the other members of my crew were long gone. Just as I walked out of the umpires' dressing room, the door of the Tiger clubhouse opened and out walked the one man in the world I really didn't want to see. Ralph Houk took two steps then stopped when he saw me.

I thought, if we get into a fight, I know I can take him.

"Hey," he said pleasantly, "where you goin'?"

"ACROSS THE STREET TO GET A #%$" '&% BEER," I screamed at him.

He cringed. "I can hear you," he said, then tilted his head in the direction of the exit. "C'mon, I'll buy."

At first I was stunned. Then I wanted to kiss him. This was one of the fiercest competitors in sports and I'd just taken a game away from him and he didn't say a word about it. It was a moment I would never forget.

Houk wants to win as much as anybody in baseball. On the field he'll fight for the slightest advantage as long and hard as anyone who ever managed a ballclub, but he never takes the game home with him. When it's over, it's done. He never holds a grudge and umpires appreciate that.

Weaver never forgets. He is convinced umpires all hold grudges against him. Once, in 1975, we got into an argument about a play at third base and he screamed at me, "You couldn't get that play right in Elmira and you still can't get it right."

If I had been clever enough, I would have asked him to at least appreciate the fact that I was consistent, but I didn't think of it. All I could think about was that this was a man who accused other people of holding grudges and he was still angry about a play that had taken place ten years earlier. There was only one thing I could say to him. Good-bye.

Managers argue with umpires for three reasons: One, they believe the umpire has made a judgment in error and should be so informed. Two, they are trying to prevent a player or players from being dismissed from the game. Three, temporary insanity.

An umpire can be wrong. Whenever I made a mistake, and knew it, I really tried to keep the manager and players in the game. I rarely apologized and only when my mistake was obvious did I admit I might be wrong—no umpire can admit all his mistakes and survive—but in those situations I took a lot more abuse than I normally would. One such situation took place in spring training in Orlando, Florida in 1970. I was at third base during a Twins game being televised back to Minnesota. As often happens during spring training, we were only using three umpires. Hank Soar was at first and Davey Phillips was behind the plate. In the very first inning Cesar Tovar hit a fly ball down the first base line. Soar went running out to right field to see if it landed in fair or foul territory. As I was supposed to do in that situation, I moved to second base in case there was a play. Tovar rounded first and went racing into second as the rightfielder threw the ball back in.

As soon as the ball landed fair, Soar turned around and raced back toward the infield. Since I was covering second, I screamed to him, "You got third, you got third," meaning he should go to third base.

Tovar had just reached second when he heard me yelling. He paused for a moment, heard me say clearly, "You got third," shrugged, and started trotting to third base. Soar called him out.

Twins manager Bill Rigney found fault with my performance and came running on the field to tell me the news. I never liked arguing with Rigney. First of all he was just as tall as I am so I couldn't look down on him, and also, he liked being on television just as much as I did. More, probably. So during the argument both of us stood on our tiptoes and kept circling so we could get on television.

The play was my fault, but there wasn't anything I could do about it. So I danced with Rigney in circles, on tippie-toes, round and round, listening to him, occasionally injecting a point of order. But Rigney was playing for his ballplayers and the camera. He wanted me to throw him out of the game to prove to Twins fans that he was willing to fight for his team. But I didn't want to throw him out since the misunderstanding had been my fault. He screamed, yelled, threatened, he did everything to get the thumb, but I wouldn't give it to him. I could see that was *really* making him angry. Finally he gave me no choice. I made him very happy; I threw him out of the game. He got his ejection and the appreciation of the Twins fans.

That was not the only time language difficulties have caused problems on the field. Since the influx of Spanish ballplayers in the 1960s and 70s baseball has become a bilingual sport. Unfortunately, I do not speak Spanish. Besides a few swear words, the only thing I can say in Spanish is Richie Garcia. But in 1975 Armando Rodriguez and I were in Kansas City for a

Royals-Oakland A's game. A's shortstop Bert Campaneris was trying to stretch a single into a double and as he slid into second, Royals second baseman Cookie Rojas tagged him. Rodriguez called Campaneris out, but then Rojas juggled the ball, so Rodriguez changed his call to safe. But Campaneris slid past the base and Rojas tagged him again, and Rodriguez called Campaneris out; then Rojas finally dropped the ball, Campaneris scampered back onto the base and Armando Rodriguez called him safe.

Now, I could see that this play was going to cause some problems. Cookie started arguing with Rodriguez in Spanish. I had absolutely no idea what they were shouting, and since it had nothing to do with me I didn't want to get involved.

Royals manager Jack McKeon reluctantly came onto the field to try to understand exactly what had happened. He stood a bit to the side listening to Rojas screaming at Rodriguez in Spanish, then turned to look at Armando when he replied. For awhile McKeon looked like a spectator at a tennis match, looking from one side to another without saying a word. Meanwhile Rojas and Rodriguez were really having a good one. At one point Jack looked at me and shrugged. Finally, after listening to them for a considerable period, he threw his hands in the air and turned around. "Screw it," he said to anyone within hearing distance, "whatever he calls it is okay."

The only language problem I ever had on the field was with a Red Sox player in 1969. This player did not speak English, he grumbled English. I'd speak to him when he came to bat and he'd reply in a voice that resembled a volcanic eruption. "How's it goin'?" I'd ask.

"Rrmmmmmm, rrmmmmmmmm," he'd reply.

We got into an argument one night and I thought

he said, "Rrmmmm$#"'$#&$#" to me, which a
player cannot say to an umpire, so I ejected him. Boston manager Dick Williams came running out to protect his player, demanding to know exactly what he
had said.

What was I going to tell him? "Rmmmmmmm?"
"I'm not gonna tell you," I said, and walked away from
him.

He followed me. "You gotta tell me."

"I don't have to tell you anything."

"You do. You gotta tell me why—" He suddenly
paused, and smiled knowingly. "I know why you
won't tell me."

"Yeah?"

He laughed. "You couldn't understand a word he
said."

Williams was one of those managers who always
insisted on getting in the final word in an argument.
Once I threw him out of a game and he stood there
with his hands on his hips and screamed, "I'm glad you
threw me out of the game, 'cause now I don't have to
put up with any more of your nonsense."

Each manager has his own arguing style. Some
plead, some try to reason, some just simply yell as
loudly and as long as they can. Weaver likes to tear up
rule books. Houk likes to kick. The one manager who
could not argue was Cleveland's Jeff Torborg. He was
simply too smart to be in baseball. He would come out
to dispute a call and carefully explain to me that "the
trajectory of the baseball was such that in relationship
to the wall there existed no possibility that a human
being could move with such velocity as to retrieve the
ball in sufficient time to put the runner out at second
base."

"Yeah?" I'd respond. "That so? Well, I once had
my arm pulled out of its socket by Big Daddy Lips-

comb!" Talk about language problems—we had an argument one day that was so complex I wasn't even sure what we were arguing about. Fortunately I knew I was going to win it.

I always knew I was going to win the argument. I was the umpire, my decision was what counted. Knowing that took the suspense out of a potentially good fight and was one of the reasons I tried to avoid them. Arguments are not fun. I rarely enjoyed them and don't know of any umpires who do. One of the very few things I wanted to do in baseball, but never had the courage to do, was to run into a team's dugout after a manager had put in the wrong player or made a dumb strategic move and jump in the air and wave my hands like a crazy man, scream at him and call him all sorts of vicious names and threaten mayhem—and then, when he ordered me out of his dugout, ask in the most surprised voice, "Me? What did I do?"

In the past few years managers have started getting physical with umpires. A manager, or player, should never, ever, under any circumstances, touch an umpire. It's not that the manager or player might catch something, it's that the umpire occupies a very special place in sports. Throughout baseball history managers have been forbidden to touch the umpire and umpires have had a limited amount of trouble from fans. But if that barrier breaks down, and it seems to be cracked right now, umpires will start having real problems with fans.

No man who has ever worked a game was surprised when a fan attacked umpire Mike Reilly during the 1981 mini-playoffs between the Yankees and Brewers. The climate is ripe for serious trouble, and if baseball doesn't crack down severely, and do it right now, there will be many more serious incidents.

On occasion I was able to avoid an argument with

a manager. That occasion took place in 1969. I had first base for the Tigers and Seattle Pilots and a Pilot hitter bounced a grounder to first baseman Norm Cash. The Tiger pitcher raced over to take the throw from Cash and touch the base, but Cash decided to take the play himself. He easily beat the batter to first. Unfortunately, as the pitcher tried to get out of the way, he ran right into the batter. I had no choice: the pitcher prevented the batter from getting to the base. That is called obstruction and it is illegal. I called the batter safe and turned around to discover Tiger manager Mayo Smith climbing inside my shirt. "How can you call him safe?" he demanded.

This was still in my early, wise-guy days. "Easy," I said, "I just put my hands out to the sides with the palms facing the ground."

Smith turned to Cash. "You touch the base?"

I interrupted. "Yeah, he touched the base, but he should've thrown the ball to the pitcher, 'cause if the pitcher had the ball when he made contact with the runner it woulda been okay, but he didn't."

Smith didn't know what to do. He looked at Cash and asked, "Why didn't you throw him the ball?"

I instantly saw my path out of this argument. "Yeah," I asked. "Why didn't you throw him the ball?"

" 'Cause I saw I could beat him to the base."

"But you saw the pitcher coming over. . . ." Smith started. Cash yelled right back at him and I quietly backed away. I saw no reason to interfere with what was shaping up to be a fine argument.

Any umpire who claims he has never missed a play is . . . well, an umpire. But the truth is that every umpire has blown plays in his career. There have been times when I stuck my hand into the air to call a player out and then just stared at that hand and wondered what in the world it was doing up there when I knew perfectly well that the player was safe. The closest I ever came to admitting on the field that I had made a mistake, except for that infamous foul home run in Baltimore, was to agree that I was out of position or that it was a "really close" play.

About the only chance a manager has to get a decision changed is to prove that the umpire misinterpreted or misunderstood a rule, and that isn't going to happen very often. The rule book is the umpire's Bible. Umpires read it, study it, discuss it. When I took the final exam at the Al Somers School I correctly answered 298 of 300 rule-book questions. Few managers could match that.

Early in my career I learned that managers don't really know the rule book very well. During my second year in the minors I had a play at first base in which the first baseman had the ball in his glove and tried to touch the base with his right foot. He missed, but somehow managed to tap it with his left foot before the runner got there. His little dance got me so confused I called the runner safe. The defensive team's manager came out to discuss my call, but before he could open his mouth I shouted, "How can you yell at me when you know he touched the base with the wrong foot?"

The manager considered that for a moment, then nodded firmly. "You're right," he said, and returned to his dugout.

A few weeks later I had his team again. He came out to discuss another close call—I had gotten this one right—and after expressing his unhappiness about that call, paused and shouted, "And another thing. It doesn't matter which foot you step on first base with!" Satisfied, he walked away.

After that I learned that managers only know the

rules with which they've had problems. If I called a
balk on a team—and that is the toughest rule to apply
because it usually relies solely on interpretation—I
knew the manager of that team was going to become
the world's greatest living expert on the balk rule before my crew had his team again. I also knew the next
time he had a balk dispute he'd quote the rule book to
the umpire and, afterward, to the press.

I always took advantage of a manager's ignorance
to get myself out of a difficult situation. If I didn't
know the correct rule to apply I'd make one up on the
spot. "How in the world can you argue about that?" I'd
ask in my most astonished voice. "You *must* know
17:23, which clearly states a runner is entitled to the
base to which he is proceeding after a fly ball is caught
if, in the judgment of the umpire, his progress is in any
way impeded by a fielder not attempting to catch a
thrown or hit baseball. I'm surprised you didn't know
that one. I thought every manager did."

As long as I spoke very quickly, and sounded as if I
were quoting the rule book verbatim, I never had any
trouble. The rule book is actually very logical: it penal-
izes the team that made the error. As long as I followed
that dictum I knew I was okay.

Those few managers who do know the rule book
sometimes try to turn it into a law book. Gene Mauch
is the worst of them. He once made me force
Glenn Abbott to put on a new sweatshirt because the
sleeves of the one he was wearing were tattered.
"Hey," I told him, "I'm an umpire, not a fashion consul-
tant," but he was right and I had to make Abbott
change shirts.

The most ingenious rule-book play I saw during
my career was pulled off by Whitey Herzog while he
was managing Kansas City. I was working third base,

and the Royals had runners on first and third with one out. The batter hit a long fly ball to left-center field and both runners got ready to tag up. According to the rule book, as long as they touch the base after the ball is caught they are free to advance at their own risk. But the runner on third left the base before the catch was made. No question about it. All the defensive team had to do was put the ball in play, by having the pitcher step on the pitcher's rubber, then touch third base, and I would have to call the runner out for leaving too soon. That would be the third out of the inning and the run would not count.

Third base coach Chuck Hiller looked at me questioningly. I nodded. He nodded. The defensive team's dugout was screaming at the players on the field to make the appeal to third base. The ball was thrown back to the infield. The pitcher took it and dutifully stepped on the rubber, then turned to toss it to the third baseman. But before he could, the runner who had tagged up at first and gone to second stunned everybody, including me, by making a mad dash for third. The pitcher held the ball and ran right at him, forcing him to stop between bases and get caught in a rundown. The pitcher tossed the ball to the third baseman, who pursued the runner back toward second, then flipped the ball to the second baseman, who tagged him for the third out of the inning. The teams quickly changed sides.

I realized what was going on, but I couldn't say a word.

When Hiller came out to coach third the next inning he was as happy as the man who married the bank president's daughter. "We did it," he bragged. "We pulled it off." That seemingly crazy dash for third was a set play, he told me. By allowing the runner to be tagged out before the other team could make its appeal on the tag-up play at third base, the Royals had stolen the run.

Not exactly. The play worked only because Herzog was smarter than the other manager. The only problem with the play is that you're not always sure that the umpire saw the runners leaving too early. But I credited that run to Herzog. I was also pleased that Torborg wasn't there to try to explain it to me.

The proof that managers do not really know the rule book is that so few protests are upheld. Umpires hate protests, not because they make them look bad, but because every time a protest is made they have to call the league office immediately after the game to explain what happened, then follow that with a more detailed night letter or telegram.

The most ridiculous protest I've ever seen was lodged by Sparky Anderson in Detroit, and my new best pal Billy Martin really turned it around on him. When Sparky first came over to the American League after managing Cincinnati to a World Championship, he'd complain about every pitch. "Where was it?" he'd shout at the umpire. "Looked good from here."

"National League strike," I'd yell right back at him on a pitch that was over the batter's head. He did not like that at all.

Sparky was a rule-book manager; when he started managing in Detroit he was determined to show the American League umpires how tough he was. We were in Yankee Stadium one afternoon and in the bottom of the third inning Yankee first baseman Chris Chambliss cut his hand sliding into second base for the third out of the inning. But while he was in the dugout having his hand taped, Lou Piniella picked up his glove and started warming up the Yankee infielders.

Anderson knows the rule book. There is a rule which states clearly that once a substitute player has reached a position in the field he is officially in the game. Sparky saw Piniella throwing grounders to the infield and told home plate umpire Bill Haller that he wanted Piniella in the game and Chambliss out of it. Haller took the proper action in that situation. He laughed. "You're not serious?" he said. Anderson was very serious. As far as he was concerned, Piniella had reached a position and had to play it. When Haller suggested to Anderson that he return quietly to the dugout, Sparky protested the game.

Haller told him that was the single dumbest protest he had ever heard, but Anderson insisted he was protesting the game.

Two innings later Detroit's catcher, Lance Parrish, made the final out of their half of the inning and, while he was in the dugout putting on his protective equipment, Rusty Staub, the Tigers' designated hitter, put on a catcher's glove and started warming up the pitcher.

Billy Martin came racing out of the Yankee dugout laughing so hard he could hardly shout. "I got it now," he screamed. "That's a protest, that's a protest." Martin insisted that Staub stay in the game and catch. "He reached the position," he insisted.

Haller must have wondered why he hadn't been smart enough to call in sick that morning. He had to forward both protests to the league office and both were denied.

The strangest protest in which I've ever been involved was lodged by Earl Weaver, although I don't think anything concerning me and Earl could really be considered strange. I believe I have made it clear that we do not get along: Once, for example, before a game, we were having a very calm discussion about managing. He tried to convince me that the most a manager can do is try to arrange things so that certain hitters will face certain pitchers. I told him he didn't know what he was talking about, because I had been watching him outmanage people in four leagues over fifteen years. He told me I was crazy. I told him he was twice as crazy as I was. Finally one of his coaches stepped in and told us to stop shouting at each other. We were in the middle of an argument and didn't even realize it.

Our serious problems started in 1976. I was out in Oakland and a local reporter asked me who my favorite manager was. Naturally I told him it was former Oakland manager Alvin Dark. Couldn't hurt, right? In fact I really did like Dark. He was an unusually moral man. Once I got into an argument with Billy North over a call at second and Dark came running out of the dugout. Here we go again, I thought. Instead Dark raced past me and said to North, "I don't know what you're arguing about because you looked out from the dugout, so pick up your hat and let's go."

I watched Dark suspiciously. I didn't turn my back on him. I wanted to know just what he had in mind being honest like that. To my amazement he was just being honest. How could he not be one of my favorite managers?

Then, unfortunately, the reporter asked me which manager I liked least. Naturally I tried to avoid a direct answer. "WEAVER," I shouted. "EARL WEAVER." I would have spelled it for him, I would have written it down, I would even have hired skywriters if necessary.

The only problem I've ever had with newspapermen is that they write for newspapers. If they would just have kept my opinions to themselves I never would have had any trouble. Weaver read my comments and did not appreciate my sense of humor. He requested that the league bar me from Baltimore's

Municipal Stadium, the State of Maryland and the entire East Coast. Lee MacPhail suggested I keep my mouth locked.

I knew MacPhail was right and did my best to avoid any more problems with Weaver. My best lasted until spring training the following year. I was in Arizona and a reporter asked me a trick question: which teams did I think would win the division races in the American League.

"It doesn't matter to me," I said. "Lee MacPhail signs my paychecks no matter who wins." When pressed further, I said I thought Oakland would win the West and I didn't care who won the East, "As long as it isn't Baltimore."

When I said it I didn't think it was a terrible thing to say. That was the way I felt as a fan, but I knew that my feelings would never and had never affected my judgment on the field. Anytime I missed a play it was simply because I missed it, not because I was partial to one team or one player.

In retrospect it was an incredibly stupid thing to say. The league fined me four hundred dollars and ordered me to apologize publicly to Weaver and the Orioles. I agreed to apologize, but not pay the fine.

Three months later my crew was in Anaheim and had Baltimore for the first time that season. I was prepared to be on my best behavior, but I could afford to be—Bill Haller was angry. Weaver had questioned his honesty by saying he should not be allowed to work Detroit Tiger games because his brother was catching for the Tigers—and the league actually removed Bill from our crew every time we had Detroit.

Haller and Weaver had had difficulties for a long time. One Saturday afternoon Haller was working the plate and looked over at the Oriole dugout and spotted Weaver on his knees on the steps. Bill wandered over there and quietly asked him to leave the premises without hesitation. Weaver couldn't believe it. "What're you throwing me out for?" he demanded. "I'm just praying. You can't throw me out for praying."

"You Jewish?"

"No," Weaver admitted.

Haller smiled. "Well, it's Saturday, and you don't pray on Saturday if you're not Jewish. So get outta here."

For the first game of this Oriole-Angel series I was at second and Haller was at third. I had a close play at second that went against Baltimore, and before I took my thumb down I knew Weaver would want to discuss it. Sure enough, I looked up and saw him coming toward me. Even before he reached me he had grabbed his hat and thrown it on the ground, and I knew he was going to go. But as I flexed my thumb I spotted Haller racing toward me from third. "I got him," he was screaming gleefully. "Lemme, lemme." I stepped aside and let Haller tell Weaver how much he had appreciated his remarks about the Tiger games.

While Haller was giving him explicit directions to the clubhouse, I looked wistfully at Weaver's cap lying on the ground and nostalgically remembered the night 6'2" Don Denkinger had eased over to Weaver's cap while I was arguing with him and first stepped on it with the very sharp golf cleats on his right foot, and then the very sharp golf cleats on his left foot, and then started twisting back and forth, back and forth.

Upon arriving in Anaheim I had announced a press conference at which I would make a formal apology for my ill-considered remarks in spring training. Before the second game a group of writers, Weaver and American League Supervisor of Umpires Dick Butler squeezed into the umpires' dressing room.

My press conference began well. "To start with,

I've got a big mouth and I said a lot of dumb things. Everyone makes mistakes and I guess I'm at the top of the ladder when it comes to saying dumb things.

"It was just a dumb, stupid statement that should never have been printed . . . Earl and his players are professionals—they know I'm not going to do anything intentionally to hurt them. I like Baltimore, and I like the Orioles team. They are a good defensive team, and that always makes it easier on an umpire."

Suddenly I heard a familiar voice from the back of the small crowd. "But you did say it," Weaver said.

"Well, sure, yeah, I did say it," I admitted, "but hey, Earl, you've said a lot of things you're sorry for, too."

"No," he said, "I'm not sorry about anything I ever said about you or to you. I've meant every word of it."

"Well, then," I replied, getting warmed up, "I haven't been too far wrong when I said those things about you, you know."

Dick Butler tried to interrupt. "Thanks, Ron . . ."

"So you meant it, huh?" Weaver snapped, "I knew it."

"No," I told him, "I didn't mean what I said about Baltimore."

"But you meant it about me!"

By this time we were shouting at each other. "Well, you're the only guy I have trouble with all the time, and you have trouble with every umpire in the league, so don't you think you're the problem?"

"I yell at you because you're biased."

"Oh, yeah? Well you're more biased than anyone!"

My attempt to apologize turned out to be a disaster. The American League had no choice but to take me off Baltimore games. I objected, but there really wasn't anything I could do about it.

I didn't work an Oriole game for an entire year. I didn't miss Weaver, but I did miss his team. The Orioles were always such a pleasure to watch—and they played quick games. To my surprise, when I received my monthly schedule for June 1979, I had been assigned to a Baltimore-White Sox series in Chicago. Haller was taking his vacation during this period and I assumed the league had gotten confused and thought I was going to be on vacation. I didn't say a word. I was looking forward to seeing my pal Earl again.

We arrived in Chicago on a Friday morning. There had been a rock concert held in Comiskey Park the previous weekend and the field had been badly torn up. New sod had been lain down, but it had rained hard during the week. When I walked across the field I sank in over my shoes. I decided that if I couldn't walk on water, certainly nobody playing major league baseball could. I declared the field unplayable and called the game.

White Sox manager Tony LaRussa objected, but I told him I wasn't going to be responsible for players getting hurt on a muddy field. Weaver agreed with me, so our first confrontation in a year went smoothly.

The sun was shining on Saturday, but the field was still in terrible shape. I still didn't think we should play, but I wasn't sure. Players on both teams signed a petition claiming the field was not playable, so I called it again. This was the only time I've known of a game called because of rain on a gorgeous June afternoon.

We played a doubleheader on Sunday. The field was not good, but life rafts were no longer necessary, either. I had the plate and Weaver started on me in the very first inning. "Looked like a strike from here." "Bend over and look at it." It took him three pitches to make me feel right at home. In the third inning I called a strike on Doug DeCinces and Weaver really let me

have it. "Wherewasitlookedhighfromherebenddown-
beardown . . ." Maybe he was right, maybe it wasn't a
strike. I had only called about 150,000 pitches from
behind the plate and he had called many more than
that from the dugout, but it looked like a good pitch to
me. I probably would not have thrown out any other
manager in baseball for complaining, but this wasn't
any other manager. This was Weaver. I turned and
looked directly at him. I carefully loaded my finger. I
pointed it right at him and shot him out of the game.
Then I calmly blew the smoke away.

He sprinted out of the dugout to confront me.
"Are you throwing me out of the game?"

I'd been waiting a long time for this moment. I
smiled broadly. "Earl," I said, "I haven't seen you in a
year. *Of course* I'm throwing you out of the game."

He then proceeded to criticize my work and concluded by protesting the game.

"Earl? What? What are you going to protest? You
lasted until the third inning. You should be flattered."

It was then he invented the strangest protest I'd
ever heard. "I'm protesting the game on account of the
umpire's integrity."

"What?"

"Umpire's integrity. And I want it announced over
the loudspeaker."

"Earl," I said sympathetically, "you know you
don't want me to do that."

"I'm not leaving the field until it's announced
over the loudspeaker." This was a man who had faked
a heart attack on the field. This was a man who had
stolen second base and wouldn't give it back. I knew
he wasn't bluffing: he wasn't going to leave the field
until that announcement was made.

I was thrilled. I knew I had him. There was no way
he was not going to get suspended for publicly attack-

ing an umpire's integrity. "Okay, buddy," I told him, "you got it." I called the public address announcer and told him exactly what Weaver wanted.

"You don't want me to announce that," he said.

"Oh, yes, I do," I chimed happily. "Oh, yes, I do."

The p.a. announcer still did not believe I was serious. He announced that the Orioles were playing the game under protest, but did not give the reason.

That brought Weaver back onto the field. "What're you doing here?" I asked him. "You're not here anymore. You're gone."

"That's not what I said I wanted," he reminded me.

I tried to be sensible. "Earl, leave it at this. It isn't going to hurt me, but it is going to hurt you."

Announce it, he insisted.

I had it announced, and play resumed.

Assistant Supervisor of Umpires Johnny Stevens was waiting for me in the umpires' dressing room at the conclusion of the first game. Fuming. He had been in contact with Lee MacPhail, he told me.

"How is Lee?" I asked.

First, Stevens told me I was not to discuss the incident with any reporters. I was not to talk to Weaver during the second game of the doubleheader under any circumstances. I wasn't to smile at him. I wasn't to tell him that I couldn't hear him to draw him out of the dugout and then when he came out give him the boot. I wasn't to allow him to back me into a corner. If the ballpark caught on fire, I wasn't even to warn him.

I began to realize this was getting serious.

At the beginning of the second game we met at home plate during the exchange of lineups. He looked at me and asked, "What's going on?"

I opened my mouth to tell him that it had taken me an entire year, but I'd finally gotten him for his performance at that press conference. But before I could utter a single syllable, umpire Russell Goetz stepped between us. "Ron says everything is fine, Earl. Now, listen, both of you, it's a new game and we're not going to talk about the first game. It's over. That's it."

I worked third base that game and only had two calls. One was a line drive hit by an Oriole that landed just foul and I called it foul at least fifteen times. The other was a sliding tag play in which a White Sox player was out. That might have been the toughest out I ever called in baseball.

Weaver was suspended for three games.

Although I didn't realize it at the time, that was the last time Weaver and I would meet between the foul lines. The following year I was up in the broadcast booth, looking down upon him. I'd like to be able to report that the three-day suspension taught him an important lesson, that from that day on Earl Weaver had acted differently toward umpires, paying them the respect that he knows they have earned by their tireless efforts.

I would really like to be able to report that. Unfortunately I can't. Weaver will be winning games and screeching at umpires on every pitch until they drag him into the Hall of Fame.

During my career on the field I got to know, and like, numerous men who managed big league ballclubs. It's an elite, exclusive fraternity, limited to a membership of twenty-six men at any one time. But as I learned, old managers never die; they just end up working for George Steinbrenner.

9

BEING AN UMPIRE
OR Even Umpires Won't Talk to You

Once a man raises his right hand to call his first strike he enters a lonely, difficult world. On a baseball diamond the umpire is a moving target. The best thing that can possibly happen to him is to be completely ignored. Unfortunately it is usually *off* the field that he is ignored. When the A's first moved into the Oakland-Alameda Coliseum in 1968, for example, they forgot to provide an umpires' dressing room. This blatant example of wishful thinking was only discovered when the umpires arrived to discuss the ground rules the day before the first game.

Umpires are the ultimate authority figures, and are therefore disliked by players and fans of all races and creeds. As I began to receive publicity I would often be stopped on the street or in hotel lobbies by baseball fans—inevitably the conversation would come around to a terrible call made by an umpire in little league, a beer league, the office softball league, or the major leagues, that cost someone a game or a bet. And these people expected me to sympathize with them.

I loved so many things about being an umpire. Nothing could be better than being in major league baseball. And certain players were wonderful. And certain managers. I got to eat in the best restaurants in

211

America's best cities. I worked with a group of fine, professional men. The only thing I *didn't* like about being an umpire, as I've said before, was making decisions. (Well, that isn't quite true. I didn't like long games on sweltering days. I didn't like certain players. Or certain managers. I hated the arguments. And the constant travel. The salary wasn't great, either.)

Baseball changed dramatically from the time I came up to the major leagues in 1969 to the end of my career in 1979. When I started, it was played by nine tough competitors, on grass, in graceful ballparks. But while I was busy trying to answer the daily "Quiz-O-Gram" on the exploding scoreboard—Question: Who in the ballpark today has played for every team in the American League? Answer: the organist.—a revolution was taking place around me. By the time I hung up my whisk brush there were ten men on each side, the game was being played indoors, on plastic, and I had to spend half my time watching out for a man dressed in a chicken suit who kept trying to kiss me.

Although I was promoted to the major leagues with eleven other umpires, it did not take me long to become well known to all the veteran umpires and many fans. I wasn't the best young umpire in that group, or the brightest, or even the most handsome. But I was the only bird watcher.

For some reason people find it strange that a man my size should enjoy watching birds. I suppose they think I should be crushing them instead, but as soon as I realized other people thought it was funny, I stopped telling anyone about it.

I've hunted all my life. I started watching birds because I wanted to know what it was I had just missed with my gun. Actually the experiences are quite different. Hunting involves other people, or a dog, while birding is a solitary experience. I go by myself deep into the woods, and listen to the silence, and think, and watch the beauty of nature. Then I'm able to go back to the ballpark.

I've been doing it for many years. In the minor leagues, if I had a rough game and needed to unwind, I'd get up at 4:00 A.M. and drive to the nearest woods and take a long walk. I'd usually be back in my hotel room and asleep before my partner was awake, but if he did wake up and ask me where I'd been, I'd just wink at him and he'd wink back knowingly and I never had to explain.

I've charted over 275 different birds. The rarest is a monk parrot, a tropical bird never seen in the north. After I spotted it I went home to try to figure out what it was, and then had a representative of the Audubon Society come out and verify it for me.

Frank Umont was the man who discovered my secret. We roomed together my first year in the majors. Early one morning, while we were in Washington, D.C., I got up and drove to Virginia for a long walk. By the time I got back Frank was out of the room and I made the incredible mistake of falling asleep without putting away my binoculars.

Binoculars were then popular with baseball players, who used them for stealing opponents' signs during games and peering through hotel windows between games. Actually no one was ever known to steal a sign. So when Umont walked into our room and found my binoculars on the dresser he assumed he had caught me with the high-powered evidence. I tried to convince him I was not a Peeping Tom. "Then what are these for?" he demanded.

I stood up to my full 6'4" and said proudly, "Bird watching."

He laughed so hard he had to sit down.

"I'm a bird watcher," I confessed.

He managed to catch his breath. "Sure, kid." He winked.

To prove to him that I was a knowledgeable bird watcher, I decided to take him to the National Zoo. Once there, I figured I would take him to the aviary and point out the various birds. Umont couldn't wait to prove me wrong. As we walked out of the hotel he grabbed my arm, pointed straight ahead, and demanded, "Okay, bird watcher, what's that?"

"A pigeon," I told him. What else did he expect to see in the middle of Washington?

When we got to the zoo we went directly to the bird cages. He pointed to a bird and asked me to identify it. I did, confidently. Then he read the identifying plate on the cage. "Nah," he said, "that's not it. You're a Peeping Tom."

I couldn't believe I was wrong. I knew exactly what it was. I pushed Umont out of the way and read the plate myself—the birds were identified by their Latin names. That was the ballgame for me. As I had proved during my teaching career, Latin was Greek to me.

It took me two weeks to convince Umont I really was a bird watcher. And once he was convinced he wanted to share the news with everybody. Wherever we would go, he'd stop people and say, "See that big guy over there? Watches birds!" He'd tell ticket-takers at the ballparks, bellboys, he'd even knock on airplane cockpit doors. "That big guy watches birds! Do you believe that? A big guy like him." Inevitably a sportswriter picked it up and wrote an amusing column about it. Then other writers picked it up. Then broadcaster Curt Gowdy invited me to be on his television program, *The American Sportsman*. I quickly became one of America's few celebrity bird watchers. Because of this publicity, within three years of being promoted to the major leagues I was better known than some of the men who had been up there doing a great job for more than a decade. No one ever complained about it or showed the slightest animosity. Most felt that what was good for one umpire was good for all umpires.

In fact, rather than being resented, at the end of the 1969 season I was elected to the board of directors of the Umpires Association. Rarely are more than two umpires promoted to the majors in any one year, but in 1968–69 eight men were brought up because the leagues expanded; two more replaced Bill Valentine and Al Salerno, who had been fired—supposedly for incompetence, though everyone knew it was really because of their union organizing efforts—and two more were brought up to replace umpires who had gotten sick. I won my seat on the board as a representative of this group of new umpires because the other men perceived me to be tough but reasonable, articulate, and loyal to the Association, in addition to the fact that I had begged for their votes.

Within the year we had our first strike.

Baseball had instituted the League Championship Series, the playoffs, in 1969, and umpires wanted to be compensated for working these additional games. When we did not receive what we believed to be a fair offer, we decided not to work the 1970 playoffs. In retrospect, we struck at the wrong time, over the wrong issues, and made the wrong demands. Otherwise we did everything very well.

Since only a few umpires were required to work the playoffs, the leagues had little difficulty replacing us with supervisory personnel and other experienced men. But when the Teamsters and other unions began supporting us—and the hot dogs couldn't be delivered to the ballparks—the league agreed to our demands. Ironically, they ended up paying more to the people who filled in for us for one game than we were asking for the entire playoffs.

During the numerous Association meetings I put my years of experience as a football player to good use. One of the most important things I had learned at Syracuse was that those who push and shove get there first. When we flew to a bowl game it was the first player off the airplane who got kissed by the bowl queens, got his picture in the newspaper, and got questioned by reporters. Once I realized that, I didn't care if I sat in first class or last class, smoking or nonsmoking, as long as I was sitting next to the door.

So, remembering that lesson, just before the end of each Association meeting, I would excuse myself to go wash up and, when I returned, take my position next to the door. As soon as the final gavel was pounded I'd be out the door ready to face the photographers and reporters. I'd tell them whatever had been said last in the meeting. If it had concluded with someone saying we were satisfied with the progress of the negotiations, I'd get out that door and solemnly tell reporters we were satisfied with the progress of negotiations.

Naturally my photograph appeared in a lot of newspapers and I was quoted extensively. The umpires who did not attend these meetings began to figure I had to be doing a great job because I got my picture in the papers so often, so within a few years I was elected president of the Association for the first of my two terms.

I also began to become known to the fans. I happen to have one of those unforgettable faces, like Gable, Mitchum or King Kong, and once someone has seen my picture or caught sight of me on a televised game, they remember me. Because I always considered myself a fan as much as an umpire, I related very well to other fans. I loved signing autographs and talking baseball and being offered food and being recognized in restaurants and walking down a street and seeing someone smile in recognition when they saw me. However, I was always careful about meeting strangers. There are a lot of people who really dislike umpires.

Once, after a game in Minnesota, Haller and I were walking out of the dressing room to our car when a young boy came up to me. "Hi, Ronnie," he said, "do you really know a guy named Charlie Arnott?"

I didn't recognize the name, but I had met a lot of people at banquets and might have met him once. I figured he had told this boy he knew me, and I didn't want to disappoint the boy. "Sure," I answered. "How is he?"

"He's right over there," the kid continued, pointing over his shoulder, "and he'd like to come over to say hello to you."

"Yeah, okay," I said, continuing to walk toward the car. I always liked to meet new people. Besides, the man might own a clothing store or, if I was very lucky, a restaurant.

Charlie caught up with us at the entrance to the parking lot. "Hey," he said, "good to see you again."

I didn't remember having ever met him before in my life. I looked at Haller and raised my eyebrows suspiciously, so he realized I didn't know the man. "Hey," I responded, "good to see you, too." Haller got into the car and I stood by the door talking to Charlie Arnott.

"Boy," he continued, "we sure had some great times together, didn't we?"

"Yeah, we sure did."

"You still bowl?"

I had never bowled a game in my life. "No, Charlie, no more."

He sighed. "Hey, we really had some good times bowling, didn't we?"

I put my hand on the door handle. I wanted to be able to make a quick getaway. "I guess we did. Well, Charlie," I said, "we gotta get . . ."

"My brother was a great bowler, remember?"

I didn't want to insult the man in front of the boy. I decided to be as polite as possible. "Sure was. How is your brother?"

"Dead," Charlie said, looking stunned. "Don't you remember? You were a pallbearer."

I began to realize this might be the beginning of trouble. I had enough of that on the field, I didn't need it in the parking lot. I tried to make him comfortable. "Uh yeah, well I . . . I forgot. Um, well, how's his wife? How's his wife doing?" I hoped his brother had been married.

He shook his head. "I didn't think the accident was that long ago. She died in it, too."

I eased myself into the car, being careful not to make any fast moves that might startle him. "Then, um . . . how's your wife?" I blurted out. "She's okay, right?"

"Nah," he said sadly, "she left me after I got sick. She got custody of the kids, too. . . ."

Haller started the car. "Well, Charlie, good seeing you again, but we've got to be going now."

He grasped the top of the half-opened window. "Why don't you come over to the house while you're in town?"

Haller began backing up. Charlie walked along slowly with us, refusing to let go of the window. "I'd like to," I said, "but we're gonna be real busy while we're here. Look, I'll call you."

"No!" he snapped. "I'll call you. Where you staying?"

I named a downtown hotel. We were staying out of town. "Maybe we'll have dinner," I suggested, trying to get him to release the window.

"Yeah," he said enthusiastically, "that'd be nice. But we can't go anyplace too fancy 'cause I just lost my job."

We drove out of the parking lot to the clubhouse exit and picked up Ken Kaiser. As we were leaving the ballpark, Haller said to me, "Hey, Ronnie, did you know that Charlie Arnott guy at all?"

I shook my head. "Never saw him before in my life."

Suddenly, in the back seat, Kaiser bolted upright. "Charlie Arnott!" he exclaimed. "I used to bowl with him!"

Haller had to pull the car to the side of the road, we were laughing so hard.

Unfortunately, because umpires do appear to have sufficient power to affect the outcome of a game, we have to be extremely careful of the people we spend time with. The truth is that the only people who could possibly make a difference in a game are the starting pitcher and the manager. But that doesn't matter— people believe umpires can fix games and attempts have been made to force them to do so. In the early seventies gamblers tried to blackmail two umpires. These men went directly to the league office with the entire story and the police were brought in. I've never been offered a bribe, or even a hint of a bribe, but that didn't stop me from getting into serious trouble.

The one thing that everyone in baseball has in common is the love of a good deal. It doesn't matter what's for sale, as long as it's a good deal. If someone gets a good price on a suit, or shoes, or even a one-winged boomerang, the word zooms through the league like a Ryan fastball. Suddenly everyone realizes the thing they're missing in life is a one-winged boomerang and the moment they hit the right city go directly to the boomerang store. Of course, within a few weeks Reggie Jackson will have bought a two-winged boomerang and the rest of us will lose interest, but while it's hot, it's blistering.

The maître d' at one of Washington D.C.'s leading restaurants was a great baseball fan, as well as the best connection in the city. He could get whatever you wanted at the best possible price, and never asked for anything in return, not even tickets. He just realized that having sports people frequent his restaurant helped business. In 1971 I was interested in buying a new pickup truck and he offered to get it for me from a place in Arlington, Virginia, for the dealer's price. That was music to my bank account and I ordered one during the season. I was supposed to pick it up in early December.

In November I was sitting at home when the telephone rang. Jim Fitzgerald, head of security for baseball, asked me to fly to Washington the following day. For some reason I decided this had something to do with a party. I don't know why I thought that, but I did. Since I didn't want to miss the party, I agreed to fly down the next morning.

Two very big men in dark, three-piece suits and sunglasses met me at the airport and drove me directly to the Pentagon. It didn't take me long to realize I wasn't going to a party. The last time I had seen these big men in dark, three-piece suits had been after the Barbaras' party in Apalachin.

Fitzgerald was waiting for me in a small office. I don't know why they were in the Pentagon except perhaps that it was close to the airport. I do know that by the time I got to that office I was so intimidated I was ready to salute everyone.

Fitzgerald was smiling when I walked in, so I knew I was in trouble. Once I was settled he showed me a photograph of the maître d'. In this photograph he had a number across his chest and he wasn't wearing a baseball uniform. Then they asked me if I knew him.

I hesitated. Before answering, I thought back to the advice an elderly man had given me when I was a very young boy. "Always respect other people," he said, "but deny everything." I said I'd never seen him before in my life.

"Take another look, Ron," he urged.

I did. "He looks familiar, but I meet so many people. . . ."

"Look again," they suggested, handing me a second photograph. This one showed me standing right next to him.

"Oh, *him!*" I said. "That's the maitre d' at . . ." I named the restaurant. I had no idea what he had done. I knew he was friendly with a lot of influential politicians, but I didn't think that was enough to make a man a criminal.

"Ever speak to him on the telephone?"

I told them I had no reason to speak to him on the telephone and firmly insisted upon it until they produced the tape recording. It then occurred to me that it would be sensible to answer all their questions honestly. I told them where I'd met him, what I'd spoken to him about, everything. It was all very innocent, I pleaded, all I'd wanted from him was a pickup truck, but in that small Pentagon room it suddenly seemed very ominous.

They already knew everything I told them. They knew things I didn't know. They probably even knew where Nina, Fonda, and Mary were, but I didn't dare ask. Eventually they told me I could go home. I snapped to attention and saluted.

Fitzgerald called me the next day and told me that the commissioner would rather I didn't buy the truck through this man. "You got it!" I told him.

Later I called a friend of mine with the FBI and asked him to find out what the situation was, and if I were in any trouble. The maître d', he reported, had been working the numbers and other rackets, although he was not a bookie and did not bet baseball games. When he was arrested, the names and addresses of a number of major league umpires had been found in his address book. My name wasn't among them, but my conversations with him had been recorded.

I never heard another word about this incident.

Of all the changes that were made in baseball during my career, the most frightening was the introduction of instant replay. Instant replay promised to take away from umpires one vital part of their equipment—the bluff. Until television developed this means of instantly rebroadcasting a live play, umpires could stand firm on their decisions, confident no one could prove their calls were right or wrong. There was no evidence. If a photograph showed a wrong call had been made, umpires could always claim it was taken from a misleading angle. By the time motion pictures of a play were developed we were usually out of town.

We knew we made occasional mistakes; we just didn't want anyone else to know it. We were really petrified replays would provoke fans and cause serious problems.

But we turned out to be wrong, because our calls were usually right. Instead of showing how many mistakes umpires made, instant replay proved that major league umpires knew what they were doing. It showed that umpires correctly called more than ninety percent of the eyelash plays, those plays that are so close the human eye can't separate two seemingly simultaneous events. Suddenly instant replay became more appealing.

It did cause some problems, however. Haller and I opened Seattle's Kingdome, and went almost six full innings before the first argument. Like most new ballparks and arenas, the dome has a giant screen on the scoreboard for showing replays. I was working second base and in an early inning I had a close play. As soon as I made my call I turned around and watched myself in action. The center-field camera caught it perfectly. I saw myself going down on one knee and shooting the runner outoutoutoutout. I felt like I was watching myself on a movie screen. I loved it.

But later in the game I had another close call. Bobby Grich, I believe, dived at sliding Seattle runner Lee Stanton to make the tag play. It was a good play by Grich and I called the runner out. Stanton got up, dusted himself off and started trotting off the field. But as he did, the replay was shown on the scoreboard. From that ridiculous center-field angle, it looked like Grich had missed the tag. Suddenly we had an argument. "You saw that," Stanton shouted at me. "He never tagged me."

"I saw him tag you," I screamed right back.

Even Grich joined in, shaking his head and saying, "That wasn't the same play. I tagged him on that play."

"That's right," I agreed, "you did."

"How can you say that?" Lee demanded, pointing to the screen. "You saw it with your own eyes."

"Yeah," I said. "I mean, no. I saw the real play, but not the play they showed up there. I mean, I saw that one, too, but that wasn't real." I was hoping to confuse him. It should've worked, I confused me.

But he kept pointing to the screen. "But that's real, that's proof."

Eventually I had to rely on the proven excuse that the camera had the wrong angle. After the game, movie star Danny Kaye, one of the owners of the ballclub, promised that controversial plays would not be shown on the scoreboard screen. He saw the problems it could create. In fact, on that play the camera did have the wrong angle.

Unless, of course, I did.

Earl Weaver immediately put the new technology to bad use. As far as he was concerned, seeing the play a second time made the umpires twice as wrong, which only made him twice as angry. The Orioles installed a closed-circuit television system in Memorial Stadium and put television sets in their clubhouse. Whenever there was a close play on the field, someone would run into the clubhouse to check the replay, signal the result to a coach standing in the corner of the dugout, who would then relay the signal to Weaver, usually already en route to his argument. They had one signal if the umpire was correct, another if he was wrong. If the replay showed the umpire had blown the play, Weaver would be all over him; but if it showed the umpire had made the right call, he'd leave after putting up perfunctory fight.

That worked very well, until the night we stole his signs. Once we knew Weaver's system we just waited for the right opportunity. With Earl we knew we wouldn't have to wait too long. The first time he charged out of the dugout the four umpires on the field looked past him into the Oriole dugout at coach Frank Robinson. Weaver started arguing, taking quick glances over his shoulder at Robinson. Finally Robinson gave him the "stop" sign, meaning the replay showed that the umpire had made a good call.

Weaver yelled his last few words, then turned around to return to his dugout—and ran right into 6'4"

Bill Haller. He turned to his right and 6'1" Rocky Roe was standing there, his arms crossed in front of his chest, smiling. He turned to his left, where 230–pound wrestler Ken Kaiser was glaring at him. Then he turned to face me. "Goin' somewhere, Earl?" I asked. "How come you're in such a hurry this time?" Once we had him trapped in an umpire sandwich, we really let him have it. We hounded him off the field. That marked the end of Earl Weaver's Instant Replay Signal System—for about two games.

The technical advance that I truly appreciated was the automatic home-plate cleaner. All I had to do to blow the dirt off the plate was step on a button and a *WHOOSH!* of air would blast it clean. That meant I didn't have to bend over at all! How could I not love it? Of course, putting that button near my foot was like dangling an unemployed manager in front of George Steinbrenner. The possibilities were just too wonderful to resist. I didn't even try.

Every once in a while a player with whom I had a good relationship would come to bat in a game that was already won or lost, and get ready to hit. George Brett, for example, would settle into the batter's box, take three or four easy practice swings, then stiffen his shoulders, cock his bat and glare out at the pitcher. His entire body would tense in concentration, his muscles would ripple and then . . . I'd step on the button.

Graig Nettles holds the backward leaping distance record. I practically launched him. Of course, I would immediately call time out, because I didn't want to penalize those players or their teams. But it sure was fun watching them jump.

Some innovations never made it into the ballpark. Like Charlie Finley's orange baseballs. Charlie firmly believed major league baseball would be a better game if it were played with orange baseballs. Bright orange baseballs. It's difficult to argue with a man who believes in orange baseballs and I never tried. I did wonder, I admit, if they would have as much value to a bartender as a white one.

Finley was convinced orange baseballs were easier to see, thus easier to hit, which would cause more scoring, in addition to being easier for the fans to follow. They were also quite lovely when used with your basic Astroturf green. One season he convinced the American League to allow him to experiment with them in two spring training games. I was scheduled to work these games and I certainly didn't mind. I figured if anyone bothered to argue with me I could always blink my eyes a lot and blame the glaring baseballs. A good umpire never eliminates a potential excuse.

The score of the first game was something like 2–1, the second game 3–1. There were seven hits in the first game and five or six in the other. There was an error in each game, and the usual number of walks and strikeouts, and no arguments. After the game I spoke to several players so I could submit a report to the league office. The pitchers claimed the ball was harder to control. The infielders said the ball seemed to vibrate as it came toward them. The outfielders claimed the orange baseball was difficult to pick up hitting the bat, which prevented them from getting a good jump on it. Finally I spoke to the hitters, who claimed it was very hard to see the rotation of the ball when the pitcher released it. The A's' second baseman, Dick Green, thought it was silly. "I don't know why we need an orange ball," he said honestly. "I still haven't figured out how to hit the white one yet."

That was the extent of the experiment, and unless baseball decides to redecorate I don't expect to see it ever again.

I didn't mind the innovations as much as I minded

the rule changes. Finley wanted to reduce the traditional four-ball walk and three-strike out to three balls
and two strikes, but he couldn't convince baseball
officials that it would benefit anyone except the
umpires. But every year, perhaps just to keep Gene
Mauch on his toes, these same officials would either
change a rule or decide the time had come to enforce
one already in the book.

One year they decided to try to enforce the balk
rule by laying down chalk "balk lines" on the pitcher's
mound. In spring training white lines were laid down
at a forty-five-degree angle between home plate and
first and third base. If the pitcher were throwing to
home plate and his foot landed behind the line, it was
to be called an automatic ball; if trying to pick off a
runner and his foot landed on the home plate side of
the line, it was a balk, and the runner advanced a base.
The problem with these lines was that they worked.
Pitchers who had never been called for balking were
getting caught a number of times each game. The balk
lines made it obvious that the rule, as then written,
was not being observed by pitchers or upheld by
umpires. So the rules committee decided to do the
obvious thing. It eliminated the balk lines.

That took care of the problem. Officially the
reason given at the time was that the balk lines discrim-
inated against pitchers who worked off the side of
the pitcher's rubber rather than the middle. Mickey
Lolich by name. He was the only one.

At various times throughout the 1970s the commissioner's office decided to speed up baseball games
by enforcing a twenty-second rule. This gave pitchers
only twenty seconds to deliver the ball from the time
they received it from the catcher, and over the course
of a two-and-a-half-hour game easily save three or four
minutes. The second base umpire was supposed to be

the official timekeeper. The penalty for taking more than twenty seconds was to have an automatic ball added to the batter's count. Now, this was a rule absolutely guaranteed to cause problems—what happened if the batter stepped out of the box after eighteen seconds had elapsed? What if the fans were watching a scoreboard clock running two seconds ahead of the umpire?—and nobody wanted to enforce it. At the beginning of the season each umpire was given a stopwatch to use in games. These watches were so badly made that Mickey Mouse had only one hand. Naturally the first time they were dropped on the floor and got jumped on they stopped working. So, to convince the league we were checking to make sure no crazy pitcher tried to take twenty-one seconds, some of us would take the silver lining from chewing gum wrappers out to second base and pretend it was a watch. The fans would see us looking at something silver and assume that's what it was. Admittedly it was difficult to determine when twenty seconds had elapsed by watching a gum wrapper, so the infraction was only called when the umpiring crew had to catch the last flight out of town that night.

The most difficult aspect of an umpire's life is the constant traveling. Umpires are never the home team. Unless an umpire happens to live in a city in his league, the baseball season is one long road trip. For this reason the divorce rate among umpires is very high. My own brief marriage is part of the statistic.

I was introduced to the woman I married by National League umpire John Kibler in Chicago in 1970. We had a whirlwind courtship. Five years after we met we rushed into it. I really wasn't ready to settle down. I didn't particularly like being on the road all the time, but I did like being completely independent, I liked doing exactly what I wanted to do when I wanted to do it.

And even after we were married I was still able to do exactly what I wanted to do. First my wife told me what I wanted to do, then I did it. Unfortunately I was away so much that the summers were very difficult. Of course, I stayed home during the winters and they were impossible.

The most positive thing that came out of my marriage was that I learned to appreciate the traveling.

The worst days on the road are the holidays. Everyone in the country is home with his family on Memorial Day, or July fourth, or Labor Day, except umpires. Even half of the players are at home for these holidays. There are few things more depressing than celebrating a beautiful July fourth by eating hamburgers in a restaurant with Ken Kaiser. There are very few arguments during holiday games because the players know the umpires are depressed; they do nothing to provoke them. The only umpire who never worked on July fourth was Gugie Guglielmo. As far as he was concerned, it was a holiday for him, too, so he took a sick day.

The one thing an umpire learns to do during his career is pack a suitcase quickly. By the time I retired I had my packing time down to fifteen seconds. All I did was open my bag, heave my clothes in it, and shut it. My belief was that as long as everything was inside, that suitcase was packed. Getting it slammed shut and locking it usually took most of the time. And as I didn't mind the wrinkled look, I never had any problems.

Umpires Marty Springstead, Larry Barnett and Joe Brinkman are the exact opposite. They are extremely neat men and pack their luggage with great care.

Obviously I couldn't let them get away with that kind of behavior.

Umpires pack their equipment and clothes in a large suitcase known as a Priesmyere bag, named after the company that originally manufactured them. On our last day in a city we would pack the bags and the clubhouse men would ship them to our next destination. Sometimes they arrived there only minutes before game time, but on other occasions they would show up a full day early, while the crew working the previous series was still in town.

Once I was in Kansas City when Marty Springstead's luggage arrived. Because I wanted to make sure nothing had been damaged during shipping, I opened his bag. As I suspected, it was magnificently packed. Everything was neatly folded and carefully placed in piles. His equipment was on the top level and his personal items on levels below that.

I proceeded to do the worst thing imaginable to the bag—I made it look just like mine. I tied knots in his shirts and shoelaces, I wrinkled his pants, I pulled bristles out of his whisk brush, tightened the straps on his shin guards and face mask. He had even bent wire hangers into domes to help his caps keep their shape, so I resculptured his hangers for him. I called this my 6-4-300 behavior, because if I weren't 6′4″ tall and didn't weigh 300 pounds I wouldn't have dared do anything like it.

Then I left town, and spent the remainder of the season chuckling over my joke. I showed him he couldn't be neat around Luciano without suffering for it.

I didn't see him, or hear from him, until the Association meeting after the season. Instead of being upset when he saw me, as I expected him to be, he greeted me with a broad smile and friendly handshake. "I sure got even with you," he said happily, "didn't I?"

I didn't know what he was talking about. "Whaddaya mean?"

"I did the same thing to your bag that you did to mine."

"Yeah?" I asked honestly. "When?" It had been in New York and, except for the fact that the straps on my mask had seemed a bit tight, I hadn't even noticed.

Besides the first game of my major league career, there were other occasions on which my equipment did not get to the ballpark on time and I had to scrounge around to get things to wear. Once, when the television program *20/20* was doing a piece about me, I ended up wearing a borrowed windbreaker, pants about four inches too short held up by a length of rope, a team cap, a catcher's mask and shin guards. The most embarrassing thing about it was that nobody noticed.

Probably the most important piece of equipment an umpire has is the whisk brush which he uses to clean home plate. These brushes are not easy to find in stores because they have to be wide, but must have very short handles so they will fit into a back pocket. Brushes last for many years and umpires become very emotional about them. If an umpire can't find his brush before a big game he might go crazy. Gugie had a brush that should be in the Hall of Fame. He must've used it for twenty seasons and by the time I worked with him it only had a few stumpy bristles left on it; because of this it took him a long, long time to clean the plate. He'd be scratching the dirt off home and the batter or catcher would suggest he buy a new brush.

To Gugie this was like insulting his best friend. "What's a matter with this one?" he'd snap back. "It's perfect. Just missing a few hairs is all."

The major change that took place in the life of umpires between the time I started and the time I finished was the creation of the Major League Umpires Association, a nonaffiliated union with fifty-two members. Because of the Association, umpires had a real voice in their own affairs for the first time.

His name is Richie Phillips.

Although I was on the board of directors my first year, I quit the Association in 1971 because I felt it was not being run for the benefit of its members. I was the only working umpire who did not belong. When we hired a new attorney to represent us, I sent in my dues and renewed my membership. This man was a fine lawyer, but really didn't have a solid sports background. When he offered to represent us for nothing, however, we hired him. To most members of the Association this was the only qualification he needed.

Finally, in 1978, we hired a tough Philadelphia lawyer named Richie Phillips, who had been representing the American Basketball Association officials and had some compassion for us.

The players always used to kid me about the Association. "I don't understand it," they would say. "How can a man like you stand being around all those umpires!"

After Phillips took over, the joking stopped. He immediately made it clear that we were willing to do whatever was necessary to gain benefits we felt we deserved. We had agreed to the basic terms of a five-year contract in 1977, to expire in 1982, but certain clauses of that contract had not yet been ratified. Early in the 1978 season, we tried to get the commissioner's office to begin negotiating those clauses. They repeatedly put us off, so Phillips organized a one-day walkout during the season. We missed one game, local officials filled in for us, and the courts ordered us back to work. But we had made our point, we thought.

The day after the walkout I went back on the field and the first player I saw looked at me and grimaced. "Oh, no," he moaned. "Don't tell me you guys are back already."

Because each umpire had an individual contract with the league we had some difficulty getting the league to negotiate with us as a union. To avoid a complicated situation, each umpire designated Richie Phillips as his personal attorney, so theoretically he was representing fifty-two individuals rather than a union of fifty-two members.

In February 1979 I was reelected president of the Association. At about the same time the league sent each umpire a letter warning that no one would be permitted to go to spring training unless he had returned his signed contract. That was a mistake on the part of baseball's attorneys because they were, in effect, locking us out. So I missed my Arizona vacation that year.

During spring training we received a second letter from the commissioner's office, this one threatening that other umpires would be hired to replace us if we didn't return our signed contracts by a certain date.

My telephone was ringing day and night. Everybody was scared. Mortgage payments were due, business loan payments were due, bank accounts were overdrawn. A lot of people wanted to go back to work, but Richie Phillips pushed and pulled and cajoled and managed to keep everybody in line. He decided we should picket the ballparks when the season opened, not so much because we wanted support from other unions, but because it would give us something to do at a difficult time.

We began picketing the day the season began. We carried signs reading, "We'd rather call safe than be out," and "Strike is not in our vocabulary." The fans were wonderful. They were constantly stopping us to talk about the strike, ask for autographs or bring us food or drink.

Richie Phillips did a masterful job orchestrating the seven-week-long strike. He told us what to say, when to say it, who to say it to and how to say it. Other than that we were on our own. But he was at his best in meetings. Once we were in Boston meeting representatives of the AFL-CIO and he gave the most impassioned speech I had ever heard. If I hadn't been out already, I would have gone on strike right then and there. He did not ask for action from any other union, just an expression of support. They gave it to us in Boston and we flew to Detroit.

We had announced to the press that we would be meeting with officials from major Detroit unions that night and picketing Tiger Stadium the following day. As the center of the auto industry Detroit is the most union-oriented city in the nation, so we didn't expect to have any difficulty getting support there.

I flew with Phillips and other board members to Detroit, and at our hotel headquarters we met the fifteen or twenty other umpires who would be picketing the next day. When we got there three television station camera crews, five radio station crews and ten newspaper reporters were waiting outside the room for a statement from the union officials we were to meet.

Once we had gotten organized inside the suite and had a few drinks and relaxed for a few minutes after the flight, Richie suggested I go get the union representatives.

"I thought you knew where they were," I said. The

only union man there was a rank-and-file member of the service union that represented ballpark workers. He had been sent down to observe the meeting and make a report, but had no authority to pledge any support or even make a statement.

We were in trouble.

Phillips remained calm and promised to think of a solution. While he was on the telephone trying to contact officers of other unions, he told us to make it sound to the reporters outside as though we were having a rough meeting. So every few minutes someone stood up and screamed, "We don't have to take that from them," and the rest of us would put down our drinks and cheer and clap and promise support.

The meeting began at seven-fifteen and by nine o'clock we were still stuck with one slightly inebriated file clerk. Finally Richie came up with a plan. Since Detroit was an American League city, the reporters did not know the National League umpires. So one of the National Leaguers would simply pretend to be a union official. As president of the Association, I would walk him out of the room, and as we passed the reporters he would say loudly to me, "Don't worry about us. We're behind you all the way." Nothing else. He wouldn't answer any questions from the reporters, but would promise a statement in the future. Soon after that I would walk out with a second National Leaguer and he would make a similar comment. That would at least enable us to get out of a potentially embarrassing situation.

We decided to sacrifice Dutch Rennert. Dutch is a small, cigar-smoking, broad-shouldered man who looks as though he really could be a union official. Unfortunately he had been in the suite for more than three hours and had emptied a lot of glasses. Richie

Phillips and I went over to him and explained the plan. "We want you to say you're behind us all the way," Richie explained.

"Damn right I'm behind you all the way," Dutch said defiantly.

"Right, we know that. But we want you to tell that to Ronnie."

"I'm behind you all the way, Ronnie." He turned around and looked directly at me.

Phillips tried to make it as simple as possible. "Dutch, you just have to say you support the Association."

"Of course I support the Association. Union all the way." He stood up and yelled loudly so the reporters outside could hear, "They can't push us around anymore."

Everybody else cheered.

"All right," Richie decided, "Ronnie will walk out with you, and if anyone asks you any questions, tell them you're a union man."

"Right. I'm a good union man."

We decided to risk it. I walked to the door with Dutch, opened it and said loudly, "Thank you for coming, sir, and we appreciate your support."

Dutch gave me a strange look. "I'm not going anywhere, Ronnie. I'm with you all the way." Then he looked at the reporters. "We're not gonna let them push us around anymore."

I shut the door. We were trapped.

Luckily an official of the AFL-CIO showed up, and apologized for being late. This was Phillips's finest hour. He sat down with the man and told him the complete truth, except for the parts he made up. The Teamsters and the service union had been there earlier, he explained, and pledged their support. This official told us that we would also have the support of his

union local and he would issue a press release after a
membership meeting the following night.

"There are three television stations, five radio stations and ten newspaper reporters outside," Phillips
explained. "We need a commitment now."

When the representative heard the magic word
television his eyes lit up. "You got it," he said.

We quickly arranged for another suite and while
the television and radio crews set up their cameras and
microphones I poured enough liquor to keep them
friendly. Finally Phillips and the union official walked
in and the bright lights went on. It was just like a scene
from a Hollywood movie. The man sat down behind a
long table and said, "There has been something done
here tonight that I have not seen in Detroit in all the
years I've been here. The Teamsters union is supporting these people . . ."

I closed my eyes.

". . . and the service union is supporting these
people . . ."

I bit down hard on my lips.

". . . and I'd like to announce right now that the
AFL-CIO will and does support these people, and that
the two and a half million union men in Detroit are
firmly behind these umpires in their struggle. . . ."

I always wondered what happened to the representative of the service union when he went to work
the next day after pledging the support of his union.

The next day we picketed Tiger Stadium. The
AFL-CIO sent forty people, but Phillips convinced the
press we had two hundred people marching in separate
areas.

A week or so later National League president
Chub Feeney, Lee MacPhail, and their attorneys met
with the Association's board and we hammered out a
settlement. In addition to an improved salary struc-

ture, we received a two-week in-season vacation. That alone will help save a lot of marriages.

The players were very happy to see us return. The quality of officiating during the strike had been very poor. "No consistency," Rod Carew told me. "They were as bad as you, but on a regular basis."

As I expected, the very first thing I heard upon our return after the very first pitch was thrown was, "Bring back those other guys."

The strike, however, left us one problem: the umpires who had worked in our place. The top minor leaguers were asked to fill in for us and had refused, and because of that many of them are still in the minors while the men who worked are in the majors. In fact, one of the reasons we were given vacations was to create spots for these men. None of them are members of the Association.

There is a strong feeling that the strike lasted seven weeks because these men worked, so, since the end of the strike, very few umpires have spoken to them off the field. During games they are treated like everyone else, because a crew has to cooperate to survive, but they are shunned when the game is over.

Being an umpire is tough enough, but it has to be even more difficult if even umpires won't talk to you.

Many people tell me the life of an umpire is not nearly as hard as I've claimed. Deep inside, they claim, people really do like umpires. I nod, I smile, then I suggest if they really believe that, next Halloween they dress their children as umpires for trick-or-treating.

They look at me as if I'm crazy. That doesn't bother me, it's a look I've seen many times before. After all, I was an umpire.

10

THE PRESS BOX
OR A Face Made For Radio

NBC Sports producer Mike Weisman is responsible for my television broadcasting career. Or, as many people who have heard me on the Game of the Week might prefer, NBC Sports producer Mike Weisman is to blame for my broadcasting career.

As the 1979 season came to an end I began to think about retiring. Now, most umpires want to retire after every season, but this time I was seriously considering it. The job takes a tremendous toll on your body—three umpires had suffered blood clots while I was in the majors and I had been carried off the field in 1972 with a perforated ulcer.

But I didn't know what I would do if I retired.

I didn't want to go back to teaching because the schools still had children in them. And I didn't think I was the executive type. I could imagine myself trying to shoot somebody outoutoutout of my office. But a year earlier I had opened a sporting goods store in Binghamton, New York—my grand-opening guest Mickey Rivers showed up six months late—and I figured some club owner would want me off the field badly enough to give me a scouting job in upstate New York. I would simply relax and hunt and take long walks—and, I realized, miss baseball very much. Perhaps I'd think better of it in the spring.

But in September 1979 Weisman called and asked me if I wanted to do color commentary during the American League Playoff series. I asked him what I would have to do.

"Talk," he said.

A perfect fit.

A number of times in the past NBC Executive Producer of Sports, Don Ohlmeyer, through Weisman, had asked me to read the starting lineups at the opening of nationally televised games. I'd agreed, because doing so enabled me to fulfill two important desires: I got to talk and people had to listen. "Mickey Rivers leads off," I'd say cheerfully, "and I love him because he swings at everything so I never have to make any calls behind the plate. Willie Randolph is next and I don't know whether he's a nice guy or not because he hasn't said a word to me in three years. . . . Reggie Jackson is going to hit a home run for us today because he knows the cameras are on him. . . . Graig Nettles is so busy spitting in his glove he doesn't have time to talk to me. . . . Dennis Werth is a young kid and he'd better not complain because I'll throw him out just to teach him to respect his umpires. . . . Tommy John is pitching and I won't have any trouble with him because he's been around so long he already knows I'm gonna miss some calls. . . ." Evidently the response to these little bits was favorable and Weisman thought I would be a nice counterpoint in the booth to people who knew what they were doing.

I couldn't resist. Baltimore was playing California, and I would be able to talk about Weaver and he wouldn't be able to answer back. But before we made it official, as a courtesy NBC decided to check with the league office and the competing clubs. California Angel manager Jim Fregosi said he's Italian, hire him. Angel General Manager Buzzy Bavasi said beautiful.

American League President Lee MacPhail said are you kidding?

It just didn't work out. Although I never found out who was against it, I suspect there was some opposition from the vicinity of the Oriole dugout. NBC made it clear to me that they were not allowing the league or the clubs to dictate announcers to them, but that they wanted to avoid any unnecessary controversy. I told them I really didn't care. I would simply go home, forget all about it, and stick my head in the oven.

In January, Weisman contacted me again and asked if I was still interested in working as the color announcer on the Saturday afternoon telecasts. I laughed. "The league won't let me do it when I'm not working," I explained. "I can't believe they'll give me Saturdays off during the season to do it."

He explained further. NBC wanted me to retire and work with Merle Harmon on the regional Game of the Week.

The opportunity of a lifetime; I would work two or three days a week, for which I would be paid a ridiculously high salary. I would be on national television and free to say almost anything I wanted to. I would be traveling first class. And I would still be in sports.

Absolutely not, I said. Talking to players on the field was one thing; talking to millions of fans was something else entirely. If things started going badly, I pointed out, I couldn't throw the fans out of their living rooms. Weisman tried to talk me into it, but I turned him down and went to spring training.

When I got to Arizona I forgot all thoughts of retirement. I was just where I wanted to be—on the baseball diamond. I was president of the Major League Umpires Association. I had a two-week in-season vacation to look forward to, my salary had become respectable, and the players were talking about a strike of

their own, which meant I would get paid for not working at all. That was even better than Weisman's two-
day-a-week offer.

Toward the end of the training season I worked a
game in Sun City; when it was over, Merle Harmon
came up to me and told me it was the last game I
would ever umpire. Merle has been one of major league
baseball's finest broadcasters for many years, and I had
known him since 1968. He owns a chain of sports
paraphernalia stores called Fanfare, and before I opened
my store I spent a few days with him learning about
the business. Now he wanted to teach me about
another business. "I've got to do twenty-six games this
season," he explained, "and I know we could do a great
job together."

"C'mon, Merle," I said. "What can I do?"

"What do you do best?"

I said I did not know there was a market for professional eaters.

Finally I gave him a good, firm maybe. Inside, one
voice was screaming, "Do it, do it," and another voice
was screaming, "If you do, millions of people will find
out you don't know what you're talking about." I really
did want to try it, but I was afraid of failing. "See
what you can work out," I said casually.

After ten years in the major leagues, umpires only
have to work two weeks during spring training, so after
my conversation with Merle I flew home. He called
the night I arrived and asked me to come to New York
City for an audition.

An audition! I knew there had to be a catch. They
wanted to know if I could do the job before hiring me.
"I don't understand," I said. "I thought I had the job if I
wanted it."

"The audition is for you," Merle replied, "not us.

If you like the way you sound you'll sign; if you don't, then you don't have to."

I agreed to do it. This was Tuesday night and I was scheduled to umpire my first game the following Saturday in California. So I packed my bags for that trip—I knew I wasn't going to like me—and went to New York Wednesday morning for the audition.

Merle and I sat in the control room and pretended to be broadcasting one of the previous fall's playoff games. Sitting in that small, dark room, I felt fine. I actually enjoyed myself. I knew there was nothing to worry about. I would do the audition, hate it, burn the tape, then get on the plane to California and be back behind home plate where I belonged. Then Haller and I would have some good times talking about the silly people in New York who actually thought I could be a broadcaster.

The following morning I went back to NBC to listen to the tape. It was just as bad as I'd expected it would be. After ten minutes I said to Merle, "That's enough. First of all, just listen to your beautiful baritone and then listen to that squeaky door of mine. Then listen to the way you pro-nounce each word so care-full-lee while I'm slurrin' everything. I know I'm gonna get . . ."

"Now just a minute," Merle interrupted. "What did you say about Belanger?"

I didn't remember precisely. Something about his moving a step closer to second base on a certain pitch. "What about it? Everybody knows he does it."

"No, everybody on the field knows it, but not the people at home. You've been on the field. You've been part of the game. That's the insight you can add."

Merle was so wonderful that morning that before I realized what I was doing, I was signing a contract.

Even then I expected someone to tell me it was all a practical joke. But it wasn't. I signed a contract and for the first time in my life, I was going to get paid for talking.

As soon as it was official, I called my brand-new former boss, Lee MacPhail, to resign. Although we had had our share of problems, I liked and respected him. I did not think he was going to be pleased to hear that one of his veteran umpires was quitting two days before the season opened. "Lee," I said, "I'm afraid I have some bad news for you. I'm not going to be in Anaheim for the opener Saturday."

There was a long silence. Then he said suspiciously, "And what's the bad news, Ronnie?"

"That is the bad news. See, I've just signed a broadcasting contract with NBC. I'm not going to be able to umpire anymore."

I could swear I heard champagne corks popping in the background. I know I heard the secretaries screaming with joy. "Ah, that's great, Ronnie," Lee said. "I'm really glad for you."

"I have one problem, though. My contract reads that I have to give you ten days' notice."

"IT'S WAIVED!" he shouted, "IT'S WAIVED. Don't worry about it. You're finished. You're done. Honest, it's waived." I couldn't ever remember him being quite so happy.

So instead of going to California to umpire, I flew to Arlington, Texas, to broadcast a game between the Rangers and New York Yankees. Mike Weisman flew down with me, and during the entire flight he was doing everything possible to build my confidence. You're going to be great, he told me, you have an insight into the game the fans have never heard before. All you have to do is be yourself and tell your stories. . . .

I didn't listen to a word he said. How could I possibly believe anyone who would hire me?

Weisman gave me only the barest instructions. Whenever I wanted to say something all I had to do was touch Merle Harmon's arm and he would give me a lead-in. That sounded simple enough. And I could say anything I wanted to, as long as I didn't swear on the air.

So that was the catch. Just like that, Weisman knocked out eighty percent of my vocabulary. I knew I was in serious trouble. I figured I would be okay for five minutes, and then I'd be out of words. Weisman kept telling me not to worry.

"That's easy for you to say," I told him.

He looked me over.

"No," he disagreed, "it's not."

I watched the opening game of the season Friday night from the press box, which was very high above the field. I've never liked heights. In fact, I don't even like being as tall as I am. I felt strange and uncomfortable, and terribly out of place. I started wandering around the ballpark. I spent some time in NBC's huge control van parked outside. That van had more buttons than Bowie Kuhn's three-piece suit. I was sure one of them was to make me explode when I said the wrong thing. Then I went into the press room and agreed to do some radio interviews after my debut the following day.

I didn't sleep very much that night and woke before dawn. My fear had been replaced with resignation. Whatever was going to happen was going to happen. I had committed myself to this and was going to see it through. But I just wanted to get it over with as quickly as possible.

It was pouring outside.

We got to the ballpark two and a half hours before

game time and Weisman suggested I go to the Rangers' clubhouse and talk to the players. "Yes, sir," I said stiffly. I was fine until I reached the clubhouse door. Then I froze. In my eleven years in the major leagues I had been in the team's locker rooms perhaps two dozen times, usually when an umpire had been hurt, and rarely when the whole squad was inside. But because of the rain the Rangers were still inside. I just couldn't go in. So I turned around and went back to the truck.

"What's the matter?" Weisman asked when he saw me.

"I can't go in there," I told him.

"Why?"

" 'Cause the team is in there."

He hesitated, searching for just the right words. "Uh, Ronnie, that's when you're *supposed* to go in there. The idea is to talk to the team. Got it?"

"I got it," I said. "I can't do it."

"Come with me." Weisman is about 5'11", 170 pounds. He took me by the hand and led me to the locker room. Then he opened the door and literally pushed me inside. I stood on the spot. Everybody was looking at me. The room suddenly became quiet. But before I could run away, Buddy Bell came over to me and put his arms around me as far as they would go. "Ronnie, it's great," he said. "I'm really pleased for you. Now I don't have to yell at you anymore."

"You mean, all those times you yelled at me, it was because I was an umpire and it wasn't because you didn't like me."

He paused to think about it. "Well . . . at least I don't have to yell at you anymore," he pointed out.

Everybody laughed, and the veterans came over to congratulate me. "You must really love baseball," Bump Wills said, "to help it out by quitting." Gaylord

Perry came over to shake hands—and his hand was covered with grease.

After spending time with the players I decided to stop in and see the umpires. For me, that was going home. I walked in just in time to hear Texas general manager Eddie Robinson trying to convince the umpires to play the game. It is the same speech heard in every rain situation. "First of all," he said, "we gotta get this game in. It's a funny schedule this year and there's no place to put it . . ."

This was the second game of the season. There were six months and 161 games to play. And Robinson was claiming the schedule was too jammed up.

". . . and we got a big advance sale today . . ."

That may have been true, but once, in Chicago, the general manager had told us the same thing. We went out and counted the crowd. There were forty-eight people in the park.

". . . and it'll clear up soon. It's not raining at the airport."

The best answer ever given to that claim was made by umpire Stan Landes. During a rain delay in the 1968 World Series, Commissioner William Eckert came into the umpires' dressing room and said he had some good news, it wasn't raining at the airport. "Great," Landes said. "Let's play the game at the airport."

After Robinson left I said seriously, "You guys don't have to listen to him, but this is my debut and I don't know if I can stand waiting another week. Let's play today, okay?"

They threw me out of the dressing room. Their very own president.

I finally went up to the announcer's booth. There were still forty-five minutes before we went on the air so I started to relax. I mumbled something to someone

about St. Anthony and the audio man turned around
and introduced himself to me. In Italian. I knew then
my voice was going to be heard. He made sure I had the
best headset. He made sure my microphone was perfect. He adjusted the tone and volume. The rest of the
world might have been collapsing, but my voice was
going to be perfect.

It was still raining when we finished rehearsing
the opening sequence, and Mike Weisman told me to
get my makeup on.

"You're kidding," I said. He was not kidding. They
put powder on my face and mascara under my eyes.
Then they told me not to move around because I'd get
makeup on my NBC sport jacket. The jacket was about
three sizes too small anyway, so I couldn't move even
if I'd wanted to.

Seven minutes before we went on the air we were
informed the start of the game would be delayed because of the rain. Weisman told me to get down to the
dugout and do the opening from there.

"But it'll take me at least fifteen minutes to get
down there," I pleaded.

"Then you'd better run."

This was not working out exactly the way I had
expected. I took off all my audio equipment and I ran
through the stands, passing the people I had seen the
previous night, down all the levels to the field, then I
hopped over the railing and ran into the dugout and
there was still one minute before air time. I was puffing so hard I could scarcely breathe. "Thirty seconds," a
technician shouted.

Mike Weisman decided I would do the opening
sequence wearing an umpire's face mask, to which no
reference would be made. I quickly put it on over my
makeup. Unfortunately the mask is heavy and fits
tightly over the mouth, making it difficult to speak
clearly.

"Don't forget to speak clearly," Weisman reminded me.

"Fifteen seconds."

"Here we go. Stand by."

Then they told me to move out of the dugout into the rain. When I was in umpires' school they told me that, unlike football, I would never be standing in the rain. They lied. They told me I would never again play in the snow. They lied. And when NBC was trying to convince me to take the job they told me I'd be up in the nice, warm announcer's booth. They lied.

I was not a pleasant sight. The rain was making my makeup run; mascara was dribbling down my face, wet powder was dripping onto my jacket. I couldn't speak clearly with the mask on. The television floodlights were so bright I couldn't see the camera and looked in the wrong direction. And to top things off, Yankee pitcher Tommy John had decided this was the time to get even with me for everything I'd ever done on the field.

From his position in the warm, dry booth Merle Harmon gave me a wonderful introduction and I started telling my story about Eddie Robinson coming into the umpires' locker room.

Tommy John started pulling down my pants.

I was desperately trying to keep my face straight and my pants up. Somehow I finished telling my story and Merle asked me how players kept their bodies loose during a rain delay. We talked about that for a few seconds, then he suggested a rainy day was perfect for Gaylord Perry. "What about it, Ron," he asked. "Does he throw the spitball?"

"Of course he does," I said flatly, "and everybody knows it."

What I didn't know was that Weisman had previously taped short clips of players talking about me. As soon as I made that statement, he cut to a clip of

Gaylord Perry, holding a large tube of Vaseline, and saying, "But you never caught me, Ron, did you?"

"Wait a second," I wanted to shout at Gaylord. "You told me where not to look." But I kept quiet. I managed to get through the segment, then we switched to Tony Kubek and Joe Garagiola, who were warm and dry inside Houston's Astrodome. I had survived. I took a deep breath. I relaxed. I sat down in the dugout. "You'd better get back upstairs, Ronnie," Weisman said. "You've got three minutes."

Our game was eventually canceled because of the rainstorm. A minute after the official announcement was made I turned around and everybody was gone. I mean everybody. Weisman, Harmon, my sound man, even the huge van was gone. I had to stay around to do interviews I had agreed to do the night before. Then the reporters wanted to talk about Perry and the spitball. Yankee announcer Frank Messer asked, "If you knew he threw it, why didn't you stop him?"

"Because baseball doesn't want it stopped," I replied. Then I began wondering if I had said the wrong thing. The absurdity of the situation suddenly hit me. I had gotten into trouble on the field when I was talking to only one player at a time. Imagine the damage I could do talking to the entire nation!

On the flight home I realized I had been awful. I knew I had destroyed my broadcasting career in one day. As soon as I got back to Endicott I called Mike Weisman to find out where I picked up my severance check.

Everything was great, he told me, we were getting great reviews. The only bad thing that had happened that day was in Houston, where Joe and Tony played extra innings and ran into *B.J. and the Bear.*

Not only wasn't I fired; Weisman told me I had done a decent job. He asked me to come to the NBC office the following Tuesday so we could spend a couple of minutes ironing out a few minor problems.

I had done such a good job that we only had to work all morning, all afternoon and into the evening. By the time we finished it was too late to drive home, so I decided to stay in New York City. The hotel where I had stayed as an umpire was full, so I took a room at a place nearby. Everything was fine, until I got my bill the next morning. Including dinner, my one night came to $290.

When I was in the minor leagues I had stayed in a hotel in Williamsport, Pennsylvania, for $1.50 a night. On other occasions I had slept a few hours in my car after driving through the night so I wouldn't have to pay for part of a day. And here I was staring at a bill for $290 for one night. That's a whole season in Williamsport. I figured this was the real test of NBC's confidence in me. When I presented this bill I was going to find out what they really thought of me.

Nobody blinked twice. Just put it on your expense account, I was told. Expense account? I had an expense account? I thought, baby, this is it. I've died and gone to Umpires' Heaven, that beautiful place where nobody ever argues and somebody else picks up the check.

Suddenly I felt confident. Maybe I actually was a little better than I thought. After all, what did I know about broadcasting? Nothing. So how could I possibly know if I was good or not?

It did not take me long to find out I knew less than I thought I did. A few weeks later we went up to Boston for the first time. I figured I would tell my best Carl Yastrzemski story. Carl and I had a little routine worked out. I once told him I believed there were really three Yastrzemskis; one was twenty years old, the second was thirty years old, and the third was forty years old. The first time I saw him during a game I'd ask him which one was playing today. "Feeling good," he might respond. "It's the kid." Or, "Long day, Ron, long day," meaning it was the forty-year-old.

I waited until Yaz came to bat for the second time that game because I didn't want to waste my big story too early. So when he got up, I said, "There are actually three Carl Yastrzemskis. One is twenty years old, one is thirty years old and the other is forty years old . . ."

But as I began this story the little voice in my ear commanded, "Talk about the hero. Talk about the hero."

I had no idea what a hero was. I thought it was a big sandwich. So I said, ". . . and the other is forty years old . . ." and shut up. End of story.

If it weren't for Merle Harmon, America might still believe there are actually three Carl Yastrzemskis. After a long pause he picked up my opening. "And I'd guess it's the thirty-year-old playing today," he said, and smoothly continued, "And as you can see on your screen, Carl banged out his three thousandth hit last season. We've got a clip of that for you right now. Let's see who the umpire was. . . ."

They cut to a tape of Yaz reaching that historic milestone. There I was, cheering him on. A hero, I learned later, was a graphic accompanied by a short film or tape clip.

That day in Boston was a particularly bad one. Usually we had one statistician in the booth with us and he fed Merle all sorts of statistics. For some reason we had two of them in Boston. In the third inning the Red Sox were winning 4–2, and my personal statistician handed me a sheet informing me that in 1924 there were six consecutive shutouts in Fenway Park, or something like that. So, I said, "Well, Merle, in 1924 they had six consecutive shutouts here in Fenway Park." Then I shut up.

A long silence followed as Merle waited for me to make my point. Unfortunately I had no point. All I had was my statistic.

At the end of the inning that voice in my ear asked, "Uh, Ronnie, what did that have to do with anything?"

I didn't know it was supposed to be relevant to the action on the field. The man had given me a piece of paper and I'd read it. They carefully explained to me that statistics were only to be used if they pertained to the situation.

Statistics continued to cause me problems. For example, Ralph Garr would come to bat and I would draw on my memories for some insight about him. I would remember that he strikes out a lot, and say that. Unfortunately the statistics didn't back me up. Garr struck out less than once every ten at bats—but for some reason he always seemed to strike out when I was working his games. I had to learn to support all my claims with statistics rather than impressions, and that took me some time to do.

If a man learns from his mistakes, I was on my way to becoming a great announcer. I made every possible mistake. I made impossible mistakes. Not only did I make the hard ones, I made all the easy ones. Every announcer has something called a cough button. When he has to clear his throat, or cough, or sneeze, he presses that button and it cuts off his microphone. Unfortunately I did not know that. We were in Detroit and I was talking about Rusty Staub. What I intended to say was that he walks like a girl, talks like a girl, runs like a girl, but hits like a man. Just before I started to tell this story I had to cough. Not knowing how the cough button worked, I took off my headset and cleared my throat. Then I put it back on and started. "Rusty walks like a girl, talks like a girl, runs like a girl . . ."

Then the voice in my ear said, "Hit the red button. Hit the red button," meaning that I should hit the red button when I wanted to cough.

I hit the red button cutting myself off, and leaving Staub running like a girl.

Merle Harmon saved me once again by finishing my sentence. I could never have survived that first season without him. From the moment we arrived in a city until we left after the game, I stayed as close to him as a label. I'd leave him at the door to his hotel room at night and when he opened it the next morning I'd be standing there waiting for him. I didn't let him move without tagging behind. Once we were watching the Friday night game and he got up, so I got up, and followed him right into the men's room.

I depended on him even more in the booth. Whenever I had something to say, or wasn't sure of something, I'd grab Merle's arm, just as Weisman had told me to. But I didn't just grab his arm, I *grabbed* his arm. One week he would sit on my right side, the next week on my left side. I didn't understand why he kept changing, and asked him. Rather than answering, he rolled up his sleeves—both arms were black and blue.

But gradually I began getting more comfortable. Not necessarily better, comfortable. I was learning how to use our equipment properly. I was learning not to interrupt Merle. I even learned to appreciate the makeup. I decided I looked so good with it on that I didn't bother taking it off after the games. Men would whistle at me. Stewardesses would ask me who did my eyes. That didn't bother me—I was holding out for a cosmetics commercial.

From the moment I signed my contract I wondered, and worried, how I would react the first time I saw an umpire blow a play. I was still president of the Association and I didn't want to criticize any of my friends or former colleagues on national television. But I knew I couldn't ignore a play, either.

It happened for the first time in Toronto. Jerry Neudecker was working third base. The Detroit Tigers had runners on first and second and the batter hit a grounder to Blue Jay third baseman Roy Howell. Howell bobbled the ball, but picked it up and dived for the bag, touching it with his glove just before the runner slid in.

Neudecker called the runner safe. There was no question that he had missed the play. Here was the moment I had been dreading. I reacted instinctively. "I know what he did!" I shouted. "I know exactly what he did." I was so happy finally to have a subject on which I was the expert that I could barely restrain myself. "I've done the same thing a hundred times myself. Watch his eyes, watch his eyes. He's doing exactly what he's supposed to be doing. You can't watch both the runner and the fielder so he was watching the runner because he expected Howell to try to tag him." As I explained this, Weisman showed the instant replay. Neudecker's eyes were riveted on the runner. I felt so good. I'd finally contributed to the broadcast. I'd gotten one right. After the game I went down to see Jerry and we discussed the play. He asked me what I'd said and I told him, and we had no problem.

As I worked more games Merle's arms started healing and I began gaining confidence in myself. When Bill Madlock was suspended and fined heavily for sticking his glove in an umpire's face, NBC sent me out to do an interview with both Madlock and the umpire for pregame shows. It was a little strange for me, because I couldn't figure out whether I was there as president of the Umpires Association or as an NBC reporter, but it worked out quite well. NBC was so pleased they started using me on the pregame show more often. I went to Evansville for a nice segment with The Bird Fidrych and the psychiatrist who was trying to hypnotize him into returning to his major league pitching form. I did another minor league piece with a young slugger in the Yankee system named Steve "Bye Bye" Balboni. But my favorite segment never made it on the air.

During my second season we taped a piece with "The Secret Spitballer," a major league veteran who agreed to show us on camera how a spitball was loaded and thrown, as long as his identity was protected. He was to wear a mask over his face, and a nondescript uniform; we had planned a delightful parody of the various crime figures who have appeared on television either masked or in shadow.

Unfortunately a reporter unmasked the "Spitballer," or "Spit," as I affectionately called him, as Don Sutton, so we never did the piece.

But as much as I enjoyed being in the booth, I missed being down on the field. I missed being part of the game, hearing the gossip, starting the fights. I remember the day Milwaukee shortstop Robin Yount asked second baseman Jim Gantner why he hadn't covered the base on a play the previous night. "I gave you the open sign," he said.

"No, you didn't," Gantner replied. "It was closed."

"Yeah, Robin," I said. "It was closed."

They both looked at me angrily. "Who asked you?" Robin said.

"Can't we even fight without you bothering us?" Gantner added. I really missed being part of that.

I remember the day Rollie Fingers was standing behind the mound kicking the grass with his spikes. I could see something was bothering him, so I asked what was wrong. "Oh," he said in a frustrated voice, talking about the catcher, "all he wants is the fastball 'cause he's afraid the runner is gonna try to steal second." I couldn't wait until the end of the half inning to run in and tell Haller that Fingers was mad at the catcher so he could share the fun.

On the field I was involved in the game. In the booth I was a spectator.

I remember a midseason game between Oakland and Milwaukee played in 1974. It wasn't a particularly important game; just a regularly scheduled game played on a beautiful summer evening in Milwaukee. The A's won, 8–7, but it was a game that had everything. Every runner who got on base scored. There were two home runs, some stolen bases, a sliding tag play at the plate, a magnificent play in the field by shortstop Bert Campaneris, a perfectly executed sacrifice bunt, and a deftly placed hit-and-run. There were no walks and no errors.

It was a game that required the managers to make a lot of strategic decisions. Oakland pitched to a Brewer hitter with a runner on second and two out, rather than intentionally walking him. Milwaukee passed up an obvious sacrifice situation to try to cross up the A's.

In the bottom of the ninth the Brewers had the tying run on third base with two out and Don Money batting against Rollie Fingers. Two talented veterans facing each other with the game on the line. How I savored these situations. The count went to 3–2 and

Fingers threw an absolutely perfect slider that just caught the outside corner of the plate. I leaped into the air. I threw out my right hand and I bellowed, "Stee-rike three, he gotcha!"

Money knew it and turned away without a word. Oakland catcher Ray Fosse went out to congratulate Fingers.

I just stood there. I didn't want to leave. I didn't want the game to be over. I wanted to shout to them, don't go, don't let it be over. I'm having too much fun. C'mon, let's play just one more inning.

I wanted to tell them all, thanks for letting me be part of it.